THE
Perfect Rule
OF THE
Christian Religion
☙

THE PERFECT RULE OF THE CHRISTIAN RELIGION

೧೮

A History of Sandemanianism in the Eighteenth Century

JOHN HOWARD SMITH

Portrait of John Glas.
By James McArdell, after William Millar.
Mezzotint, mid 18th century
14 in. x 9 7/8 in. (355 mm x 251 mm) paper size
NPG D2440
Given by the daughter of compiler William Fleming, MD, Mary Elizabeth Stopford, 1931-06-25

© National Portrait Gallery, London

Published by State University of New York Press, Albany

© 2008 State University of New York Press, Albany

All rights reserved

Printed in the United States of America

No part of this book may be used or reproduced in any manner whatsoever without written permission. No part of this book may be stored in a retrieval system or transmitted in any form or by any means including electronic, electrostatic, magnetic tape, mechanical, photocopying, recording or otherwise without the prior permission in writing of the publisher.

For information, contact State University of New York Press, Albany, NY
www.sunypress.edu

Production by Ryan Morris
Marketing by Anne M. Valentine

Library of Congress of Cataloging-in-Publication Data

Smith, John Howard, 1968–
  The perfect rule of the Christian religion : a history of Sandemanianism in the eighteenth century / John Howard Smith.
      p. cm.
  Includes bibliographical references and index.
  ISBN 978-1-4384-2507-8 (hardcover : alk. paper)
  ISBN 978-1-4384-2508-5 (pbk. : alk. paper)
  1. Sandemanianism—History—18th century. 2. United States—Church history—18th century. I. Title.
  BX9747.S65 2008
  289.9—dc22

                              2008020827

                    10 9 8 7 6 5 4 3 2 1

Contents

Acknowledgments	vii
Introduction	1
1. "I Thought Myself a Sound Presbyterian"	9
2. "The Perfect Rule of the Christian Religion"	37
3. "He Becomes Possessed of a Truth"	65
4. "May God Preserve Our [Churches] Amidst All Attacks"	93
5. "Spirited Conduct"	121
6. "Mine Eyes Must Flow with a River of Tears"	153
Epilogue	177
Notes	183
Bibliography	211
Index	231

Acknowledgments

I am an Alan Alda fan, and when I bought a ticket to see *Sweet Liberty* in the late spring of 1986, I thought I was going to spend a couple of hours enjoying what I expected would be a good comedy. Little did I know that it would change my life. In the film, Alda plays an early Americanist professor of history, and when I saw the scenes of him teaching a course on the American Revolution, suddenly a casual interest in eighteenth-century America, which began with an oral presentation on Thomas Jefferson in 1976 for a Cub Scout merit badge, forced its way to the surface. As I gazed upon the screen, I knew I wanted the kind of life that Alda's character had, and, though I took many exciting detours along the way, I inevitably found myself becoming an early Americanist. I owe Mr. Alda a heartfelt note of thanks for making a good movie, and for showing me the way ahead.

This book began, as all such things must, with a question. I was a doctoral student at the University at Albany, State University of New York, taking Sung Bok Kim's seminar in early America, and I was writing an historiographical essay on Benedict Arnold biographies. James Kirby Martin's *Benedict Arnold, Revolutionary Hero: An American Warrior Reconsidered* (1997) mentioned an incident when Arnold, leading a group of Danbury, Connecticut, Sons of Liberty, was "'mobbing the Sandemanians,'" quoting Samuel Peters's late eighteenth-century *General History of Connecticut*. A parenthetical note only identified the Sandemanians as "a small Scottish religious sect in New Haven," which did not satisfy my curiosity. If they were suspected Tories, why note their religion as though that had some bearing on their political orientation? And anyway, what is a Sandemanian? I took my second question to a selection of eminent scholars and specialists in New England history in a series of emails, and the only response came from Laurel Thatcher Ulrich, who directed me to the Massachusetts Historical Society's Sandeman-Barrell Papers. I then discovered Williston Walker's short article in the American Historical Association's Annual Report for 1901, and a 1987 article by Jean F. Hankins in the *New England Quarterly*, none of which explained fully what the Sandemanians believed or where they came from except that an immigrant Scot, Robert Sandeman, founded a few primitive Christian churches in New England in the 1760s. I went on to write a seminar paper on the Sandemanians during the years leading up to and through the War for Independence, which was published in the *Historical Journal of Massachusetts*, and that in turn grew circuitously into a doctoral dissertation, and finally evolved into the present book.

When I began my doctoral studies, I intended to concentrate on the social and political dimensions of loyalism, but gradually found myself gravitating toward the history and culture of early American Christianity. I was—and continue to be—interested in those Loyalists who were so out of religious convictions, and the first incarnation of my dissertation was a study of religious loyalism throughout revolutionary America. The Sandemanians, however, repeatedly demanded my attention, and Professor Kim suggested that I narrow my focus to that group, applying substantive flesh to what seemed to be mainly bone and sinew. That the Sandemanians have for the most part been ignored in the major scholarly literature is a mystery, and I hope that in years to come others will give them the pride of place they deserve in the history of Christianity in Britain and North America.

I have incurred a great many debts as I have made my way through various projects that culminate in this book, and to name them all would take up too much precious space, but several must be acknowledged. First, I want to extend my gratitude to Professor Ulrich, who inadvertently kicked off my career with her kind response to a novice historian's out-of-the-blue question. I owe a debt to the many archivists and librarians I have had the pleasure to work with as I conducted my research, especially the staffs at the Massachusetts Historical Society, the Yale University Library, the Boston Public Library, the Danbury Historical Society, and the David Library of the American Revolution. A number of people have encouraged my academic ambitions over the years since I set out to become a historian, and without whom I would never have achieved the realization of my dream. Thanks to Julia K. Woodcock, Milton Ready, Kathleen Nilan, the late Jeanne Marty, Teddy J. Uldricks, Robert F. Yeager, Nadieszda Kizenko, John Monfasani, Candis Murray,

Acknowledgments

Gary L. Loura, Dennis Brennan, Mary Linnane, Alice Malavasic, Jeremiah Patrie, Rosamond Hooper-Hammersley, and Jeannine Chandler for their friendship and support. I thank the participants at an Omohundro Institute of Early American History and Culture Spring Colloquium in 2002, with whom I discussed eighteenth-century American Christianity, and who were gracious—and vigorous—in their comments and criticism. I am especially indebted to Ron Hoffman, Fredrika Teute, and Christopher Grasso for their insights and hospitality.

I have been privileged to have the comradeship and support of several scholars who have been most helpful in the development of this project. Chris Beneke and Karen O'Brien have been great friends and frequent co-panelists at several academic conferences, where they have both been subjected to my fixation with fringe religious groups, unorthodox theorizing, and penchant for Indian cuisine. I also thank the many fellow panelists at conferences in the United States and Great Britain who have commented on my work, especially J. R. Pole, Andrew Colin Gow, Christine Leigh Heyrman, Stephen A. Marini, Nancy L. Rhoden, James Leamon, Seth Cotlar, and Richard W. Pointer. Pauline Maier offered a note of encouragement at a critical juncture. The history department at Texas A&M University-Commerce has provided a nice environment in which to work, and my thanks go out to Scott Downing of Gee Library's interlibrary loan department, who is a skillful wizard at procuring obscure texts. I am also grateful to James Klein, formerly Dean of the College of Arts and Sciences at A&M-Commerce, for approving course reductions so that I could revise the manuscript. Nancy Ellegate and Ryan Morris at SUNY Press have been extremely helpful and accommodating. Rosemary Wellner is a thorough and gifted editor.

My wife, Charlene D. Gentry-Smith, has been an unfailingly patient supporter and sounding board, contending with the precarious life of someone establishing a career in academia. She was also an able research assistant during my many trips to Boston. This project could not have been completed without her accommodating grace.

Most of all I thank my mentor, Sung Bok Kim, who taught me so much more than just how to be a historian. He has been a stern, yet good-humored father figure since I first began working with him in 1998, and I dedicate this book to him. Its strengths are the result of his guidance, and the comments and criticisms of many of these wonderful people, while its weaknesses remain entirely my responsibility.

☙

Thanks to the Massachusetts Historical Society for permission to quote from the Sandeman-Barrell Papers and the Winslow Family Papers.

Introduction

> [M]ine eyes must flow with rivers of tears, whenever [I] think on the goodness of God manifested to his people in that place, and the ill returns made Him, whereby he has been provoked to remove the candlestick out of his place; and, oh! what a large share of the guilt is chargeable on me ...
> —Edward Foster to Robert Ferrier, 1 May 1782

Edward Foster stood on the deck of a British transport ship, looking mournfully out at the cityscape that had been his home. It was March 1776, and the Patriot siege of Boston had finally forced the military governor of Massachusetts, General William Howe, to abandon the city when his efforts to dislodge the Continental Army's artillery emplacements atop the Dorchester Heights failed. He reluctantly conceded that his position was indefensible, and resolved to evacuate before any more Patriot cannon-shot could rain down upon his troops' positions and the Royal Navy ships in the harbor. Those ships sat moored at the docks, taking on not only his troops and their supplies, but also those panicked residents who refused to live under what they considered to be mob rule. The American rebels showed an unexpected tenacity in defense of their supposed rights under the British constitution, to the point of turning on their fellow citizens who dared to question or challenge them. Foster, the proprietor of a blacksmith shop, had been a victim of Patriot abuses, and it hardened his resolve to uphold British imperial authority. When a mob failed in its attempt to burn down Boston Light the previous year, he volunteered his services and those of his workers to repair it, accomplishing it in record time. For his cooperation with the occupiers of Boston and the military government of Massachusetts, Whig newspapers accused him of loyalism and urged the boycotting of his business at the insistence of the city's prerevolutionary leadership. Poised on the brink of financial ruin, it took all that he had left to make arrangements to join the British army as it left Boston for Halifax, Nova Scotia.[1]

Foster's loyalist sympathies were not the only source of the Whigs' rancor against him. He was a Sandemanian, a member of a small primitive Christian sect, which held doctrinal beliefs that clashed with those of the Congregationalist majority who surrounded them. Their liturgical practices and aspects of their personal behavior elicited disdainful public comment, gossip, and harassment. Founded by a maverick Scottish Presbyterian named John Glas (1695–1773), whose followers were originally known as "Glasites," it had been brought to New England by Glas's son-in-law Robert Sandeman (1714–1771) in 1764. By then Sandeman had eclipsed his father-in-law as leader of the sect, and his name became attached to the movement. Sandeman and his ideas immediately caught the wary interest of none other than Ezra Stiles of Connecticut and other New England divines, who thought the Sandemanians enough of a threat to publish treatises criticizing their doctrinal errors. As the sect grew, he began to write letters to his fellow clergymen, drenched in distrust and warning them about these peculiar sectarians who thought themselves the only true Christians. At a time when New England's— especially Connecticut's—churches seemed to be undergoing a period of decline on account of a "dividing, party-Spirit," the numbers of those seeking membership and approaching the Lord's Table shrinking in proportion to the rapidly growing population, Stiles and his colleagues regarded these religious *arrivistes* with grave suspicion and dismay in spite of certain appealing aspects of Sandemanian theology.[2]

Why the Sandemanians seemed to pose such a threat when their numbers were so marginal is at first perplexing, and is the central question this work seeks to answer. New England has a history in the seventeenth century of railing against and persecuting non-Congregationalist Dissenters, particularly Quakers, but the radical Puritanism of that century had given way in the eighteenth century to a more roundly tolerant, rationalist and Arminian Calvinism[3] despite the New Light fundamentalism of the First Great Awakening. Baptists, Anglicans, and Quakers still chaffed against church establishment and ministerial taxation, which Stiles and his colleagues staunchly defended, and these Dissenters were still perceived as threats, but only on account of their impressive growth rates.[4] The Sandemanians should have come across as barely worth noticing, much less deserving of the intense scrutiny and surveillance Stiles recommended. The egalitarianism of Sandemanian ecclesiology and rationalism of their theology should have appealed to Patriot Congregationalists who feared Anglican institutionalization in the 1760s, and the whiff of aristocracy inherent to it. However, a sense of embattlement pervaded New England's religious culture, divided as it still was in the 1760s between Old Lights and New Lights who continued to bicker over obscure aspects of soteriology and ecclesiology, interrupted only by the Revolution. Sandemanianism was, in the end, too egalitarian, too rationalist, and too exclusionary, thus constituting yet another obstacle to what Stiles thought should be a redefinition of New England's religious identity. The answer to this question can only be found in the history of theological exchange between Britain and its colonies, beginning in 1630. What Sandemanianism lacked in numbers of adherents it compensated for in intellectual heft and theological impact, as fully involved in the debates that ran parallel to and suffused the First Great Awakening as was the incipient Methodist movement, which was every bit as marginal in the 1760s.

⁜

In the field of Christian theological history, the vast bulk of work is tightly focused and wary of synthesis.[5] The scholarly literature is concerned either with the Protestant, Catholic, or Orthodox traditions, or with denominations and varieties of one or another of those traditions, and generally limited to specific countries or geographic regions. In terms of the history of theology in Britain and the United States, comparatively few works exist that underscore the close ties between the two countries and mutual influences.[6] The history of theology in America during the colonial and revolutionary periods emphasizes a process of steady maturation based on a close and essentially derivative relationship with Britain. However, Sydney E. Ahlstrom identified a daunting "multifariousness" in American Christianity, influenced during the colonial period by myriad varieties of European expression that may account for scholars' reluctance to tackle what is admittedly a colossal subject. This was fully remedied in 2003 with the publication of E. Brooks Holifield's magisterial *Theology in America*, though he conceded that in our current milieu when synthetic history is derided as passé, "most students of American religion have turned their attention away from literate elites, the history of ideas, the abstractions of intellectuals, and the activities of leaders." He explains that for the greater part American theologians borrowed from their European (mainly British) counterparts and not vice versa, although there were a few Americans who influenced Europeans in the 1700s, namely, Jonathan Edwards and Jonathan Dickinson. Others have highlighted the existence of an expanding clerical communications network across the Atlantic Ocean as a consequence of the Great Awakening, but, in the colonies, the connections were largely between New England and Britain. New England alone was densely populated enough in the 1600s to allow for intellectual networks to grow, and had the means to print treatises and books that were read by students, clergymen and laymen alike.[7]

The body of work on denominational theologies in America is impressive, though generally conflated with denominational history and overwhelmingly tilted in preference away from Catholicism and toward Protestantism. As regards the latter in the seventeenth and eighteenth centuries, New England Puritanism/Congregationalism emerges as the favored subject, with Baptists and Methodists well represented.[8] The deluge of works concerned with New England has abated in recent years, but the region continues to dominate the religious history of early America; a dominance defended by Holifield as stemming from the unavoidable fact that "Theology as an enterprise of sustained reflection on claims of Christian truth began ... with the Calvinist clergy of seventeenth-century New England [who] produced the first substantial corpus of theological writings." They, he avers, "set the agenda for a debate that continued more than three centuries." Additionally, "While the middle and southern colonies produced a few isolated instances of seventeenth-century theology, most of it came from New England." Part of this is attributable, however, to a greater interest in and deferential reverence for New England following Union victory in the Civil War, reinvigorated by criticism of a presumably socially retrograde and intellectually stunted South during the Civil Rights era of the 1950s and 1960s. That the following work is partially set in New England is therefore not the product of any filiopietistic inclinations, but rather of the inscrutable vicissitudes of history.[9]

To reach a fuller understanding of the early modern Atlantic world, one cannot focus solely on dominant groups and movements. Just as the astronomer must block the light from the brightest stars in order to discover nearby bodies lost in the glare that nevertheless influences those stars' motions,[10] so also must the historian do likewise in order to "see" phenomena that otherwise might be lost and forgotten. Those historians who have studied marginal groups such as the Moravians, Mennonites, Huguenots, and Shakers, among others, have not only illuminated those particular groups, but also the ways that the major Christian denominations were influenced by them.[11] The result is a clearer, more three-dimensional view of the past. The Sandemanians are at once the product of a synthesis of eighteenth-century Enlightenment rationalism and contemporary interpretations of Calvinism, and they arose at a watershed period in British-American history. That alone makes them worthy of close study, but they also allow for a better understanding of the relationship between religion and politics in what R. R. Palmer dubbed the "age of the democratic revolution."[12]

The published historical literature concerning the Glasites and Sandemanians is scant at best, apart from scattered references and the occasional footnote. Williston Walker presented the first systematic study of either group in "The Sandemanians of New England" (1902), being a general overview of the sect in America. Charles St. C. Stayner offered an essentially genealogical examination of certain members of Nova Scotia's Sandemanian population for the Royal Nova Scotia Historical Society in 1951 which hardly touches on theology or the actual founding of the churches there. Jean F. Hankins expanded upon Walker's work in a 1987 article for the *New England Quarterly* and in an essay on Connecticut Sandemanians for *Loyalists and Community in Revolutionary America* (1994), edited by Robert M. Calhoon. Geoffrey Cantor studied arguably the most famous Sandemanian in his biography of the English scientist Michael Faraday in 1991. I expanded upon aspects of Hankins's work in an article published in the *Historical Journal of Massachusetts* in 2000. However, considering the attention the Glasites and Sandemanians attracted in the eighteenth century, especially Robert Sandeman's impact as a theological writer and the controversy the sect aroused in the Anglo-American world from the First Great Awakening to the American Revolution, their virtual absence from the historiography of religion in America is puzzling. Neither has there been any published analysis of Sandemanian theology within the context of Anglo-American religious history, which this work provides.[13]

In studying the Glasite-Sandemanian movement in detail, it is the purpose of this book to shed more light upon the intimate connections between Scotland and the British American colonies in the eighteenth century. Ned C. Landsman, who demonstrated that the ties were political and economic, as well as ethnic and cultural, explored these connections to their greatest extent, but the intellectual connections remain comparatively unexplored.[14] The emphasis here is on the tightly interwoven threads of politics and religion in the Atlantic World. J. C. D. Clark, who demonstrated how the drive for religious freedom was indistinguishable from the drive for individual political freedom in Britain and its American colonies, has done very important work in this area. In characterizing the American War for Independence[15] as a "war of religion," Clark reinforces the intertwined nature of religion and politics in colonial and revolutionary America as an inheritance from Britain.[16] Finally, and most important, the reputation of Robert Sandeman—whose name eventually became more tightly bound with the Glasites than that of the sect's founder—as a highly influential theologian has long been overlooked despite overwhelming evidence to the contrary, and his status is reasserted in this work. His apparent failure as a sectarian leader, due mainly to the fundamental tenets of Sandemanianism, does not compromise his place as a prominent religious thinker.

The foregoing work chronicles the origins and development of the Glasite-Sandemanian movement in the eighteenth century from its beginnings in Scotland and growth throughout Britain in developing a variant of commonsense Christianity, to its transmission to New England and travails there, and finally to its general removal to Nova Scotia—a "New Scotland"—where it found more fertile ground in which to grow. Using a variety of primary sources—mainly treatises and letters—left behind by the founders and members of the movement in both Britain and North America, the book is organized into six chapters. Chapter 1 describes the advent of John Glas's movement in a storm of controversy within the Scottish Church arising out of its sixteenth-century Reformation, and that highlights unresolved issues concerning the relationship between church and state, and an argument over which precipitated Glas's expulsion from the ministry. Chapter 2 details the further development and solidification of Glasite doctrine and liturgical practices. Chapter 3 introduces Robert Sandeman and his provocative work *Letters on Theron and Aspasio*, the impact it had among British and American theologians, and the spread of the movement in England and Wales. Chapter 4 follows Sandeman to New England, where he struggled to build congregations, and the resistance he encountered as a result. Chapter 5 deals with the difficulties the American Sandemanians faced during the imperial crisis and the Revolution, and chapter 6 sees the loyalist Sandemanians off to Nova Scotia, and offers an analytical summary of the Glasite-Sandemanian movement, assessing its impact and the reasons for its ultimate decline. A concluding epilogue catches up with a couple of Sandemanian exiles in Nova Scotia, and tracks the theology in the United States into primitive Restorationism under John and Alexander Campbell.

The story of the Sandemanians in the eighteenth century is not merely a sidebar in the larger histories of Scottish Protestantism, New England society, the First Great Awakening, or of religion in the American Revolution, but an important thread in all of these interwoven histories. The issues that impelled John Glas to break from the Church of Scotland in the late 1720s persisted as topics of vigorous debate among Robert Sandeman's supporters and opponents in Connecticut and Massachusetts in the 1760s. The same forces that cast the Glasites as outsiders in the 1730s and 1740s similarly placed the Sandemanians in that position in the 1760s and 1770s, especially as the storm of the American Revolution broke all around the incipient New England churches. Factors inherent to Glasite-Sandemanian theology and ecclesiology rendered the American Sandemanians incapable of weathering the storm of persecution they faced in an increasingly polarizing revolutionary environment, and only when they exiled themselves to Nova Scotia were they able to discover a hospitable environment that allowed the denomination to flourish once again as it did in Britain. Treated mainly as a curious footnote in Anglo-American religious history on account of the relatively small numbers of Sandemanian churches, and the paucity of some churches' membership, the Sandemanians and their theology remain worthy of close study for the light they shed on religion and politics in the eighteenth-century British-American Atlantic world.

☙ 1 ❧
"I Thought Myself a Sound Presbyterian"
John Glas's Break from The Church of Scotland

> This young man seems to be Independent in his principles, and against all pouer in spiritual Societys beyond a single congregation.... He is not for any Society, and can bear no contradiction, without running to hights. It's designed by smooth methods to keep him quiet.
> —Robert Wodrow, *Analecta*

On 17 October 1727, John Glas waited anxiously, steeling himself as he prepared to stand before the Synod of Angus and Mearns to answer the charges of heterodoxy levied against him. The thirty-two-year-old minister of the Church of Scotland[1] had grown increasingly impatient with the weight of Presbyterian authority, particularly the synods, which exercised powers he thought bore marks of worldliness and clerical despotism. Individual churches, he averred, had gradually lost the ability to govern their own affairs, being forced to submit proposals even on minor decisions to local presbyteries for approval on matters having little or nothing to do with church doctrine. He criticized the Presbyterian establishment from his pulpit, and published critical polemics charging its leaders with corruption. He defiantly rebuffed a preliminary examination, and the matter shifted to the Presbytery of Dundee, which demanded that he renounce his opinions and reaffirm his Confession of Faith and the Formula. He stood his ground, and the presbytery suspended him from preaching until the matter could be decided by the Synod of Dundee, which stripped Glas of his license to preach; this penalty was ratified in 1730 by a Commission of the General Assembly sitting in Edinburgh. The result was the creation of a new Christian sect, the influence of which radiated throughout Britain and to America for over two hundred years.

The controversy into which John Glas threw himself concerned Presbyterian church polity and its relationship to secular authority, as defined by covenants made between the church and the monarchy after the Scottish Reformation in the latter half of the sixteenth century. In order to understand fully the origins and later development of Glasite doctrine and church organization, it is necessary first to summarize the origin of the Covenants in the milieu of Reformation-era Scotland, and how issues spawned by them intermittently threatened the stability of the church establishment and led to various schismatic movements, of which John Glas's was but one of many. However, the vast majority of these movements' influence never extended beyond Scotland, and in some cases not beyond certain regions, while the Glasites[2] spread throughout southern Scotland and far beyond. It would be quite impossible to understand the genesis of the Glasite movement, and its theological underpinnings, without first encompassing the Scottish Reformation, particularly in the context of the stormy relationship between Scotland and England.

Reformations Religious and Political

Scotland was touched by Martin Luther's reform movement not long after Luther had posted his *Ninety-Five Theses* in 1517. The Scottish parliament, anxious to prevent Lutheranism's spread beyond England, passed laws banning the printing and possession of books by Luther or otherwise propagating Lutheran doctrines. King James V (r. 1513–1542), while cognizant of the need for reform within the Catholic Church, nonetheless feared for the stability of his country, resolving to keep militant antiauthoritarian radicalism at bay. Rather, he quietly encouraged dissent and warned Scottish bishops that, if they disagreed on the necessity of moderate reform, he would send them to England to be dealt with by his uncle, King Henry VIII. However, one critic, Patrick Hamilton, a priest from St. Andrews, believed that more sweeping changes were needed, and his preaching against the Church made it impossible for him to remain in Scotland safely. He left in 1527 for Germany, where he conferred, returning to Scotland the next year. He was promptly arrested and convicted of heresy by Cardinal David Betoun, Archbishop of St. Andrews, and burned at the stake. The sudden death of King James V in 1542 made his infant daughter, Mary, queen of Scotland. The Catholic factions moved quickly to tie Scotland diplomatically to France while the Protestants urged reconciliation with "the auld enemy" England in order to complete the process of reformation. The reformers were split into two competing factions: a moderate wing that took the gradualist approach that James had embraced, and a radical wing under the leadership of John Knox (1505–1572). This unstable situation worsened with the assassination of Archbishop Betoun by the radicals and their occupation of his castle in 1546. French troops stormed the castle, dispersed the radicals, and captured Knox. The moderates pushed their agenda through a series of Provincial Councils, resulting in the nobles signing the First Covenant in 1557 and taking Scotland's first step toward establishing Protestantism. Then progress stalled as a 1559 council at Edinburgh failed to reach an agreement between the clergy, nobility, and the gentry over the election of bishops and the appointment of parish priests. Knox, who had been released and made his way to Geneva to study at the feet of John Calvin, was summoned by the reforming nobles and returned to Scotland.[3]

On his arrival, there was a long-expected confrontation with Mary of Guise and her government. She issued a preemptive proclamation banning anyone from preaching or administering the sacrament without a bishop's authority. The extreme reformers ignored this and soon afterwards Knox was scheduled to preach in St. John's, Perth. Once his sermon was completed, a priest prepared to say Mass. This caused a riot in the congregation, opening a floodgate of iconoclastic fury that Knox failed to prevent, and which drowned southern Scotland in waves of destruction that damaged or ruined churches and monasteries. When French interference again loomed on the horizon, Knox negotiated with the English government to secure its support, and in October 1559 he approved of the lords of his party suspending their allegiance to the regent queen. Mary's death in June 1560 opened the way to a cessation of hostilities and an agreement leaving the settlement of ecclesiastical questions to the Scottish estates, rather than to the throne. John Knox and the party of reformers, called the Lords of the Congregation, drew up a petition proposing the abolition of Roman Catholic doctrine, the restoration of purity of worship and discipline, and the transfer of ecclesiastical revenues to the support of the ministry, the promotion of education, and the relief of the poor. This document, called The Confession of Faith Professed and Believed by the Protestants within the Realm of Scotland (more commonly known as The Confession), was presented to the Scottish parliament and ratified on 17 August 1560. Soon afterwards, Knox and three other ministers drew up a plan of ecclesiastical government, known as the *First Booke of Discipline*, which was approved by the General Assembly and subscribed to by a majority of the members of the Privy Council. As codified in the *Booke*, authority rested not with individual clergymen, but with conciliar bodies called presbyteries with the prerogative of assembling synods to handle issues pertaining to church discipline and doctrine. Thus was Presbyterianism established. When Mary Queen of Scots, widowed by the untimely death of King Francis II in 1560, arrived from France to assume her crown, she pledged to leave Protestantism undisturbed. An incredulous Knox stubbornly defied Mary's authority and thundered against her religious hypocrisy, as well as French influence in Scottish affairs. Mary was forced to abdicate the throne in 1567 in favor of her young son, the future James VI, before becoming the ultimately doomed prisoner of her cousin Queen Elizabeth I of England. All the acts of 1560 were then confirmed, establishing Presbyterianism as the state church, though it would not be codified fully until the ratification of a *Second Booke of Discipline* (1581) in 1592. This set the Scottish Church on a firm Calvinist foundation.[4]

King James VI, however, on his ascension to the English throne as James I in 1603, maintained the validity of episcopacy in church government in a campaign to bring the churches of England and Scotland into uniformity with each other. He was determined to rid Scotland of the radical "fiery spirited men in the ministry" who "fed themselves with the hope to become *Tribuni plebes*" by preaching "that all Kings and Princes were naturally enemies to the liberty of the church." Initially James had acquiesced to the moderate Presbyterians and left their system undisturbed, but after 1595 he took control of the General Assembly, successfully manipulating church affairs remotely for five years, but in 1600 his attempts to subordinate the church to the assembly were frustrated by an inability to influence his hand-picked commissioners. He then resorted to the course of action he preferred in the first place, the reestablishment of episcopacy. The tentative reintroduction of bishops who shared authority with the presbyteries went much more smoothly than might have been expected, primarily because the nobility generally supported episcopacy. Weary of conflict and instability, some Presbyterians grudgingly accepted the new order while a small minority continued to resist. James acted forcefully to punish recalcitrant clergy and compelled the creation of estates for the bishops. Nevertheless, the constant undercurrent of resistance and criticism among elements within the clergy and the laity forestalled anything more than an uneasy truce with the presence of episcopacy, and sustained internal debates over the issues of church government and its relationship to secular authority. When King Charles I and his Archbishop of Canterbury, William Laud, attempted to introduce the *Book of Common Prayer* into church practice in 1634, a firestorm of popular and clerical protest led to the total rejection of episcopacy. This was conclusively stated and confirmed by a mass subscription to *The Confession of Faith of the Church of Scotland*, better known as the National Covenant, which was drafted in 1638 and signed by over 300,000 Scots the following year.[5]

When the English Civil War broke out in 1642 between the Royalists who supported the Stuart sovereign, and the Puritans led by Oliver Cromwell, the latter sought Scottish military and political assistance. The Scots agreed, but only after the English pledged to reform their church along the lines of that in Scotland. Desperate for their support, the Puritan-dominated English parliament agreed and a "Solemn League and Covenant" was passed by a Convention of Estates in 1643. With the defeat of the Royalist forces and the surrender of the king in 1646, the Puritans proceeded to ignore their end of the Solemn League and Covenant, and further shocked the Scots by executing Charles I in 1649 and establishing the Cromwellian Protectorate. Here marks the emergence of the radical Presbyterian faction known as the Covenanters, who affirmed their respect for legitimate authority by agreeing to endorse Charles Stuart's claim to his father's throne and that of Scotland on the condition that he subscribe to the National Covenant, which he did in 1651. He was duly crowned "King of the Scots" at Scone that same year. Cromwell responded by invading Scotland, which was subdued by 1652, and while England and Scotland were tenuously united, the Church of Scotland remained riven by factionalism between rival General Assemblies and synods divided between supporters and opponents of Charles Stuart, and between ministers who wished to separate church and state and those who argued in favor of state-sponsored Presbyterianism. Attempts by Cromwell's government to reestablish the unity of the Church of Scotland between 1653 and 1659 were signally unsuccessful, and when it became clear that the Restoration was going to happen, the future Charles II would be sure to remember who his friends and his enemies had been.[6]

When Charles II finally ascended the English throne in the Restoration of 1660, he indicated a desire to mediate a healing of the divisions in the Scottish Church, but only as a delaying tactic while he consolidated his authority in England. It was well known that he advocated episcopacy, however, and anxiety among the Covenanters ran high. The nobility, whose authority had been compromised during the Interregnum, embraced the Restoration and sought to subordinate the National Church to the Scottish parliament via Charles II. At the first meeting of Parliament on 1 January 1661, an act was passed requiring the members to swear an Oath of Allegiance that contained a clause stating that "I acknowledge my said Soverane only Supream Governour of this Kingdome over all persons and in all causes." This raised the thorny issue of the role of the king in church affairs, heightened by the passage of an act that illegalized the making of leagues without royal permission, as well as an act that annulled the Convention of Estates in

1643 that had passed the Solemn League and Covenant. It was then decided that renewal of the Solemn League and Covenant could not happen without royal permission. This was followed by Charles II's annulling his subscription to the National Covenant and attempting to restore episcopacy in Scotland by revoking all legislation passed by the Scottish parliament between 1640 and 1660. The outraged Covenanters rebelled, left the established church, and resorted to "conventicles" in the countryside, with their ministers preaching in the open air. Armed rebellion soon followed, especially in the southwest of Scotland and in Ayrshire. Between 1661 and 1688, it is estimated that 18,000 died both in battles and persecution, creating a succession of martyrs and lasting bitterness. Eventually some degree of order was restored in 1690, after the accession of William of Orange and Queen Mary to the English throne. Even so, some extreme Covenanters, known as Cameronians, followers of Richard Cameron who disliked William of Orange because he had refused to sign the Covenant, continued to object despite King William's passing the Act of Settlement in 1690 through Parliament which secured the establishment of the Presbyterian Church in Scotland.[7]

The publication of John Locke's *Letters Concerning Toleration* in 1689, coupled with William and Mary's passing the Act of Toleration through Parliament that same year, gave encouragement to schismatic movements that justified themselves on the basis of a new wave of religious freedom. James Hogg of Carnock rejoiced that

> The heavy yoke of persecution by a chain of wonders was now taken off, and hereby many were inclined to easy courses; and an excessive aversion from what they apprehended might be irritating, and bring us into trouble, proved a snare ... [O]ur settlement was in a weak and infant state, and our adversaries were many and strong; hence, such methods were thought advisable, that we might not too much provoke them.

Few in Scotland expected the relative stability to last, as tensions between the various religious factions continued to build underneath the placid surface of the first several years of the Revolution Settlement. When the Act of Union was passed in 1707 formally uniting the kingdoms of England, Scotland, Ireland, and Wales, outrage and violence erupted throughout Scotland, with rioting in Edinburgh, Glasgow, and Dumfries. The "democratic hierarchy" of Presbyterianism was somewhat undermined by the reintroduction of patronage by the English parliament in 1712 as a means to eliminate Jacobitism and reinforce episcopacy in the selection of clergy to fill pulpit vacancies, but, despite the General Assembly's objections the power of the presbyteries was never seriously compromised. The Scottish clergy were required to swear an Oath of Abjuration that same year that compelled them to "support, maintain, and defend the succession of the Crown ... as settled by the English Parliament," and at least one-third refused to take the oath, mainly in the north and west of the country. A flood of petitions inundated the Scottish parliament protesting the union, coming mostly from the southwest, and several presbyteries accused the commission of "national perjury" for endorsing the union with a nation that had broken the covenants. One radical Presbyterian faction led by John Hepburn of Galloway, the Hebronites, condemned England as "a Nation deeply Guilty of many National Abominations, who have openly Broke and Burnt their Covenant with GOD and League with US."[8]

The Act of Union recognized the coexistence of the separate Churches of England and Scotland, the former catholic and Arminian, the latter Calvinistic and Presbyterian. The dissolution of the Scottish parliament resulted in local government being conducted through parish kirks that constituted the lowest level of the National Church, which functioned through a system of church courts. These began with the local congregational kirk-session made up of the minister and the lay elders, progressed upward through the presbytery consisting of regional representative elders and ministers, continued on through the synod representing several presbyteries, and culminated in the national General Assembly. The church courts were intended to be representative, based on popular election, with the General Assembly fulfilling the role of a supreme court. However, the Presbyterians of southeastern Scotland, under the influence of Anglicans in northern England, gravitated toward a policy of moderation in religious practice that tended toward Arminianism and the abandonment of traditionally Scottish practices and doctrines in the National Church. A direct result of English efforts to extend its influence into Scotland after the Act of Union, "Moderatism," as this movement was called, constituted the next great controversy in the Church of Scotland as orthodox Presbyterian clerics sought out and accused those who exhibited symptoms of "moderate" beliefs. John Simson, a highly regarded Professor of Divinity at the University of Glasgow, was brought before the General Assembly in 1714 for preaching Arminianism, but was acquitted due to lack of evidence. He would be hauled up again in 1736, this time for propagating Arianism. This "damnable heresy," his opponents alleged, had been exported into Scotland by "pretended Protestants in neighbouring nations," and the assembly convicted him, though punishing him only with a written reprimand and a short suspension. In the wake of Simson's acquittal on the first charge, Thomas Boston of Simprin, a town in Berwickshire, in the

Borderlands, distributed among a circle of his friends and ministerial colleagues an old evangelical and traditionalist work, *The Marrow of Modern Divinity* (London, 1645), which had been reprinted by Hogg, one of Boston's friends, in 1718.[9]

Composed of a hodgepodge of Reformation theology from Luther and Calvin to the Puritan theologian Richard Hooker, though essentially Calvinist, *The Marrow of Modern Divinity* asserted the gospels' power to offer salvation to the distressed sinner, and lead such a one to Christ. Written in the form of an allegorical dialogue, much of it hints at universal redemption. Boston declared that on first reading the book it was "a light which the Lord had seasonably struck up to me in my darkness." In his sermon, "Christ Gifted to Sinners," Boston stated that Christ offered salvation "not to the elect only but to sinners indefinitely ... sinners of the race of Adam without exception, whatever they have been, whatever they are." It was eagerly read by anti-Moderates, who submitted the book to the General Assembly in 1720, but when that body rejected it as "Antinomian," Boston, Ebenezer Erskine of Stirling, and his brother Ralph Erskine of Dunfermline—who became known as the "Marrow Men"—defended the book and condemned the assembly in the most vociferous terms. They withdrew from the Synod of Perth and Stirling to form an "Associate Presbytery" in 1733, which by 1737 became known as the "Secession church." The General Assembly formally deposed the Seceders from the church in 1740. The Moderates identified with the landed gentry of Anglicized southern Scotland who embraced the Enlightenment and rational Christianity, whereas the evangelical Secession Church gained wide popular support as well as that of the ecclesiological descendants of the Covenanters, who by the eighteenth century called themselves "Reformed" Presbyterians.[10]

Southern Scotland in the early eighteenth century was rife with religious tension and open conflict over the Covenants, Presbyterian doctrines and practices, pressures toward Anglicization, and Anglican Church influence, and it was in this milieu that John Glas was educated and spent his formative years in the pulpit. The controversy in which he became embroiled was not in itself a particularly unique phenomenon. His was but one of several schismatic movements assailing the Presbyterian Establishment at the time, but the Glasites became something very different. Glas never saw himself as a radical in the mold of a Richard Cameron or a John Hepburn. His break from the Scottish Church began over the most trivial of matters, but escalated into a major argument over issues of authority between ministers, presbyteries, synods, and the state. Attacked by colleagues with whom he had personality conflicts, and charged by church authorities he thought unwilling to allow his self-defense, Glas found himself pushed gradually and inexorably away from Presbyterianism and into a radical independency.

THE RELUCTANT RADICAL

Alexander Glas, Presbyterian minister to the parish of Auchtermuchty in County Fife, and his wife Christian celebrated the birth of their only son, John, in September 1695. Five years later Alexander accepted a pastorate in Kinclaven, and there John received his elementary education before going on to attend the grammar school in Perth, where he studied Latin and Greek, at which he excelled. Bookish and spiritually disposed, the young boy believed that he was destined to become a minister, having come from a long line of clergymen beginning with his great-grandfather William Glas, who had been a favorite of King James VI. He enrolled at St. Leonard's College at the University of St. Andrews, receiving his Master of Arts degree in May 1713. He continued his education at the University of Edinburgh, where he studied philosophy and theology, and it was there that he developed an immediate distaste for the secularism that had been gaining in popularity at European universities influenced by Enlightenment philosophy.

Raised by his father in accordance with stern Calvinist orthodoxy, John's early disposition and intellectual focus made him a natural candidate for the ministry. However, holding the pastoral office in the highest regard, he doubted his talents and believed himself inadequately prepared to take on a minister's duties. He was also plagued by a deep sense of spiritual uncertainty. While his studies had confirmed his belief in the doctrines of the Scottish Church, his feelings of spiritual and intellectual inadequacy restrained him from pursuing a ministerial career. His friends and several well-respected figures in the church encouraged him to seek the ministry, and take the "trials" as a licentiate. He continued to dither, however. "My uneasiness in all respects," he later wrote, "was evident to me, and I was therefore truly averse from it." His friends maintained their encouragement, and Glas underwent the trials administered by the Presbytery of Dunkeld, receiving his probationary license on 20 May 1718. According to Robert Wodrow, who chronicled this early phase of Glas's career as part of a larger history of the Scottish clergy, Alexander Glas disapproved of his son's apparently lackluster performance in the trials. Nine months later John was called to succeed Hugh Maxwell as pastor to the church and parish at Tealing, and was appointed to the post by the Presbytery of Dundee on 4 March 1719, formally receiving ordination two days later.[11]

Tealing was in 1719 and remains a disparate parish measuring three miles long and two miles wide, lying on the south side of the Seidlaw (or Sidlaw) Hills approximately five miles from Dundee. At the time Glas assumed his duties, the population of the parish numbered between seven hundred and eight hundred people settled in the hamlets of Churchton, Newbigging, Balkello, and Todhills. Setting aside his earlier doubts, Glas entered his new position in hopes of proving himself a faithful minister of the Church of Scotland and a worthy successor to his paternal line's glittering clerical reputation. Spiritual religion had long been declining in early eighteenth-century Scotland, and what interest it did elicit manifested itself in concern for the externals of religion, the maintenance of the Covenants and the Establishment, the security of the Presbyterian polity, and the rights of the people as opposed to patronage, rather than evangelical zeal and the pursuit of spiritual culture. Glas closely followed these issues, and considered himself an orthodox Presbyterian and supporter of the National Church, believing that Presbyterianism was more in accord with the New Testament than either episcopacy or independency. Glas began his ministry with a determination to make the Word of God his sole rule of conduct, and it never occurred to him that adherence to such a rule could ever bring him into collision with the laws and standards of the church.[12]

Glas immediately noticed the underdeveloped spiritual condition of his parish, due to the advanced politicization of Presbyterianism. He also confronted substantial hostility against the National Church, principally from those who held to Cameronian theology, and these Covenanters gave him the most trouble. They exhibited a frosty suspiciousness of him, attending his sermons not out of any genuine desire for religious edification, but to confirm their prejudices and discover the new minister's doctrinal inconsistencies. Establishment ministers who demonstrated the greatest zeal in maintaining the binding obligation of the Covenants attained for themselves some popularity, but Glas did not manifest such fervor and was consequently regarded as lukewarm on matters of critical magnitude. His main concern was the spiritual wellbeing of his parishioners, whom he had heard described as "an ignorant and ungodly people"; an assessment he reluctantly concurred with and blamed on the inadequacy of his predecessor. When queried as to his apparent refusal to preach against episcopacy, he averred that "if they were once Christians, it were then perhaps time to speak of that." Through special sermons and private catechizing he attempted to educate his parishioners in the truths of the Christian faith as he understood them. He began a course of evening lectures on issues pertaining to the Shorter Catechism, which in their turn prompted him to much introspection. This led him to reevaluate his conception of his faith and the ministry as necessarily depending on a simple reliance on the example of Christ.[13]

This resonates with a movement then gaining prominence in central Europe known as Pietism. Rooted in a rejection of the steady influence of scientific rationalism in Protestant theology that encouraged the reconciliation of faith with reason, Pietism reasserted the mystical spirituality of the Christian religion and insisted that faith superseded reason, and that Christians embrace those aspects of religion that seemed most irrational. Groups of Pietists sought to recapture the flavor and core ecclesiology of first-century Christianity, gravitating toward higher and higher levels of mysticism and millenarianism as they established experimental communities grounded in strict spiritual egalitarianism. A parallel movement looking back to a medieval mysticism, sectarian groups called *collegia*—mainly of Anabaptists—gathered to indulge in free prophecy, apocalypticism, and an ecstatic form of *imitatio Christi* that bordered on perfectionism. The mysticism of the Collegiants fed into a movement that came to be known as theosophy, innovated by Valentine Weigel (1533–1588), who emphasized the indwelling of the Spirit of God in the heart of the believer to the extent that he argued on behalf of an almost literal unity between God and the individual at the highest level of religious experience. In what would become a characteristic of Pietism, Weigel exhorted "true" Christians to put off worldly concerns in absolute surrender to God and the cultivation of the spiritual life. Jacob Böhme (1575–1624), a devotee of Weigel, distressed by the outbreak and viciousness of the Thirty Years War (1618–1648), declared the argument between reason and revelation to be a dead letter, when true life could only be discovered in the "vital piety" of the heart that calmed the spirits of a people traumatized by the experience of war. Certain pockets of persecuted English Puritans likewise found refuge in a form of Pietism, the greatest expounders of which were Lewis Bayly (c.1575–1631) and Richard Sibbes (1577–1635), who variously exhorted Christians to devote themselves entirely to living their lives in as faithful an *imitatio Christi* as could be humanly possible. The culmination of English Pietism came with Jeremy Taylor (1613–1667), whose books *The Rule and Exercises of Holy Living* (1650) and its sequel *The Rule and Exercises of Holy Dying* (1651) argued that the ideal Christian life (and death) is and must be beautiful, the essence of which "was sweetness, reasonableness, and implicit trust in a good God of whom all creation speaks to the devout spirit." In Germany, Philipp Jakob Spener

(1635–1705) and his disciple August Hermann Francke (1663–1727) harnessed the individualism and populism of the Reformation to campaign for spiritual regeneration and social justice, innovating an activist form of Protestantism at Halle.[14]

Given the inhospitable environment into which he assumed his duties, it comes as no surprise that Glas's preaching originally met with little positive response—so little, in fact, that he began to question the wisdom of his entering the ministry. The Cameronian faction in his church continued to impede his efforts, and constituted a perennial source of disciplinary problems. Cases of chastisement were numerous, and some parishioners openly begrudged his sternness. Determined to make a favorable impression, he began to succeed through the intensity of his preaching, his personal character, and ministerial compassion. His growing fame and reputation as a preacher gradually silenced his critics, and won some of them to his side. People from neighboring parishes began traveling to hear his sermons, and on occasions when he journeyed to more distant places to assist fellow ministers, the churches would be filled with people who came specifically to hear him. Despite his rising reputation, the Cameronians remained a thorn in his side, and Glas "resolved, if possible, to be at the bottom of this controversy." This led him to a deep consideration of Question 26 of the Shorter Catechism, "How doth Christ execute the office of a king?" The result would change his ministry and his life.[15]

He came to the conclusion that the kingdom of Christ is essentially a spiritual one, and must be completely independent of state authority and control, as well as of the support of secular government. He declared that he "had done with national covenanting," and his preaching and catechizing revealed this new perspective, which set him at even greater odds with the Cameronian faction, and made many others uncomfortable. It was not his intention to spark controversy, and it would have remained purely a local matter were it not for another contentious episode. James Traill, the minister at Montrose, subscribed to a public donation to construct a proposed Episcopal church there. The Covenanters stridently denounced him as a defector to the Episcopalian cause, and charged before the presbytery of encouraging malevolent elements seeking to build what they considered a "synagogue of Satan." The Covenanters made a great deal of hay out of the issue, and at a synod John Willison, minister at Dundee, and James Goodsir, minister at Monikie, pressed the issue in a manner that strongly favored the Covenanters. The presbytery attempted to prevent a threatened mass defection to the Cameronians by appealing to the General Assembly for a renewal of the Covenants. At this critical moment Glas was called to assist James Kerr of Dun at a sacrament in his parish, where he took the opportunity of urging the people "to submit to their Minister and strengthen his Hands," so anxious was he to avoid further controversy and preserve the unity of the church.[16]

The movement toward secession was forestalled by the death in 1723 of John Hepburn, the ardent Covenanter who had come into conflict with both ecclesiastical and secular authorities, and whose Hebronite faction maintained a doctrinal position very similar to that of the Cameronians. However, in 1725, the presbytery required its members to sign the Formula of 1711, which bound subscribers to that document as a confession of their own faith, and was meant to reassert the authority of the presbyteries and synods of the Church of Scotland. Francis Archibald, the minister at Guthrie and a Cameronian sympathizer, refused to sign and submitted a paper listing the deviations of the church from the Covenants. A petition was drafted and circulated at Angus and Mearns supporting the option of secession. Glas harbored grave concerns about a movement that he considered "the most effectual way to ruin the interest of the gospel in this country." He resolved to speak his mind on the controversy, declaring that "[I] thought myself bound no longer to forbear, and reckoned it my duty to give the people, as far as I had access, some information upon that point; even as I myself had been taught."[17]

His thinking about the nature and constitution of the church subsequently underwent further refinement as a result of the Covenanter crisis. Stemming from a belief in the essential spirituality of the church, he came to the conclusion that such an institution must be composed of true believers who possessed a real experience of saving grace, who, in compliance with the will of Christ, felt an inevitable compulsion to separate themselves from the world. These happened to be the ecclesiological principles of the English Independents—the Congregationalists—who upheld the necessary establishment of "gathered churches" composed of "visible saints" as separate from "mixed" congregations. Alexander Glas, as he lay dying, confided to John that he had always thought his son an Independent at heart, and predicted that, like Ishmael, "his hand would be against every man, and every man's hand against him." Thomas Black, John's father-in-law, likewise advised him that "he was fighting in vain, for what he aimed at never would or could take place." John's reply was that if he could find a dozen shepherds at the foot of "Seidla-hill [sic]" to join with him that he would be contented. While some counseled Glas to keep his views to himself and not risk censure or the official revocation of his ministry, his wife Catherine and a handful of his parishioners encouraged him to stand by his principles and be unafraid to express them. He formed a fellowship—an *ecclesiola*—of approximately a hundred like-minded individuals from within his church and from other parishes on 13 July 1725. They "agreed to join together in Christian profession, to follow Christ the Lord, as the righteousness of his people, and to walk together in brotherly love, and in the duties of it, in subjection to Mr. Glas, as their overseer in the Lord." They also pledged to observe the sacrament of the Eucharist once every month. At their next meeting on 12 August the principle set down in Matthew 18 was adopted to punish offenses, and in December they established a fund for the relief of impoverished members. Later they decided to hold weekly meetings for prayer and mutual exhortation that eventually evolved into formal worship services. Though Glas did not think that he had formed a church within his church—a charge his opponents began to hurl at him with venomous abandon—it was the beginning of the Glasite movement.[18]

That he had strayed dangerously close to independency was certainly not lost on Glas himself, and this impelled him to study the differences between the Independents and Presbyterians. It gradually dawned on him that his doctrinal beliefs lay with the former and no longer with the latter. He made little effort to hide this fact, as evidenced by increasing and very public conflicts with several of his colleagues. At a fast-day service near Dundee, James Goodsir firmly upheld the Covenants, and in private conversation with John Willison, Glas complained about the highly political tone of the sermon. In his own sermon the following day he considered "the mistaken notion of the nature of Christ's kingdom, as if it were of this world, and came with observation, and as if his servants were to fight for him, taking him by force to make him king." Later at Dundee he declared that the setting up of any covenant other than Christ's promoted factional divisions among God's people. This sermon certainly appeared to some to be an attack on the Covenants, particularly by Willison, who soon proposed to Glas that the issue should be discussed in writing.[19]

Francis Archibald, a minister at Guthrie in the Presbytery of Arbroath, was at this time leaning toward Cameronian beliefs as a result of the presbytery's requiring him to sign the Formula of 1711, which he refused to do, and in December 1725 he wrote to Glas asking for a further explication of his views on the Covenants. Glas's reply began the controversy for which he was hauled before the ecclesiastical courts, and indeed it was so explosive that his friends persuaded him not to send it, but to invite Archibald to a private meeting to discuss the issues raised in it. They could not come to terms of agreement, and in the meantime the letter was circulated privately among a small circle of friends. During the winter of 1725–1726, Willison informed Glas that he was willing to ignore the question of the Covenants if Glas would support him on other issues, to which Glas retorted that he was not going to be drawn into cliques and factions within the church. Willison became vehemently antipathetic to Glas, making dark intimations and harshly critical remarks about him, even to some of Glas's close friends. Intramural politics so outraged Glas, a fury exacerbated by continued overtures promising to overlook his doctrinal nonconformities, that he resolved to expound upon the subject of the Covenants in a sermon delivered at the Strathmartine parish church on 6 August 1726. He proceeded to speak of Christ in his threefold role as prophet, priest, and king, reminding his audience that Christ's kingdom was a spiritual one and not of this world, meaning that secular governments have no authority to govern in religious affairs anymore than church bodies have authority to rule in secular affairs. He proclaimed his unwavering loyalty to the witness of the apostles who had insisted on the spiritual nature of Christ's kingdom against the "Judaisers" who advocated on behalf of a temporal kingdom. However, referring to the early church leaders, he added "as far as they contended for any such national covenants as whereby Christ's kingdom should be of this world, his Church and the world mingled together, and his people who are of the truth, and hear his voice, divided from one another, and such as he hath not appointed under the New Testament, but set aside; so far they were not enlightened."[20]

Willison proceeded to the pulpit upon the completion of Glas's sermon. He adamantly avowed his support for the National Covenant, which he depicted as "the glory of Scotland," the product of an effusion of God's Spirit upon all people; that it was for the Covenants the martyrs had fought, suffered, and sacrificed their lives. He went on to lament that the martyrs were obviously so lightly esteemed, and not just by certain laymen, but by certain Church of Scotland clergy as well. Any opposition to the Covenants, Willison averred, constituted opposition to the National Church and a national confession of faith. He concluded his sermon with "an exhortation to pray for a revival of God's work through a renewal of the Covenants." Due to Willison's broadcasting of his antagonism to Glas, people from all around Strathmartine parish packed the church to hear the combatants duel, and they were not disappointed. Willison had pushed Glas into a spotlight, even if he did not have to put much effort into doing so, since Glas had become increasingly dogmatic and pugnacious in his self-defense and justification of his opinions.[21]

The Presbytery of Dundee met precisely one month after the sermons at Strathmartine, and Willison presided over the opening of the proceedings there, taking the opportunity to reprove those in the church who were dissatisfied with the Covenants and had introduced novel doctrines. National covenanting, he averred, is sanctioned in both the Old and New Testaments, though he chose to defer to the judgment of church authorities on the issue. Willison made clear to everyone in attendance his intention to advertise before the presbytery the controversy that had pitted himself against Glas the previous month, and when Glas was called to offer his opinions, he bristled at the thinly veiled references to himself in Willison's address. Once the ordinary business of the presbytery had been concluded, Willison and Glas were invited to elaborate upon their positions in greater detail. Willison referenced an Act of Assembly requiring the expulsion of those who spoke against the Covenants. However, he suggested magnanimously that Glas might only merit censure rather than a humiliating deposition. Glas's reply noted that by charging him with opposition to church doctrine Willison had mentioned the National Covenant without reference to the equally binding Solemn League and Covenant, and that if Willison ignored the obligation of the latter, he too was guilty of opposition to the church. Challenged to declare himself on this point before the presbytery, Willison refused on the grounds that he was under no obligation to answer Glas's question, and that the presbytery should act in a judicial capacity. This was refused; the consensus among the presbyters was that the matter should go before the judicatories, after which Glas accounted for his doctrines espoused at Strathmartine, thus sparking a heated exchange between him and Willison. Glas decided that friendly, or at least rational, discussion was no longer possible with Willison, and the latter stormed out of the meeting along with his supporters.[22]

Ministers throughout southeastern Scotland began aligning themselves along pro- and anti-Glas lines, with his opponents waging a campaign to discredit him and call into doubt his Presbyterian orthodoxy. Here Willison and Goodsir stood at the forefront, baiting Glas into a war of words over the nature and authority of the Covenants. The presbytery ordered Glas to hold his peace on the issue in the hope that the controversy would either sort itself out or simply fade away, but Glas refused to keep silent, and publicly defended his preaching as neither contrary to the gospels nor inconsistent with the principles of the Establishment. He also rejected the order of silence, which he argued gave his enemies free rein to libel him and destroy his ministry without recourse to self-defense. Willison contended that Glas had started the controversy and accused him of perpetuating it to his advantage—in essence, running a smear campaign against Willison and his supporters—while Glas laid the blame solely on Willison. The presbytery resolved in

November 1726 to use "smooth methods" to "keep him [Glas] quiet." They were not destined to be successful.[23]

James Adams, minister of Kinnaire in Gowrie, addressed twenty-six queries on the issue of the Covenants to Glas in a pamphlet published in early 1727, which received by way of reply three anonymous letters of which Glas was the suspected author. While Glas admitted that he was familiar with Adams's queries, he disavowed authorship of the letters, and believed that their author was not in fact a minister in the Church of Scotland. Concerned that a stranger had volunteered to speak for him, Glas replied directly to Adams in a series of sixty-three counter queries.[24] This exchange came to the attention of the presbytery of Dundee, and Willison supplied the body with a copy of one of the letters Glas had written to Francis Archibald that argued that the Covenants were incompatible with the nature of Christ's kingdom. Willison insisted that Glas represented merely the tip of a dangerous iceberg of anti-Establishment sentiment, and that the church could suffer devastating schisms if the dissidents were not dealt with quickly through official action. The Synod of Dundee, meeting at Arbroath in April 1727, proved itself reluctant to force its ministers to sign new confessions of faith that reaffirmed the Covenants, preferring to see the controversy as a minor one involving principally two quarrelling ministers and their small bands of supporters. The synod solicited Archibald for his thoughts on the matter, and he confirmed that disaffection with the National Church had led to separatist movements, and that he agreed with Glas's criticisms of the Covenants, though both he and Glas professed not to be nascent schismatics. Glas formally addressed the synod after Archibald, and suggested that the Covenants be clarified through redefinition. Did they entail only the National Covenant and the Solemn League and Covenant, or did they also include the Confession of Faith and the Formula of 1711? Also, what exactly was the relationship of the church to the government, and was any such relationship in conformity with the dictates of the gospels? Glas's questions served to bring more ministers critical of the Covenants out into the open, and there ensued a flurry of pamphlet- and letter-writing on the subject between the dissidents and the defenders of the Covenants. The latter began accusing Glas of adhering to independency, and Willison published a book, *The Afflicted Man's Companion* (1728), which in its preface impugned Glas and his supporters (though not by name) as "breaking down the excellent forms of our reformation, viz. our covenants, confessions, and [the] magistrate's power, &c." Glas and his clerical supporters often addressed the controversy in their sermons, further identifying themselves in contrast to their opponents, with an inevitable hardening of positions. At this point, church leaders began to scrutinize Glas and call him to account for his apparent dissident opinions.[25]

Argument and Judgment

The Synod of Angus and Mearns, meeting at Montrose in October 1727, set out to investigate those ministers suspected of expressing views contrary to the purity of church doctrine. A committee requested Glas's presence and informed him that various rumors of his heterodoxy had been swirling about him, most of which Glas managed to dismiss. The committee then examined him with regard to his teaching and ministry, asking him whether or not he had argued that "the covenant of grace was substantially or essentially different under the Old Testament and under the New." He refused to answer on the grounds that the questions were ignorantly put, and when the committee members rebuked him for his reticence, he offered that he would gladly answer any relevant questions. He further announced that he was not ashamed of his principles and had prepared himself to defend them to whatever degree necessary. Convinced that he had no intention of answering their questions satisfactorily, the committee suggested that the synod instruct the Presbytery of Dundee to "make strict inquiry concerning the deportment of the said Mr. Glas," and if there existed sufficient grounds "to proceed against him," then it should apply to the Commission of the General Assembly for counsel, and then report to the next synod at Brechin in April 1728 "until the said affair be absolutely finished." Glas opined that he considered the investigation a personal slander, but that he expected to be exonerated in due course.[26]

On 26 March 1728 the presbytery of Dundee, acting on the advice of a subcommittee of the Commission of the General Assembly, cited John Glas and required him to subscribe his adherence to the Confession of Faith and the Formula of 1711, and to renounce publicly in writing the errors of which he had been accused. "I am not careful to answer you in that matter, let the consequences be what they will," he began, but "if I were made sensible of any errors that I have vented or taught, I would reckon it my honour judicially to renounce them, but until that be, I must be excused from renouncing them." He went on to declare that while his faith was contained in the Confession, he would not subscribe for two reasons. He argued that the Formula required him to affirm that the government of the National Church by church sessions, presbyteries, provincial synods, and general assemblies is founded on biblical precedent, whereas his study of the scriptures led him to conclude that the Presbyterian order as then defined lacked the warrant of divine authority, though at the same time he did not disclaim the legal establishment, "seeing, as he takes it, that establishment does not settle [the constitution of the National Church] upon the foundation of the word of God." His second justification for his refusal to subscribe he based on the Confession, which acknowledges the authority of the civil magistrate in the maintenance of church order and doctrine and the suppression of heresies and abuses, with power to call and to attend synods for that purpose, none of which was sanctioned by the New Testament. Therefore, he insisted, the magistrate has no authority over the kingdom of Christ, which is spiritual and not temporal. He did, however, express his openness to conviction from the gospels on these matters.[27]

The Presbytery of Dundee then read out the formal list of charges of doctrinal error against Glas and called him to answer them, to which he replied that the time for his statement would come only after the court had examined his accusers. He added that he had publicly doubted that the Formula had the sanction of Christ as a test of admission to the ministry. A report was prepared by the presbytery and presented to the synod at Brechin in April 1728, and the synod prepared a list of twenty-six queries for Glas to answer in time for the synod's next session. Although the questions are quite comprehensive and must have taken considerable time to compose, Glas was only given a few hours to prepare his answers. They were intended to bring the whole controversy to a head, and to force Glas to state his position clearly and unequivocally. The queries related to matters such as the power of the civil magistrate within the sphere of religion, the use of the secular arm in the defense of the church, the inherent nature of the church, the biblical sanction for national covenanting, the place and authority of the local congregation, the membership of the church, the qualifications for admission to Communion, and the religious education of children. They left absolutely no room for ambiguity or equivocation, and Glas's answers were just as clear, forming the solid foundation of what became Glasite and Sandemanian doctrine.[28]

Glas maintained that as the kingdom of Christ was not of this world, the civil magistrate as such had no authority in the Church; that the kingdom of Christ could not be advanced by earthly power or defended by arms or civil sanctions; that the Covenants had no warrant in either the Old or the New Testaments, and that the first Christian churches were congregational churches; that the members of the visible church were those whose Christian character was revealed in obedience to the law of Christ; that none should be admitted to Communion without the consent of the congregation, and that the admission of known unbelievers tarnishes the fellowship; that "A congregation, or Church of Jesus Christ, with its presbytery, is, in its discipline, subject to no jurisdiction under heaven." The last query read, "Do you think yourself obliged in conscience, to teach and publish these your opinions, differing from the received doctrine of this Church, unto the people?" To this Glas replied,

> I think myself obliged in conscience to declare every truth of Christ, and keep nothing back, but to speak all the words of this life, and to teach his people to observe all things whatsoever he commands, so far as I can understand; and that, notwithstanding of others their differing from me, and my being exposed to hazard in the declaring of them.

When asked about his scruples in renewing his subscription to the Confession of Faith, Glas icily answered that "I have not freedom to refuse any thing in our Confession, but what relates to the passage already mentioned in the chapter concerning Christian liberty, and liberty of conscience, and in the chapter concerning synods." Some of Glas's supporters later questioned his wisdom in answering the queries, that by so doing he only encouraged his opponents, namely, Willison, to which he replied that although he considered the Court's procedure illegal, he believed it his duty to confess his principles.[29]

The synod read the queries and Glas's answers to them, and ten ministers were assigned to meet with Glas in the hopes of recovering him from his doctrinal errors before the court passed a sentence of censure upon him. Five other ministers weighed the evidence for or against censure. Upon the completion of the interview with Glas, the synod reassembled, rendering a judgment that Glas had abrogated his ministerial duties and insisted upon maintaining his heterodoxy, as well as refusing to keep silent about it. The synod resolved to censure Glas because his opinions "tend to make a rent in the church of Christ and to overturn our constitution." Following a prayer seeking illumination on the matter, Glas was asked if he had anything further to say on his behalf before the sentence of censure was passed, to which he answered that he could not in good conscience take back or amend anything he had already said. A majority vote resulted in his suspension from the ministry until the next ordinary meeting of the synod. In the meantime an informal effort to recover Glas from his errors continued. It was hoped that the prospect of a relaxation of the suspension might encourage Glas to recant and thus recover him from heterodoxy. Adamantly, Glas declared his intention to appeal the ruling at the next General Assembly, which was to meet in Edinburgh on 2 May. The parish church in Tealing was informed of the suspension on 28 April.[30]

The General Assembly read Glas's nine-page appeal on 11 May 1728. In it he took exception to the manner in which the issue was brought before the synod; that proceedings against him should have originated in the presbytery of which he was a member; that his judges gave undue weight to his opponents' presentations of evidence without proper investigation; that the Synod of Brechin had not followed accurate procedure in suspending him so quickly; that the suspension emanated from political concerns and not doctrinal matters, about the latter he affirmed his correctness; and that Episcopalian clerics after the Revolution Settlement had not been suspended or deposed on account of their principles. He and a few of his supporting parishioners attempted to have the suspension rescinded, yet despite filing petitions signed by colleagues and parishioners, Glas remained intransigent in repeated interviews with members of a subcommittee exhorting him to retract his theologically wayward opinions. He had also continued to preach, the synod learned, demonstrating a defiance of the Establishment that led the synod to consider a sentence of prohibition against him. "While the vote was passing, I could not tell which of the two [suspension or prohibition] I should choose," Glas confided to his journal. He went on to say that

> I desired to reverence the Providence, that I should not continue in this church, but, being thus thrust out, I might have liberty to follow the institution of Christ, which I now saw they would not allow me to follow, and live at peace, and preach among them. What will be the issue, He only knows who has all power in heaven and in earth.... My mind was kept rankling against my enemies, and was more light and easy after this determination of the commission; and I saw nothing from the word of God to hinder me going on to preach.

He was brought before a committee of the Synod of Dundee on 30 July 1728, where he challenged the authority of the committee to adjudicate as though the full synod were present. The committee rejected his objection and adjourned to consider the evidence until 7 August, at which he was to attend. He chose not to appear, but wrote a letter restating his objections and abjuring the necessity of his attendance. In the meantime, he had begun to compose an account of the affair in *A Narrative of the Rise and Progress of the Controversy about the National Covenants*

(Dundee, 1728) and *A Continuation of Mr. Glas's Narrative* (Edinburgh, 1729) to publicize his cause.[31]

On 8 August a subcommittee examined more thoroughly Glas's answers to some of the queries that they found to be contrary to the Confession of Faith. Concerning the other matters remitted to the committee it decided not to proceed but to suggest that it "request the presbytery of Dundee to consider Mr. Glas's practices in contemning the sentence of the church against him, form a libel thereon, lead probation thereof, and have that affair ripe against the meeting of the synod." The committee approved the report in the first week of September, and determined that there remained no further requirement to hold any continued discourse with Glas on the matter, but unofficially offered to meet with him, provided he resigned himself to submission to the synod's sentence and hold his peace until an overall consensus could be reached. Glas responded with an admission that he remained open to consultation, but that he had grave concerns about the censorious remarks the committee made in reference to his answers to the queries. He had defied the synod in continuing to preach and in refusing to consider their admonitions, relegating what followed to foregone conclusions.[32]

Glas's behavior at subsequent meetings of the synod and its committees reveal a man growing increasingly defensive, using his knowledge about the rules of procedure against the various bodies' actions in a futile attempt to avoid the inevitable. He refused to stop preaching, "resolved," according to Robert Wodrow, "to breake all squares with the Church, and set up upon his own leggs on the Independent way." He also hinted that he would not recognize a negative judgment of him, even as he told the synod that he was willing to speak with individual ministers and listen to their entreaties for him to return to orthodoxy. His words suggest that he was teetering on the edge of independency, while his actions clearly demonstrated that he had already abandoned Presbyterianism. In his dealings with the synod he pressed his contentions that church and state authority could not dictate to congregations and that ecclesiastical courts—such as the one trying him—had no foundation or warrant in the gospels. He depicted the case against him as a persecution that belied the politicized nature of the National Church that threatened its existence as a true church of God. He trusted that the authority of Christ would always outweigh the authority and prestige of any church, and insisted that the National Church as a whole indict him in order for all of Scotland to witness the church's heterodoxy.[33]

The libel case was brought before the presbytery of Dundee on 5 September 1728 and ran for a month. It asked Glas if he had complied with the sentence of suspension passed against him, to which Glas replied that the current process against him should properly begin at the synodical level, but, even so, the facts had to be cleared according to the rules of the church. The presbytery drew up the libel charge, which consisted of Glas's refusal to stop preaching and the administration of the sacraments at Tealing and in neighboring parishes, for which he merited censure. At the next meeting on the 18 September, Glas presented some answers to the new charge, along with a request for representation by George Miller, the Perth town clerk, which was granted. Miller took advantage of mistakes made in drawing up the documents to invalidate the libel charge, while Glas read a lengthy statement raising his objections to the proceedings against him. He admitted to not being learned on matters of ecclesiastical law, but insisted that the rules of the church should be based on the Bible. If such were the case, Glas declared, the foundation of the charges against him would not exist, and that the ecclesiastical courts had failed to prove that his stated opinions—particularly his answers to the queries—were doctrinally erroneous. He pointed out that the Commission of the Assembly had admitted that insufficient means had been used to reclaim him from his supposed errors, even as it proclaimed his answers to the queries inconsistent with the Word of God and the Confession.[34]

Concerning the issue of doctrinal error, Glas affirmed that even if he happened to be in error, Christ could not be shown to have authorized the suspension or censure of a minister on such an account. He confessed to an ignorance of the prospect that the Church of Scotland's ministers expected or even claimed infallibility, though obviously it seemed that they were reaching for it. Until the Presbytery was convinced that it had divine authority to inhibit him on account of doctrinal error, he hoped that it would not consider the synod's sentence warranted by the gospels. Moreover, instead of preventing him from espousing only those opinions that appeared inconsistent with church doctrine, the sentence attempted to cease the exercise of his ministry altogether, which also had no gospel authority. To forbid a messenger of Christ from performing his duties must involve rigorous examination of the evidence and judgment by a unanimous synod, and the sentence passed against him involved only a small majority acting against strong opposition. He generously harbored no ill will against the ministers comprising the Presbytery of Dundee and the ecclesiastical courts, some of whom he admitted were good men acting in the best interests of the church, but he uttered an ominous warning against the rise and growth of a persecuting spirit intolerant to any differences of opinion. His ultimate responsibility, he reminded them, was to God and not to men, and that he must see the entire presbytery judge him rather than a single party within it. The presbytery considered

Glas's statement, but decided to sustain the libel charge against him, to which Glas retorted that he felt no obligation to acknowledge any alleged facts presented during the case, essentially challenging the presbytery to secure witnesses against him.[35]

His strategy worked, as the Presbytery of Dundee had great difficulty compelling Glas's parishioners to testify against him, finally calling upon the power of local government officials to bring in a handful of witnesses. They were questioned on 23 September 1728, but the testimony of the first several was unsurprisingly weak, while one Bailie Lyon refused to testify and thereby assist in the "quenching [of] a great light in the corner." The rest followed Lyon's example, and the hearings were adjourned until 9 October, when twenty-one additional witnesses were assembled but refused to be questioned. The matter was handed over to the Synod of Dundee, which met the following week, and there Glas remained steadfast in his conviction that the proceedings were not about silencing him for holding unorthodox ecclesiological views, but about destroying his career and reputation in order to eradicate dissent of whatever stripe. The synod appointed yet another deputation to "reclaim" him, and Glas refused to meet them on the grounds that it was a contradiction for the synod to try to bring him back into the fold even as it was preparing to censure him. The synod dropped the proposal, and composed a summary of the case so far and its justifications for censuring him, charging him with seven specific offenses: (1) that Glas asserted that there was no scriptural foundation for the government of the national church; (2) that he refused to subscribe to the Confession of Faith, owing to his doubts respecting the magistrate's power in church affairs, and the passage regarding liberty of conscience and synods; (3) that he maintained that the Old Testament examples did not furnish a warrant for magistrates acting for the reformation of religion and the suppression of false worship; (4) that he held that the kingly office of David and his successors was ecclesiastical; (5) that he asserted that there was no warrant for covenanting in the Word of God; (6) that he held there was no authority in the New Testament for a national church, and that a single congregation with its presbytery and discipline were subject to no jurisdiction under heaven; and (7) that he regarded it as unwarrantable to take parents engaged to educate their children, when baptized, according to the Confession of Faith. The synod concluded that Glas had never retracted his alleged errors, and that any hope for his reclamation had been lost.[36]

The synod called Glas to stand before it and hear its judgment on 15 October 1728, where he was offered one last opportunity to speak for himself. He declined, apart from declaring his readiness for whatever the verdict might be, though by this time he and everyone else knew what to expect. The members of the synod read him the letter of the Act of the Assembly of 5 August 1648 stating that "If any suspended minister, during his suspension, exercise any part of his ministerial calling, that he be deposed." The synod then voted to "depose the said Mr. John Glas from the office of the holy ministry, prohibiting and discharging him to exercise the same, or any part thereof, in all time coming, under the pain of the highest censures of the Church" despite four negative votes and several abstentions. Glas immediately filed an appeal with the Commission of the General Assembly, but it buried the case for a year until it agreed to hear his case on 11 March 1730. Before the assembly and many of his opponents and supporters he delivered a lengthy discourse on his differences with the National Church, which he justified using a deluge of biblical references. The vote of the commission, though close, upheld the deposition on the grounds that he held to doctrinal errors that he insisted on propagating despite the original suspension, as well as formed a schismatic group within his parish that attracted disciples from other parishes. Glas blamed the entire affair on the infiltration of politics into the church, believing that "all of them in this thing, were one way or another influenced by the spirit of persecution."[37]

Four of the elders from Glas's Tealing churches submitted a signed protest that very day against the sentence of the commission, declaring that they and the rest of the membership did not consider themselves as "in the least measure loosed" from their adherence to Glas's ministrations, and that parishioners from other districts were in accord with their rejection of the commission's decision. The next day, four ministers offered a more formal protest. It affirmed that the manner in which the answers to the queries, and later Glas's deposition, had been extracted and used as grounds for the suspension was contrary to established procedures. They complained that the commission had failed to take sufficient steps to allow adequate time to reclaim Glas, and that the synod should have dealt with this case in a superior ecclesiastical court. They insisted that the charges against Glas had not been conclusively proven and the sentence had been passed by a minority of the synod due to the abstentions from the vote. Finally, and most ominously, the deposition endangered the souls in Tealing parish thus deprived of a worthy minister.[38]

What had so alarmed the commission was not so much the doctrinal errors Glas had developed and preached, being only one man, but that he had attracted an impressive following that began to look increasingly like a separate church, complete with elders and an emerging ecclesiological structure that threatened the coherence of the National Church.

These "Glasites," as they were beginning to be called, had organized a few societies around the nuclear society at Tealing, and confirmed for many of Glas's opponents that his goal was to break away from the church altogether in a schismatic fashion. The deposition of Glas is also notable for being the first instance of such an action taken against a minister in the Reformed Church of Scotland. However, in 1739, the General Assembly revoked the sentence of deposition in order that he may remain "a minister of the gospel of Christ," but that "until he shall renounce the principles embraced and avowed by him, that are inconsistent with the constitution of this church," he not be esteemed a minister in the Church of Scotland. Despite the efforts of a few sympathizers who attempted to petition the assembly to restore his ministry in the church, Glas resolved not to recognize it, even were it to be forthcoming. The Glasite churches had grown impressively, and his doctrines and church discipline underwent the final stages of development.[39]

Glas maintained his ministry after his deposition, moving to Dundee where he began to draw up the rules of order and discipline for the Glasite church. The lack of a ministerial salary put him and his family in dire financial straits, but friends and members of his new church helped him keep poverty at bay with regular donations. He opened a bookstore in Dundee, and was gradually able to restore his fortunes. The Dundee church was attended by members from as far away as Perth and Edinburgh, which placed a hardship on those who had to travel the greatest distances.[40] Glas wanted to establish churches there, but there was no one who could serve as an elder or pastor apart from Francis Archibald, Glas's close friend and supporter. Standing on such relatively unstable ground, the first Glasite church suffered a shock that nearly destroyed it. In the summer of 1730, Glas went to Dunkeld for a brief sabbatical, and when circumstances prevented his returning to Dundee in time for the Sabbath, questions were raised whether the Communion could be observed without the presence of the pastor. Although the membership included men who had held the office of elder in the National Church, certain members insisted that they were ruling elders and not teaching elders; only the latter were qualified to administer the sacrament. Others contended that any elder has the authority to perform sacramental duties. According to Dr. John Owen, a member of the Dundee church, "such was the leaven of human authority on the minds of many, that it was kept up at intervals the whole day, without either party being convinced; and such was their state of mind at parting in the evening, that few expected they were ever to meet together again." Representatives from the two sides of the controversy were selected to find Glas in Dundee and confer with him. Glas returned with them to

Dundee without making a statement on the matter, resolving to consult the New Testament. An examination of Acts 20:17-18, I Timothy 3, and Titus 1 convinced Glas that the essential qualification of an elder was that he be "apt to teach," and that "ruling" elders who lacked this gift had no warrant in the New Testament. The majority of the congregation accepted this ruling, while those who dissented were separated from fellowship.[41]

Glas also concluded that there is no scriptural warrant for a learned ministry, and that any among the brethren who possessed high moral character, piety, and ministerial ability, regardless of education or prior status in another church, may be elders. This infuriated the established clergy, who defended the necessity of professional ministers and pronounced untrained teachers and preachers to be "unlearned babblers." John Willison, in a sermon before the Synod of Angus and Mearns, railed against this "sect which is lately risen among us, who decry the knowledge of human arts and sciences, and of the languages, as unnecessary for gospel-ministers, and therefore made choice of illiterate men for that office." Glas responded by pointing out several instances when the Church of Scotland acted in the same fashion, and that Glasite elders made no claims to being ministers of the National Church. Two weeks after Glas's letter to Willison, Alexander Morice, a weaver in the parish of Kettins, was cited before a kirk-session to answer a charge of inviting two Glasite elders "to make a shew of preaching" in a local barn. The summons, signed by the session clerk declared "That by the wholesome constitutions of this national church, and by the word of God itself, no man ought to intrude into the sacred office of the ministry, without being called and sent of God; nor ought they to be received into Christian houses, nor bid God speed."[42]

Reaction to the Glasites was not confined to clergymen, and did not always express itself in mere words. In 1733, a Glasite church was formed in Perth, and Glas, accompanied by a few friends, traveled from Dundee to attend the opening services. When the party, who had come by boat, landed at Perth they were met by an angry mob that not only greeted them with verbal abuse, but also pelted them with mud, rocks, garbage, offal, and a variety of other missiles. The local clergy were incensed at the founding of a sectarian meetinghouse in their midst, and one of their number went so far as to urge the magistrates to suppress the society. He went on to preach a sermon denouncing the Glasites with such inflammatory rhetoric that the agitated congregation proposed burning down the Glasite meetinghouse. Only the timely intervention of George Miller, the town clerk and Glas's advocate, prevented the incident. One overzealous woman became so enraged by the appearance of Glas on the street and the apparent lack of concern among passersby that she called out, "Why do they not rive him to pieces?" Such episodes of menace and violence were very rare, however, and once a Glasite church was founded in Edinburgh in 1734, there seemed to be as many such churches as there were ever likely to be.[43]

☙

John Glas never intended to break from the Church of Scotland when the long controversy over the Covenants erupted. He believed he was defending Presbyterianism against the contagion of politicization that clouded the true mission of Christianity as he thought Jesus Christ and the gospels defined it. However, it became increasingly clear to him that established Presbyterianism had inevitably fallen prey to worldliness and its corruptions, and thus abandoned its essential duty to humanity. Consequently, he rejected state-sponsored Christianity or any overlap or collaboration between church and state, which to his mind perennially compromised Christianity throughout its history. His drift into Independency, initially unconscious and later deliberate, allowed him to become the minister he originally imagined he would be, while his early doubts reflected uneasiness with the externals of religion that brought him into conflict with the Establishment. Expelled from his pulpit in Tealing but settled into new duties in Dundee, he delved deeper into study of the New Testament churches, fully developed his theology, and modeled the Glasite congregations on the apostolic example as gleaned from the Book of Acts.

⌘ 2 ⌘
"The Perfect Rule of the Christian Religion"
Glasite Doctrine and Ecclesiology

> [T]he Scriptures of the Old Testament as Christ and his apostles received them from the Jews, and gave them to Christians, with the scriptures of the New Testament, as we have them handed down to us, contain the complete revelation of the whole counsel of God, and are the perfect rule of the Christian religion; which is still to be found pure and entire in these.
>
> —John Glas, *Some Observations upon the Original Constitution of the Christian Church*

John Glas thought it unnecessary to codify his concepts of Christian doctrine and church discipline in a formal platform, since, as he interpreted, it the New Testament set it down definitively. Consequently, the student of Sandemanianism must derive them from Glas's theological writings and letters exchanged between him and his disciples. The experience with the ecclesiastical courts of the presbyteries and synods quickly disabused him of their validity in light of the scriptures, with the result that the Glasite churches were essentially Congregational in structure, and strictly Calvinist in theology. Since Glas considered the teachings of Christ and the practices of Pauline Christianity to be his ultimate foundation and rule, the Glasites qualify as "primitive" Christians.[1] Rather than developing in isolation, however, Sandemanianism was part of the broader North Atlantic phenomenon known as the First Great Awakening that began in the 1720s and flourished until the 1770s in the northern American colonies and in Great Britain.[2] It is noteworthy, however, that they were not evangelicals or enthusiastic Protestants, much less Pietists. In order to understand these sectarians, particularly when Robert Sandeman established Glasite congregations in prerevolutionary New England, it is necessary to devote this chapter to Glasite theology, church organization, and practice.

Theological Development

John Glas spent the majority of his life pondering the question of how a sinful person can obtain salvation and peace with God. He found solace in a realization of the sufficiency of divine grace manifested in the redemptive work of Jesus Christ, perfected in his atoning death on the cross. Therefore, Glas based his soteriology[3] on the premise that the sinner is justified before God only through Christ's perfect righteousness. "The whole scripture-revelation," he wrote, "centers in the death of Christ, that great fact whereby the counsel and purpose of God, for the declaration of his justice and mercy in the salvation of sinners, is executed." He delved into a deep study of the differences between the doctrines of John Calvin (1509–1564) and Jacobus Arminius (1560–1609) and concluded that the tenets of Arminianism were entirely unsupported by the scriptures. He went on to become a staunch advocate of salvation by sovereign grace, maintaining the Calvinist doctrine of particular redemption (limited atonement) as opposed to that of universal redemption, which was gaining popularity among liberal clergy. His study of the New Testament led him to argue that while there are passages in the apostolic writings that imply universal redemption, "the Apostles never intended the universal way of speaking of Christ's death should lead any to think he died for every one of mankind who fell in Adam." In their own day, the apostles saw comparatively few "partaking of the common salvation and blessedness," and so far from predicting that in the future the majority of any nation would become partakers thereof, they anticipated a repetition of what had happened among the Jews—that the greater majority would be blinded and fall, while the elect obtained the promised redemption.[4]

Glas buttressed his conclusion with reliance on the ninth chapter of Paul's letter to the Romans, in which the evangelist argued that God is absolutely free to either elect or reject nations or individuals as he pleases, and that no one can question the divine choice or the justice of it. "The gospel silences man's reason on this subject that is quite above it, by that humbling question 'Who art thou, O man, that repliest against God?'" Here Glas was echoing Calvin, who in the *Institutes of the Christian Religion* (1536) stated, "The will of God is the supreme rule of righteousness, so that everything which he wills must be held to be righteous by the mere fact of his willing it." God's power over his creation is not less than that of the potter over his clay. He may follow his own counsel as he wishes: "If God have mercy on whom he will, then he has not mercy on every one; and there must be some on whom he has not compassion, as Paul's brethren who were not called, like him, but separated from Christ." For Glas, the fundamental truth is the absolute sovereignty of God, and the doctrine of redemption, he argued, must be interpreted in light of this fact.[5]

In rejecting Arminianism, Glas reiterated the fundamental Lutheran doctrine of justification by faith alone (*solo fide*), that salvation cannot come through any action on the part of the individual (good works), which Arminius believed is a necessary component of spiritual development and salvation. In *Notes on Scripture Texts No. II*: "A Description of Justifying Faith" (1748), Glas expounded upon his defense of fideism. "God, who condemned all men to death for one transgression of his law, will never justify any man by what he can work in obedience to a law which he in any point transgresses." One can find neither fitness for nor hope of salvation within oneself, but must rest any hope solely on the testimony of Christ. This testimony is presented in the gospels and must be received by faith. "It is the business of faith to hear God's voice in revelation; and justifying faith comes by hearing, and hearing by the word of God." In *The Scheme of Justification by Faith* (1753), Glas held that this doctrine of justification, once central in the apostolic testimony, had long been dimmed and obscured. Even Paul complained about professors of the faith who adulterated the gospel, and Glas noted, "these perverters of the gospel were only a sample of that grand apostasy from the faith, under some profession of it, that was to come." The blame for this he placed squarely on the Roman church in the early centuries of officially sanctioned Christianity, and that not until the Reformation did the long-obscured doctrine of justification by faith alone resurface. Even among nominal Calvinists, Glas protested, the truth had been watered down, as churches relaxed restrictions on and requirements for church membership, as well as access to the sacraments. Glas maintained that despite differences on election and the perseverance of the saints, the Calvinists and Arminians were really at one with regard to justification, since they looked for grounds of confidence within themselves rather than from "the answer of a good conscience toward God by Christ's resurrection, as the spring of the Christian religion," which was the testimony of the apostles.[6]

While justification for Glas was a simple matter of faith, the matter of saving grace was quite a deceptively complicated one. It is neither more nor less than a belief of the truth or testimony of God concerning Jesus Christ passively received by the understanding. Therefore, it is not an act of the human will but the production of the divine spirit. In his early influential work *The Testimony of the King of Martyrs* (1729), Glas enunciated and expounded upon the conception of faith, which Robert Sandeman afterwards forcibly and militantly advocated in

Letters on Theron and Aspasio (1757). The truth of God's revelation in the incarnation of Jesus Christ imparted divinely, and reinforced by the testimony of the apostles, and that "this persuasion of this truth, upon the evidence of the divine testimony in it, is indeed that faith whereby we are justified, and eternally saved.... Thus the scripture-notion of faith agrees with the common notion of faith and belief among men, a persuasion of a thing upon testimony." According to Glas, this scriptural view of faith has frequently been deeply obscured by numerous attempts to describe it. Some definitions of faith have been so comprehensive as to include the whole of "gospel-obedience." Thus, faith has not only been confused with its concomitants or effects, but also represented in such a way as to make it a "work," an act on the part of the believer, whereas faith is the outcome of God's operation on the mind of the believer.[7]

In Glas's judgment, such a conception not only produces confusion in the minds of serious inquirers who are thereby led to look within themselves for evidence of faith, but also tends to militate against faith by begetting doubts and fears. The truth of the gospel is not dependent on an individual's inward state or feelings, but rests entirely on the divine testimony presented for acceptance. What the gospel offers is evidence of truth, which remains the truth even when not believed. The gospel is a testimony to be credited because it comes with divine authority. "Whosoever is verily persuaded of this truth that Christ bears witness unto, and that upon the credit of his testimony, and the evidence that it carries in itself, is of this truth; and this faith or belief is the fruit of the soul's being cast into the mould of that doctrine, without which no obedience can be given unto it." In his treatise on *The Usefulness of Catechisms Considered* (1736), Glas passed severe strictures on the definition of faith contained in the shorter catechism. This is one source of much confusion, for that definition "is the darkest of all, and doth not so much as make any express mention of that which the New Testament calls faith." One should obtain their definition of faith from the gospels, for there it "is more clearly and plainly described ... than in any catechism."[8]

Glas went on to assert that the common use of the words "receiving and resting, or coming or embracing, and trusting," imparts more into the idea of faith than the scriptures allow. These terms imply love and hope, "if they do not comprehend the exercise of all the graces of the gospel." He admitted that love and hope, also good works, are inseparably connected with faith, for in the scriptures they are clearly distinguished from it. "As I dare not, therefore separate those things which God hath conjoined in his word, so I am afraid to confound the things that he hath expressly distinguished. For this reason, I cannot approve of the definition of faith in the assembly's catechism." Faith may be described as "receiving," but as the receiving of a testimony as set out in I John 5:9–10, but this is very different from the sense implied in the shorter catechism, and in the common interpretation of it, which "takes in the exercise of all the graces that may be found in them that believe on his name," for "they would make it to signify any good disposition of heart toward Christ that you can name, rather than believing, or receiving the testimony of God concerning him." Glas summed up his view of faith as that represented in the New Testament rather than that concocted by the church, thus indicating his farther drift away from Presbyterianism and into Independency.[9]

Glas's critics accused him of Antinomianism,[10] of preaching a doctrine equivalent to the "faith of devils" as found in James 2:19, to which he responded by pointing out that there is a distinct contrast between the faith of the elect and the faith of devils as defined by James:

> I cannot find that James distinguishes the faith of God's elect here, from that of devils, by placing the nature of it in anything beside the belief of the truth of the gospel; but it is easy to perceive that he would have us shew our belief of the truth, to be of a different nature from their belief, by the fruits of it, good works.... [T]he true saving faith of the gospel, in the souls of men that are born of God (i. 18, 21), must be very different from the devils belief; because it produces good works, fruits of a very different nature from the fruit of the devils faith; and he would have the root distinguished by the fruits, as he says, "I will shew thee my faith by my works."

Glas interpreted James to say that religious profession without corresponding practice is worthless, but where zeal for unadulterated religion does correspond with zeal in profession, there can be no comparison with the "faith of devils." True faith will inevitably produce good works, being a natural by-product of proper Christian devotion, and no greater exemplar can be found than Jesus himself, whose life "was a work of grace and mercy to miserable sinners, to the worthless and wretched; for the end of it was to reconcile them to God. He went about always doing good, relieving the distressed." Glas insisted that "good works ... as the fruits and evidences of faith, are works of mercy and almsdeeds, to be done to all men, but especially to the household of faith." However, Glas did not limit the fruits of faith to works of mercy and almsgiving, but represented them as full conformity to Christ's example. The true Christian will take Christ as the ultimate model of the effects of faith and the sanctification it bestows. Thus, Glas boiled faith down to seven basic precepts, as typified by Christ's attitude and behavior: (1) the profession of the truth he believed, even at the cost of the world's hatred and contempt; (2) his dependence on the Father's revelation in the Word, which led him to despise the traditions of men; (3) his love of the truth and hatred for everything opposed to it; (4) his absolute sincerity manifested in the "perfect agreement betwixt the belief of his heart and the confession of his mouth"; (5) his humility and self-denial; (6) his hope of the joy set before him—a hope that sustained him in every affliction; and (7) his unfailing patience. Glas concluded that these effects are evident in the lives of all true believers in Christ, and the absence of them exposes those who are not of the elect.[11]

Alongside the issue of justification stood the tortured question of assurance: how could one be sensible of his justification and therefore assured of his salvation? Glas affirmed the strict Calvinist tenet that Christ died only for the elect, and that knowledge or assurance may be inferred from the promise of the Holy Spirit as the Comforter, the pressing exhortations to seek after assurance, and the directions given for its attainment. He was careful, though, to distinguish between the assurance of faith and the assurance of hope, declaring that it is useless to expect the latter until faith—the essential component—has been exercised. The foundation of hope is the assurance of faith, which can be nothing else than what is proposed in the gospels for acceptance of salvation. The assurance of hope is the fruit of faith, which originates not from any persuasion of personal interest in Christ or the certainty of salvation, but from the truth believed. The scriptural representation of such assurance as "the full assurance of understanding, to the acknowledgment of the mystery of God, and of the Father, and of Christ, Col. ii. 2. And what is that, but a full persuasion of the truth of which Christ speaks, when he says, 'Every one that is of the truth, heareth my voice?'" Glas denied any knowledge of justification except by the works or labors of love. The evidence on which the first Christians based their assurance of salvation was not the possession of any special gift or theophany, but the "charity, the fruit of faith, and the work and labor of that charity or love, without which there is no Christianity."[12]

Glas warned against the shadow of pride that threatens to make the Christian delight in his or her worth and distinction. Assurance cannot arise from the possession of any special powers, against the notion of which Jesus preached when he warned about false prophets speaking in his name who did not possess saving grace. Similarly, Paul acknowledged that some may possess great gifts without charity or grace, and in those instances of apostasy in the early church, it is clear that men are deceived by themselves and by others. Assurance cannot spring from the testimony of the gospels concerning the common salvation, for not everyone who hears the gospel is destined to be among the elect. It cannot come by reflection on the soundness of one's belief, without the love of the truth manifested in good works. Splendid outer works are no sign of assurance, for they are indicative of spiritual pride and self-righteousness, and the recollection of prior acts of devotion and charity constitute no basis for assurance unless one continues to perform them diligently and unselfishly. Those who continue "steadfastly in the work of faith and labour of love ... are in the straight way to the full assurance of hope." This, Glas added, dispels all doubt by the concurring testimony of two witnesses. First, one's conscience testifies as to whether one is walking in faith and love. However, as the testimony of conscience may waver, "the Holy Ghost comes in as another witness, corroborating the testimony of our spirit, and finishing the proof, by adding his own testimony; as the apostle says, 'The Spirit himself beareth witness with our spirit, that we are the children of God.'"[13]

Rather than allow one to develop a haughty self-righteousness in spite of the aforementioned pitfalls, Glas admitted that while the knowledge of personal justification is attainable, and that the Word of God testifies to the sufficiency of Christ's righteousness to justify the sinner, "we must not think that he who is thus certain of the sufficiency of Christ's righteousness to make him just, is yet assured, that this righteousness is imputed to him, and that he is made just by it." Glas suggested that the Christian's persuasion of Christ's power in justification is comparable to the faith which Jesus required in those who came to him for healing—a persuasion of his ability to heal. For instance, the leper said, "If thou wilt, thou canst make me clean." Though he believed in the power of Jesus to heal, he did not think that Jesus was under any obligation to heal *him*, and consequently placed himself at Christ's mercy. "He was fully persuaded of his ability to do it; and by this faith he was healed; for Jesus said, 'I will, be thou clean.'"[14] Robert Sandeman would echo this as well in his works, which to some extent recapitulate his mentor's writings, but incited enormous controversy.

GLASITE ECCLESIOLOGY

The system of Glasite church organization is essentially identical to Congregationalism—then known as Independency—though with some significant deviations. It most closely resembled the Puritanism espoused by William Bradshaw (1571–1618), and can be labeled as Presbyterian Independency due to the status accorded to church elders. However, the authority of the elders did not carry as great a weight among the Glasites as it did in other Independent denominations, and bore earmarks of patriarchal egalitarianism. This undoubtedly resulted from John Glas's negative experience with church hierarchies. Glas himself struggled with the question of just what the Glasites thought themselves to be, and ultimately rejected any efforts at self-identification or external definition beyond the terms "Christians" or "Disciples of Christ." He devised a system of church organization based on his close study of the New Testament, and the structures of the early Christian churches. He insisted that, according to New Testament usage, the term "church" applies only to the "mystic body of Christ" and to the visible expression of that body in a company of believers locally gathered and organized. Likewise, "church" and "congregation" are identical terms, hence "The whole nation of Israel is called a church ... [and] The catholic church of Christ, his holy nation and kingdom, the anti-type of that church of Israel, is also a congregation, having one place of worship, where they all assemble by faith, and hold communion." The coming of Jesus Christ abrogated the temporal covenant with Israel, so that "the church had passed out of the state of earthly nation ... and is now a glorious general assembly out of all nations; typified by that national assembly: for it is also a nation; but not earthly, not of this world; and so it very far exceeds the earthly nation." It was this conception of the spiritual nature of Christ's kingdom that led Glas to alter his views on the nature and constitution of gospel-churches.[15]

In the same way that the Puritan clergy sought to separate the "sheep" from the "goats"—the regenerate from the unregenerate—so also did Glas seek to distinguish between the church visible and the church invisible. Not all in a congregation are destined for redemption, and the true "one holy catholic church made up of all of them in heaven and on the earth that are born of the Spirit" will not be revealed "till Christ [re]appear[s]." Visible church members nonetheless enjoy access to the sacraments and Christian fellowship, and while the invisible church may exhibit itself in the humble and pious natures of its membership, Glas confessed that he did "not know of any visible face or form of a church upon the earth." Consequently, in Glas's estimation, there is no larger visible entity like that of the National Church or a worldwide ecclesiastical corporation: "We may have a metaphysical view of the universality of the visible members of the mystical body of Christ; but that this universality of visible members is, or ever was at any time, one visible church in a political sense, or one visibly organised body, is so far from being a truth, that it is evidently false in fact." Each New Testament church existed as its own independent entity within the mystical body of Christ, in Glas's interpretation, and he asserted that each congregation does not submit to an overarching secular or ecclesiastical authority. The local congregation alone has divine sanction.[16]

Glas never presumed an ability to know absolutely who the members of the church invisible are. "We cannot discern betwixt the common and special operations of the Spirit in others, or betwixt a temporary believer, who may fall away, and them that believe to the saving of the soul." The requirements for church membership cannot be too stringent, for one may honestly yearn to join a church and yet "fall away." If one can "shew a hearty agreement" in the confession of the one faith and desires to join a church congregation, he or she should be received, for the early church did not wait for the evidence of a good life before receiving its members, and thus accepted applicants on a confession of faith. A member's sincerity manifests itself among the fellowship by walking in fraternal love and observance of the institutions of Christ, and it was the fellowship's duty to maintain church discipline, including the admission and excommunication of members. Though every congregation must have its own officer-bearers, elders and deacons, the New Testament makes no mention of church representatives to whom are delegated the powers, which belong to the whole company of disciples who constitute a church.[17]

Given his difficulties over the Covenants and the ruling body of the Church of Scotland, Glas defined the church as a purely spiritual society, having no immediate concern with questions of civil government, and the state as a civil institution with no right to exercise legislative or executive functions in the sphere of religion. Here Glas differs not only from the standards of the Church of Scotland respecting the magistrate's authority, but also from the views of the early Puritans who held that the magistrate as such has authority in religious matters. Further, Glas declared that as Christ did not appropriate civil sanctions to his laws, his kingdom cannot be advanced by earthly power, that religion may not—like natural or civil rights—be defended by force of arms, and that the magistrate has no direct concern with the administration of the churches.[18] This marked a revolutionary turn of thought in an era of close alliances between religion and politics that rendered them indistinguishable in places, being two halves of a whole. Glas's problem with the National Covenants of 1638 and the Solemn League and Covenant of 1643 rested on their assumption that the nation occupied a position similar to that of ancient Israel, which was a covenanted church-state, and religion maintained by civil sanctions and the power of the sword. This was contrary to Christ's dictum that his kingdom was not of this world. The Christian must "render unto Caesar" and obey the magistrate as is necessary, but the magistrate cannot exercise religious authority.

In the letter that originated the controversy about the Covenants, Glas wrote that his "scruples then with respect to our Covenants ... take their rise from the view I have of the new testament church, and its distinction from the church of the old testament." Christ substantially revised and expanded the covenant between God and Israel, and in Glas's interpretation identified the kingdom of heaven as consisting "not of any one earthly kingdom, nor of many commonwealths joined in one; but of a society gathered out of all nations into one." The Scottish Covenants, Glas contended, imitated the Old Testament covenants by privileging Scotland above other nations. The consequent blending of politics and religion thus brought about spiritual and doctrinal laxity, as evidenced by the gradual corruption of the Roman Church after it had become the state religion under the emperor Constantine in 313 C.E. The same process had infected the National Church; the Covenants had enlarged the visible church beyond the limits intended by Christ by allowing many to take the Covenants without giving any evidence of true faith.[19]

Most troubling to Glas was the intrusion of the coercive power of the state, which by laws and penalties enforces the national form of religion. By subordinating Christianity to the political realm, the act of owning the National Covenants "was not a profession of subjection to Jesus Christ and his authority, as was the professed subjection of men to the gospel at the first: but a profession of subjection to the magistrate instead of Christ." Moreover, in the absence of submission, the magistrate has recourse to force, and in Scotland, the Covenants only countenanced Presbyterianism. This insistence on uniformity in creed and church government led to intolerance and persecution. Those who could not conscientiously subscribe to the Covenants were deprived of church communion and the privileges of the commonwealth, while those who actively resisted them were met by force of arms. Coercion is a violation of one's natural right to liberty of conscience, as well as of the founding principles of Christ's kingdom, and the civil power is never justified in compelling orthodoxy by external force. Obedience obtained in such ways is useless. Neither can the cause of Christ be defended nor propagated by the sword. The state's power extends only to the defense of civil liberties and freedom of conscience, and any society that claims Christ as king while employing force in his interest, betrays itself as a kingdom of the world and not a kingdom of Christ. Thus, the secular arm must never support the church.[20]

Another entanglement caused by the mixture of church and state is one of divided loyalties. Where the law establishes a church, the state will naturally claim some voice in ecclesiastical affairs, so that it becomes difficult—and sometimes impossible—to maintain a consistent loyalty to Christ with a consistent obedience to the civil power. Christ exhorted his disciples to "render unto Caesar what is Caesar's, and unto God what is God's," and Paul's letter to the Romans echoes this dictum concerning obedience to the magistrate, but in a church-state

> the maintenance of the ministers of the church is provided for, and their authority over the people of the nation raised and secured, this must, in the nature of things, be an allurement to worldly men to seek into the ministry, that seek nothing but their own honour, gain, and ease, and to lay out themselves for it, as men do for any honourable, gainful, and easy worldly employment. And whatever professions or subscriptions be required of them, when connected with such temporal advantages, these will be complied with by multitudes that have nothing but these advantages in view.

Not only are the acquisitive encouraged to enter the ministry for the sake of the perquisites and status accorded to them by the Establishment, but also they are afterwards prone to regard the maintenance of the ecclesiastical system as their chief business, irrespective of higher calls or duties. Based on his interpretation of the gospels, Glas thus advocated the complete separation of church and state, a concept known as the Principle.[21]

Glas's extensive study of the first three hundred years of Christianity brought him to some important conclusions regarding the ministry, which he detailed in a treatise titled *Tradition by the Succession of Bishops*, published in 1752. In it he traced the progression of the New Testament churches' leadership from a simple pastorate up through its development into a clerical caste, and on up to a monarchical episcopate. His intention was to justify his opposition to any form of ecclesiastical hierarchy, but the deep respect for the ministerial office that had daunted him as a youth and nearly persuaded him not to seek it led him to place so much emphasis on the pastor and the elders that critics averred that the Glasite churches retained the leaven of clerical domination. Glas spoke in many of his works about the necessity of a constituted presbytery—meaning the body of elders and deacons in a congregation—for the proper functioning of a church, which he called the "permanent ministry" and included deaconesses and ministering widows. "The written tradition," he wrote, "establishes a plurality of bishops in every church, and we may as well seek for one chief deacon, as for one chief presbyter in any church there."[22]

Everywhere in the New Testament, the church officers are spoken of in the plural, and Glas held that, without such a plurality of elders, congregational discipline and Christian order cannot be maintained. He rejected the Presbyterian office of pastor as superior to the elders and deacons, as well as the Congregationalist vesting of authority among the lay membership, and blurred the distinction between teaching elders and preaching elders. Each church must have at least two elders to form a presbytery, and Glas adhered to the qualifications for elders as set down in I Timothy 3:1–7 and Titus 1:6–9, which, beyond the ability to teach, required a good personal reputation and character traits of temperance, sobriety, charity, generosity, and justice. Selection from among the membership was by the unanimous decision of the church after giving evidence of their qualifications. Character and ability were the criteria for candidacy, not academic skills or social position:

> No man can take this office to himself without being duly called according to the word of God. But it is not in the power of any church to limit access into that office any otherwise than it is limited in the word of God. As little is it in the power of any church to put men into that office by means of any other qualifications, or by any other rules than those that are insisted on in that word.

Having been called and approved, an elder is solemnly set apart by prayer and fasting, with the laying on of hands by the presbytery who also give the right hand of fellowship. Candidacy cannot be conferred by sole nomination, and neither can a single person perform ordination, since there are no instances of such to be found in the New Testament churches.[23]

Glas adamantly maintained that the ordination of an elder did not confer any special status on the recipient that elevated him above the congregation. He denied any distinction between the clergy and the laity, abhorred the use of ecclesiastical titles, and rejected the professionalization of the clergy. There was no scriptural warrant for what he considered a "hireling" clergy, and vigilantly warned about the potential for corruption and abuse inherent in a professional clergy. Glasite church elders were to hold ordinary occupations and not expect support from their flocks, except in cases when dire necessity required it. The office of deacon was confined to the common administration of church affairs and ministering to the poor. The ordination process for deacons was similar to that for elders, with the exceptions that there was no mandated period of fasting, and no extension of the right hand of fellowship. One wonders, then, why Glas maintained the offices of elder and deacon if they were so hollow. Certainly, specific tasks relating to church maintenance were delegated to those individuals who showed the greatest willingness and aptitude for the work. However, it is with regard to church discipline that the elders and deacons were most necessary, and, as will become clear, the maintenance of discipline proved to be most difficult.[24]

Glas's interpretation of the administration of the sacraments was characteristically wide in some areas and narrower in others. Regarding baptism, he defined it as "the great Christian truth, concerning salvation by the death and resurrection of Jesus Christ, the Son of God, in whom the Father is well pleased, and the purification of sinners by his blood." Its warrant is the command of Christ to his disciples to baptize all nations, but it has been progressively perverted and opposed. Some, supposing that baptism itself makes people into Christians, argued for the baptism of nations as such, whether or not the people have become disciples through the influence of the gospels upon their minds. Others have interpreted baptism as a temporary arrangement at the time when Christianity first appeared in the world, applicable to the first converts among Jews and Gentiles, but not intended to continue beyond that period. Others, such as the Quakers, emphasized the Baptism of the Spirit and denied the obligation of the external rite of water-baptism. The Anabaptists limited the subjects of baptism to adults on confession of faith, denying that children fall within the scope of the ordinance. Glas widened access to baptism to believers and their children as an institution of permanent obligation, though he did not administer it indiscriminately.[25]

Most Christian denominations extended the sacraments exclusively to church members, but Glas contended that baptism precedes admission into the fellowship of a particular church, establishing a relationship to the Universal Church, but not conferring membership in a local church. The subjects of baptism are those who confess their faith in Christ, as well as their children, who are to be "judged of according to the parents confession while infants, but according to their own profession when come to years." In tune with fundamentalist Calvinism, baptism to Glas was the sign and seal of the New Testament covenant even as circumcision was a sign of the Old Testament covenant. It belongs to the Church, which, drawn from all nations, has superseded the nation of Israel as the covenanted people of God. The children of believers may be members of this covenanted church, and though Glas could not find scriptural warrant in favor of infant baptism, he did not conclude from their incapability of hearing the Word and confessing their faith that they should be barred from the rite. Glas believed that antipedobaptism arose from the fundamental mistake of making baptism "to lie in something else than the thing signified; even that, whatever it be, which distinguishes the adult Christian from his infant: though our Lord expressly declares, that we must enter his kingdom even as infants enter it." When Jesus rebuked his disciples for attempting to turn away the children brought to him for blessing, he secured the church-membership of infants before his institution of baptism. In terms of the method of baptism, Glas preferred to "wash" recipients rather than immersing them: "The common way of baptizing is not by sprinkling, as has been always falsely alledged [sic] in this controversy; but by pouring water from the hand of the baptizer upon the baptized." In the scriptures, different figures are used to represent washing or cleansing, but that did not indicate that any one form of baptism is or should be mandated. "If we look at the will of the institutor expressed in his word, as the sole ground of the relation betwixt the signs in baptism and the Lord's supper, and that which is signified by them; we will not look for any such similitude in these instituted signs, as we do in pictures or images." The scriptures do not stipulate that any one particular mode of baptism must be used as opposed to others. Thus, Glas did not concern himself with whether one was immersed, "washed," or sprinkled. The means were unimportant, so long as the spiritual transformation elicited by baptism took place.[26]

The sacrament of the Lord's Supper Glas considered "the most solemn outward action of religious worship instituted in the New Testament." Appointed by Christ as a memorial to his atoning sacrifice, and as the bond of communion with him in his death, the rite is perpetually obligatory to his disciples until his predicted return. As baptism marks a relation to the Universal Church into which all believers are baptized, so the Lord's Supper marks a relation to the particular visible church, which is the body of Christ. The distinction between baptism and the Lord's Supper is that baptism is administered to individuals, while the Lord's Supper must be partaken of in the company of fellow Christians. Moreover, those who partake must be one body; consequently, membership in a church is necessary to admission to the Lord's Table. Glas deplored the lax standards by which most churches, Presbyterian and otherwise, granted access to the Lord's Supper, and identified the same process of corruption that had degenerated the church since the fourth century C.E. as leading to such indiscriminate access. He admitted the difficulty of preserving the purity of communion, that "in the purest external communion that can be expected in a visible church there will be hypocrites, foolish virgins with the wise ... [,] and branches in Christ not bearing fruit." Promiscuous communicating destroys true fellowship in the mystical body of Christ, and thus "it is our duty to forbear communion in the Lord's supper with them that have no appearance of being disciples of Christ."[27]

As to times and frequency, Glas considered that the practice of the apostolic Church in observing the rite at least weekly is binding on all Christians: "We say, Christ has made it once a-week at least. He has solemnly ratified from heaven the constant practice of his churches assembling to his supper every first day of the week, without making one Sabbath more solemn thereby than another." If there are objections that weekly observance is too common, the answer is that where the discipline is rightly maintained it serves as a fence from unworthy communicating. The early Christians met to observe the supper on the first day of the week, but there is no precise time of the day specified for its observance. Glas decided that the rite must be performed in the evening, since Christ instituted the Eucharist at the Jewish feast of Passover, and that one does not eat supper in the morning or at lunchtime. Glas's doctrine of the Lord's Supper emphasized the commemorative and declaratory aspects of the rite. While the sacrament is a real communion of the body and blood of Christ, the sign must not be confused with that which is signified, specifically the sacrificial death of Christ. The consumption of bread and wine does not constitute the act of Communion. Rather, it is the spiritual partaking of Christ whose body and blood are represented by the bread and wine that marks Communion, as well as the communal nature of the rite.[28]

Glas placed great importance on the social character of Christianity. Only in fellowship can the duties of Christian discipleship be fulfilled and the Christian character developed properly. To neglect the fellowship is, on the one hand, a failure to observe the ordinances of Christ, and, on the other, a failure to fulfill the duties of brotherly love whereby the Christian shows his love of Christ. The first Christians assembled regularly on the first day of the week for fellowship in prayer and praise, mutual exhortation, and the observance of the Lord's Supper. In so doing, they acted not from any sense of obligation to an external law, but from a desire for communion with one another in Christ, and to express their common faith and hope in the gospel. Glas considered it the duty as well as the privilege of the Christian to give constant and regular attendance on the teaching, the fellowship, the breaking of bread, and the saying of prayers. Those whom God has called to the ministry expound the doctrine, but exhortation was not confined to the teaching elders in Glasite churches, as congregants were expected to exhort one another.[29]

By "fellowship" Glas meant the regular contribution of members to the requirements and services of the church, especially the relief of needy brethren. This is the sense in which the word appears frequently in the New Testament, and refers to "communicating as to giving and receiving." Whereas praise and exhortation were important elements in Glasite church services, the focal point was always the administration of Communion. "This ordinance is not occasional, but continual and binding, in the constant assemblies of the people of God.... The union of the people of God with Christ and with one another in him ... is especially manifest in the Lord's supper." Another important practice instituted by Glas—though not as part of the worship service—was the *agape*, or "love feast," which, unlike the Lord's Supper, takes place in the home as a common meal in which the poorer brethren may share. This usually occurred after the conclusion of the Sunday morning service, and all members of the church contributed a dish, as in the modern potluck supper. This more social gathering strengthened bonds between individuals in the churches, as well as fulfilled the dispensation of charity.[30]

The typical Glasite church service followed a standardized order:

1. Psalm-singing (Praise)
2. Recitation of the Lord's Prayer by an Elder
3. Praise
4. Prayer led by one of the brethren (either spontaneously offered or solicited by an elder)
5. Praise
6. Prayer led by another of the brethren
7. Praise
8. Prayer
9. Praise
10. Prayer
11. Opening of the church to the public
12. Prayer, followed by a reading of three chapters from the Law and three from the Prophets
13. Praise
14. Invocation and Sermon
15. Prayer
16. Praise
17. Benediction and Dismissal

The congregation then convened at one of the brethren's houses for the *agape*, which concluded with a hymn. The afternoon service followed essentially the same order, with the exception of the omission of prayers by the brethren, and the reading of three chapters from the New Testament. Once the sermon was completed, the nonmembers departed while the members remained behind to take Communion. The "fellowship offering" was received, and an elder consecrated the elements, which deacons carried around to each communicant.[31] A hymn was sung, and an elder invoked a blessing on the Exhortation in which the male members took part one after another. The assembly was then dismissed with the Blessing.

Other practices sanctioned by Glas and associated with sociability among church members were the "kiss of charity" and foot-washing. Long abandoned, these earliest Christian practices generated much consternation and derisive comment from non-Glasites, but Glas insisted that the many references to them placed them as central to Christian social interaction. The kiss of charity is mentioned no less than five times as the proper Christian method of greeting,[32] and was, as far as Glas was concerned, an "expression of brotherly love among the first Christians, wherein they followed the example of their Lord and Master, who condescended to allow his disciples this familiarity and freedom with him in saluting him." The custom had been faithfully observed until "the great apostasy from the primitive profession of the faith and love that is in Christ.... But as 'charity never faileth', so neither should any of the duties or expressions of it be allowed to fail."[33] Foot-washing was exemplified and enjoined by Christ himself when he bathed the feet of his disciples, saying, "If I then your Lord and Master, have washed your feet; ye also ought to wash one another's feet. For I have given you an example, that ye should do as I have done to you."[34] That the early church followed this example is shown by what Paul said of the qualification of the ministering widow or deaconess, that "she have washed the saints' feet."[35]

The foundation of Glasite church discipline was a constantly reinforced sentiment of brotherly love and mutual support among congregants and church members. Glas based his understanding of discipline—as he did all other matters pertaining to Christian worship—on the words of Christ and the practice of the first churches. He recognized that errors and disputes would arise in the churches, and preferred a degree of forbearance in correcting errant brethren, but did not shrink from harsher punishments to ensure unity. A generous forbearance must never defeat the ends of discipline, for Christ did not fail to chastise his disciples for their infractions, and neither should the Glasites. While Christ set limits upon the exercise of discipline, Glas warned "against hurting discipline by forbearance, or forbearance by the discipline," even to the point of excommunication in the most extreme cases. He grounded the rule of discipline in a particular or visible church on the prescription in Matthew 18:20: "It cannot be the universal church that the offended brother is to hear: but a particular visible church, wherein they are concerned, and which they have access to speak to, and hear."

Glas considered this rule to apply primarily with private offenses committed by one of the brethren against another:

> The Lord himself gave a rule of discipline to his disciples, for the preservation of brotherly love in purity among them, notwithstanding offences arising, and mutual provocations, through pride remaining in them.... And it appears from the occasion of it, and from the discourse against pride and ambition that introduces it, ver. 1–14, that it respects only those trespasses of his disciples against one another, that flow from pride, and such offences as are removed as often as the trespasser humbles himself to confess his fault and profess repentance; and though he trespass often in this way, he cannot be put away from among the brotherhood, if he still hear the church admonishing or rebuking him for his trespass by professing his repentance.

However, this unlimited forbearance did not apply in cases of heinous sins. "We must distinguish the case of a man taken in such faults, who must be restored in the spirit of meekness ... from the case of one who lives and walks in them, so far as to be denominated a fornicator, or a drunkard, or covetous man, and by his practice declares (however he speak) that he does not repent." Those proven guilty of persistent sins were treated according to the apostolic directions in I Corinthians 5, which deprived such wayward brethren of all fellowship, even to the extent of not being allowed to eat and drink with the faithful.[36]

Only the church as a whole exercised the rule of discipline. The persons concerned were the brethren, and on them devolved the responsibility of decision-making without the aid of any external authority. Though the elders presided and pronounced in the church's name, they could not act independently of the church, which alone had the power to bind or loosen. Unanimity was essential in church discipline as in all other decisions, for a "majority of voices has no place in this discipline.... And there is nothing like a warrant for it in the New Testament, as there is for the way of doing by agreement and consent of the whole." The exercise of discipline was simply to enforce adherence to Christ's law, and was never intended to be permanent or to leave a permanent mark on the chastened. Excommunication, the most extreme punishment, Glas regarded as a salutary reminder of the final judgment at the latter day, calculated to inspire fear and repentance in the sinner's heart, and also to move the whole church with fear. Discipline thus leaves room for repentance and may be the means of producing it.[37]

One outstanding case in the Glasite church during the 1750s involved a woman in Arbroath who had been excommunicated for intemperance no fewer than eleven times. Despairing of her reclamation, the church ultimately decided to have nothing more to do with her. Glas wrote to James Cant of Perth about the situation, wondering if there was any scriptural warrant for permanent excommunication:

> After this doubt had settled awhile on our minds ... it became a formal question in the church, where it was found very ridiculous to say the church should go on in their ancient practice, unless the Scripture expressly forbade it; or that the church should at her pleasure, exercise her power of binding and loosing, except where the Scripture expressly limited her.... It was next alleged that whatever difference be betwixt Matt. xviii. and I Cor. v., yet when it comes the length of cutting off, there is no difference; the one being putting away a wicked person as well as the other.

This case led Glas to amend his interpretation of the doctrine of "Second Absolution," noting that in the Ephesian Church

> *they imposed the course of repentance never but once. And whoever fell into his vitious transgressions the second time, could never be reconciled to the church, and was to expect his pardon from God alone:* because they had no precedent for a second absolution from excommunication in the scripture, which gives a very plain direction as to the first.

Although he had earlier stated that though an offender "trespass *often* in this way, he cannot be put away from the brotherhood, if he still hear the church admonishing him for his trespass by professing his repentance," this case led him to alter the discipline of the first Glasite churches.[38]

Glas interpreted the apostolic injunction "Be not unequally yoked together with unbelievers" as referring to religious fellowship, and thus held intercommunion with members of other denominations impermissible. Genuine Christians are called to separate themselves from the unbelieving world, which Glas thought to be filled with charlatans and misguided professors of religion who did not share with him the unity of a common belief and discipline. This did not mean that Glasites were antisocial. The injunction is not concerned with civil communion, "for separation in this respect would be to go out of the world, or turn monks, and transgress many commandments of Jesus Christ." However, there stood strict prohibitions against joining in the worship, either public or private, of those who rejected Glasite faith and order. Such intermingling, in Glas's opinion, undermined the foundation of Christian union in obedience to Christ. In his early writings, Glas insisted that Christians can and will have different interpretations of the truth, yet remain part of the one body of Christ. Uniformity was neither expected nor required, as long as all confessed to Christ's lordship. A member of one church was eligible to be a member of any true church in the world, "and this was the catholicism that took place in the beginning of Christianity."[39]

Glas's relative lenience on this matter of forbearance shifted to intransigence in a matter of only a few years. In a letter written in 1740, he admitted that his mind was changing, and in a treatise on "Catholic Charity" written as a response to George Whitefield, he insisted on full conformity with the commandments of Christ and the apostles, the original intent of whom he had come to believe he firmly understood. He declared that any and all who proclaimed Christ's commission to preach the gospel are "obliged to teach the disciples to observe all things whatsoever he commanded his apostles, which things they taught the first Christians to observe; and, if they acknowledge any as disciples, who will not be taught to observe all these things, they are then plainly acting contrary to his instructions." Relaxed views on charity and forbearance are dangerous, tending to make people cool or indifferent respecting the true faith and negligent in their duties. Therefore, all who concerned themselves with obedience to Christ's laws will be "hateful to the charitable forbearing world, as enemies to the Catholic charity; even as they were before hated and persecuted as enemies to the Catholic uniformity."[40]

Glas limited forbearance as enjoined by the apostles to the difference between the Jewish and Gentile Christians respecting food ways as well as ceremonial observances of the old law. He denied that it extended to any deviation from the explicit precepts of Christ and his apostles concerning truth and church order. True charity is essentially love of the truth, and in practice it "must be precisely regulated by the New Testament." Forbearance that ignores the truth is not Christian charity:

> Christians love one another for the truth's sake, for which the world hates them. But we have been much dunned with a great noise and cry for charity, especially by those who have been most remarkably opposing the truth wherewith charity rejoiceth. And if the truth be taken from us, how then shall we love for the truth's sake? The charity that is so loudly called for, in this case, must be love without faith, yea and love to the world hating the truth.

Christ's true disciples are thus distinguished from mere professors by the observance of all the Christian laws and institutions. Therefore, Communion can only be held with those who are one in the faith and order of the gospel. Though ready to do good to all men, the Glasites could not unite in the worship of other religious societies that failed to recognize its obligations.[41]

Glasite Practices

The published works of John Glas contain little relating specifically to Christian ethics. His interests were primarily theological and ecclesiological. One cannot presume, however, that he was indifferent to the practical side of religion. Both he and his disciples maintained a high standard of personal conduct despite the early libels of those who charged them with Antinomianism. It was not long before the Glasites garnered for themselves the respect and even admiration of their neighbors on the force of their integrity and character. They considered themselves under an obligation to obey all of Christ's commandments, which included all the practical and moral precepts of the New Testament. Though opposed to self-righteousness, they assumed that common virtues such as benevolence, honesty, purity, temperance, and passivity would naturally follow from a true profession of the Christian faith. The churches always dealt sternly with offenses against common morality. There are four aspects of Christian practice, as understood and propagated by Glas, which bear closer examination.

Glas's study of the New Testament led him to revive a dietary restriction that had fallen out of practice among Christians—that against "blood-eating." He contended that this Hebraic abstinence from eating blood or "things strangled," which was binding on the first Christians and had never been lifted, must continue to be observed. In his judgment, the question was not one of ceremonial but one of moral importance, which cannot be set aside:

> It is odd, to say, that by "these necessary things" we are to understand, these indifferent things, made necessary at that time, only by the present disposition of the believing Jews; the same of which that church in Jerusalem then consisted, who, it seems, were well disposed to give up circumcision, and the keeping of the law of Moses to the believing Gentiles, but could by no means be prevailed with to give up the article of blood! They who incline to talk at this rate, must say further, that, by "these necessary things", we must understand, partly such indifferent things, and partly things necessary in opposition to indifferent: for some of those things that are here declared necessary, are owned to be very far from indifferent, and affirmed, to be binding on all Christians, in all ages, to the end of the world.

Abstinence from blood-eating continued to be observed long after the apostolic era, and was noted among the Christian confessors and martyrs. Glas cited Tertullian as evidence of the view held by the early church, that Christians do not regard the blood of animals as food, but abstain not only from things strangled, but also from those that have died of themselves, lest they partake of secreted blood.[42]

Glas saw in this prohibition an anticipation of the Atonement. Blood is the sacred symbol of sacrifice, made dramatically more significant by Christ's institution of the Eucharist and self-sacrifice. "This precept about blood ... declares the sinful mortal's dependence on God, as redeeming him from sin and death by atoning blood; and disobedience to this precept, imports disregard to that blood, as being in effect a renunciation of dependence on the Lord God." The basis for this was in Mosaic law as set down among the Levitical prohibitions, and was instituted by apostolic decree to the Gentile Christians. "But the true atonement was not by the blood of beasts, which could not take away any real sin, and the respect due to it, was on the account of the true atonement, prefigured by it, which is only in the blood of Christ shed for the remission of sins." Glas held the rule against blood-eating as a precept of the divine law, and made it one of the terms of Communion, and this reinforced his views against worshipping with outsiders, since they pollute themselves by eating blood. "Therefore, when the Gentiles are admitted to share in the salvation that is by [Christ's] blood, without the typical sacrifices of the law, they are commanded to abstain from blood: for still the true reason of the prohibition remains."[43]

While Glas never discouraged his disciples from achieving financial success, it was imperative that those who prospered would share their wealth with their less fortunate brethren. Glas considered covetousness as evidence of unbelief and also an offense against the spirit of fraternal love, which should animate all Christians. "We are surrounded," he wrote, "with temptations to the fulfilment of this lust in all the situations wherein we are placed in the world and we must watch against it, as a most crafty enemy lying in wait to surprise us, and take away our life; for we can never be truly happy without the victory over it." Glasites took very seriously Christ's dictum that believers must "Lay not up for yourselves treasures upon earth ... but lay up for yourselves treasures in heaven," and therefore they placed almsgiving in a place of utmost importance in Christian daily devotional practice. An example of this is provided by Glas in the fourth petition of the Lord's Prayer, "Give us this day our daily bread," which, for Glas, "is opposed to thoughtfulness for the future, and is inconsistent with our reckoning anything we have of our own, while the children of God, with whom we pray for daily bread, are in want of that bread." Consequently, Glasite-Sandemanianism did not demand poverty of its adherents, and thus maintained an appeal among artisans, tradesmen, and merchants. Nonetheless, almsgiving is a Christian duty devolving upon all who have the capacity to give. Christ "does not absolutely forbid us to lay up treasures of these things to ourselves. On the contrary, he bids us lay them up. But that which he forbids is, laying them up on earth.... Almsgiving, then, is lending to the Lord, who hath obliged himself to repay what is so lent."[44]

Glas stressed that God commanded people to "do good to all men, especially unto them who are of the household of faith." Such is the natural fruit of grace, "the evidence of our faith and knowledge of his grace.... By this we shew the subjection of our confession to the gospel of Christ" in "pure and undefiled religion." Some people reckon almsgiving as "but a low evidence of faith, in comparison with the impressions they feel on their hearts by the word of God," but such forget that all feelings that do not issue in works of charity are worthless and deceptive. "The practice of this pure and undefiled religion, then, is laying up for ourselves treasures in heaven; yea, the giving of our money, our food, our raiment, to all the poor, especially such as are of the household of faith." No one may rightly lay up treasures for oneself alone, or amass a fortune to increase one's own wealth or secure his or her future, for such is to betray a spirit of covetousness and a lack of trust in God. Christian benevolence should manifest itself in the fellowship of the church. Fraternal love requires that every member should be prepared to support, according to his or her abilities, those who are brethren in Christ.[45]

It should be qualified that Glas did not institute communalism in the strictest definition of the term. Glasites did not hold property in common, nor were members compelled to contribute their money or property into any kind of common fund for even redistribution. While Glas acknowledged, that during the apostolic period, the Jerusalem church had a "communion of goods," which was an extraordinary circumstance, it not being "the case ... in other churches; where the disciples laboured, for the most part, in their ordinary employments throughout the week." This did not create a conflict with Christ's warning about laying up treasure on earth, for "the scripture no where makes the retaining of any part of what we possess, in every case, to be a proof of idolatry, or that our hearts are where what we have is." However, Glas maintained that every member is bound to consider all his worldly wealth at the service of the church, especially in its ministering to needy brethren, but, under normal circumstances, liberality manifested itself in contributing to the "Fellowship" at the Lord's Supper. Glasite charity was not confined to their own churches, for while they secured provisions for the impoverished, the sick, and the elderly among their number, they also generously supported various philanthropic and humanitarian institutions for the relief of the poor and the sick, without regard to religious connection or creed.[46]

On questions regarding social diversions, Glas did not adhere to the puritanical spirit that prevailed among evangelical circles of eighteenth-century Protestantism. Though strict in his requirement that full obedience be given to every precept of the New Testament, he objected to making laws where Christ had not made them. He perceived no detrimental effects in playing games and socially acceptable recreations, or in attending balls, the theater, or other places of entertainment. Prohibitions against what he considered harmless and innocent diversions were reminiscent of Pharisaism:

> We cannot find ground to condemn the amusements or diversions of music and dancing; or even the reading or hearing of plays, though the Methodists and such like plead much religion in abstinence from all these more than in strictly following every command of God, and the testimony of Jesus; crying out on all the diversions of the grand polite world, and damning them to the poor people who cannot get at them, and so are easily moved by envy to shew their great zeal against them.

The only exceptions, however, concerned games of chance, "because the whole disposal thereof is of the Lord, whose providence is not to be played with." Nevertheless, the world is one that God has made wonderful partly because of a person's ability to find pleasure in it, but only so long as enjoyable pastimes do not distract one into worldliness. Those church members who clearly wandered into intemperance were sternly disciplined, as has been shown. Glas's relatively liberal view of the lawfulness of common pleasures brought down upon him and his disciples, from the more puritanically religious, charges of moral laxity and worldliness throughout their history.[47]

A critical facet of Glasite doctrine, and one with far-reaching effects, concerned the relationship of the Christian to the secular government. Although Glas refused to allow the civil magistrate any place or authority in the church, he insisted on the duty of recognizing civil power within its own sphere as enjoined by the apostle Paul. Glas reinforced God's ordination of the authorities for the government of society, as the guardians of law and order, and consequently they may claim the allegiance of all citizens in matters that come within civil jurisdiction:

Government and magistracy is the valuable pledge of the divine goodness and forbearance to this wicked world, that, without it, would be filled with violence.... This is pointed to, and explained by the apostle, Rom. xiii., where he calls the power that is, and the ruler, the ordinance of God, and the minister of God to us for good, who bears the sword as a revenger to execute wrath upon him that doth evil to his neighbour; and he declares tribute to be due to these powers and rulers, as the ministers of God. The peaceable life that men enjoy at any time under the powers that be, which God hath ordained, is the effect of the divine goodness, upholding the power, and blessing it to the end for which he ordained it.

The Glasites, in emulation of first-century Christians, espoused a twofold duty to the state that entails primarily obedience to its laws, and secondarily to pray for rulers and all who are in positions of authority.[48]

The Glasites were thus enjoined to live peaceably and in an orderly manner, neither troubling the state by breaking its laws, nor by calling on its sanctions. If internal disputes should arise over temporal concerns, they must endeavor to settle their differences, not by recourse to the civil courts but by reference to the laws of Christ and the claims of fraternal love. The magistrate is appointed for the restraint of evildoers, but these should not be found in a society of Christian brethren. True Christians should seek to give due honor to rulers, refraining from rebellion or active opposition to constituted authority. Even a corrupt administration does not release the Christian from his or her obligations, for tyrannical government "must still be better than none; and the divine long-suffering appears more in any government, than it can do in anarchy, which must fill the earth with violence." Christians are also commanded to pray for kings, rulers, and magistrates, irrespective of their characters or policies: "When we are bidden pray for kings, and all in authority, we have no other question left us to ask, but this plain one, Who is the authority? For, if we should enquire further, whether they be in authority according to right? we shall not find a solution of that question in the gospel. And therefore it commands us to be subject to the 'powers that be', to pray for them, and to pay them tribute." It does not matter that Christians may question the legitimacy of the ruler's claim to authority or his fitness to govern, since God accorded these for his purposes, and are inscrutable to the human mind.[49]

The ends of constituted authority must be attained under any government, as was the case in the early days of the church. Even under Nero it was better that there was some form of government than none at all, tyrannical as it had been. Allegiance cannot be suspended until satisfaction with the ruling administration is achieved, or on account of mistreatment at the hands of the government. If Christians are oppressed and persecuted for their religious principles, they must never resist by force of arms, but bear with meekness and patience the hardships imposed on them, praying for their rulers that God may change their hearts. "The Christian spirit will lead us, as it did the first Christians, to trust God with our prayers for the powers that be, and not meddle with those that are given to change." Christ would have his followers surpass the men of the world in patient endurance of injuries. Such was the spirit of the early Christians who, though arguably the greatest sufferers under the Roman imperial policy before Constantine, took no part in the insurrections of their day. John Glas insisted on a similar lofty, detached standard of behavior for his followers, believing that the same dynamic that attracted so many to convert to Christianity in its formative century would likewise attract adherents to his brand of commonsense Christianity.[50]

There is much here that is reminiscent of seventeenth-century European and English Anabaptist theology, particularly the emphasis on egalitarianism and the rejection of a ministry apart from the office of elder. In terms of ecclesiology and doctrine, one distinctly recognizes ritual foot-washing and the *agape* meal, as well as frequent exhortations to spiritual detachment from the material world. However, Glas's theology was deeply influenced by the Scottish Enlightenment, in which he had been steeped during his student days at Edinburgh, and thus is eminently rationalistic and redolent with the commonsense moral philosophy of Francis Hutcheson. By asserting what John Locke called the "reasonableness" of Christianity, particularly the natural receptivity of the mind to the essential truth of apostolic Christianity as opposed to the instability of the heart, Glas tried—as had others—to reconcile natural law and ethics with Calvinism. This inevitably led to widespread confusion with Arminian doctrine that sparked a wave of anti-Calvinism in England that spread to New England in the 1740s, as so-called "catholick" Calvinists there similarly linked their theology more closely to moral virtue. It also explains Glas's and Sandeman's opposition to the antirationalist, evangelical revivalism that had begun to sweep the Atlantic world.[51]

☙

John Glas's experience with church authority drove him into Independency, though, as his own father noted, it marked a milestone toward which he had been traveling since before he entered the ministry. Like most idealists, he took the Scottish Church more or less at face value, assuming that it had rid itself of most—if not all—of the political elements that plagued the Anglican and Catholic churches. The intimate relationship between church and state he found most disquieting, which formed his espousal of the Voluntary Principle. The Glasite church that he founded, and which proliferated throughout southern Scotland and England during the 1740s, 1750s, and 1760s, attracted adherents from a wide spectrum of British society, but by and large they came from the middle and lower classes. The church grew rapidly in the mid-eighteenth century under the influence of Glas's son-in-law, Robert Sandeman, who gained notoriety from his pivotal treatise, called *Letters on Theron and Aspasio* (1757), which engaged the nascent Methodist movement's theology. This and the revivalism of the First Great Awakening convinced him to export Sandemanianism to the British North American colonies in 1763. Simultaneously dismayed and energized by enthusiastic evangelicalism, Sandeman believed that he was engaged in a redemptive enterprise as well as a missionary one when he disembarked at Boston in 1764.

❦ 3 ❦

"He Becomes Possessed of a Truth"

Robert Sandeman, Glasite Proselyte

> Many popular preachers ... make offers of Christ and all his benefits unto men, upon certain terms, and to assure them of the benefits on their complying with the terms.... But anyone who reads the New Testament with tolerable attention, may see that there is little foundation for any such offer.
>
> —Robert Sandeman, *Letters on Theron and Aspasio*

The *George* bobbed gently in the Glasgow harbor as Robert Sandeman, accompanied by a handful of companions, strode aboard to embark on the voyage to America. The success with which he espoused Glasite theology and established Glasite churches in England and Wales made him the foremost among John Glas's disciples, and a combination of circumstances led him up the gangplank of the *George* in September 1764 to establish Glasite churches in the British colonies in America. Having interposed himself in an argument between John Wesley and James Hervey over Wesley's apparent conversion to mainstream Calvinism, Sandeman made a rather impressive splash in what had only been the intermittently turbulent religious waters of eighteenth-century England. The attention he garnered as a result, and the interest in Glasite theology likewise generated, led to Sandeman's traveling all over Britain, cultivating the establishment of Glasite churches. His influence grew to such an extent that the movement gradually came to be known as "Sandemanian" instead of "Glasite," though neither Glasites nor Sandemanians used the term self-referentially, preferring to call themselves Christians.[1]

The context in which Sandeman's rise to prominence resides is peculiarly double-layered. On the one hand, it was the height of the Scottish Enlightenment, at the forefront of which at the time of Sandeman's debut stood philosophers and scientists such as David Hume, Francis Hutcheson, and Henry Home, Lord Kames. On the other hand, there was a growing rejection of rationalism in religion, which evangelical critics blamed for precipitating a dramatic decline in popular piety, clerical vigor, as well as the fundamental doctrines of Protestant Christianity itself. One such group in England emerged, eventually becoming the Methodists. Seeking to restore the piety of earlier generations, enthusiastic preachers in Britain and its North American colonies fostered revivals in the churches and out of doors, and the energy of the response was such that it drew proponents and detractors. The blaze of revivalism burned for about thirty years, and then petered out, but the controversies aroused by the movement continued in the presses as clergymen published books, treatises, and pamphlets on theological issues raised by the revivalists and their opponents. Sandeman, opposed to religious enthusiasm, made a name for himself in this respect when he engaged emergent Methodism, consequently playing an integral part in its theological refinement. This led to the establishment of Glasite churches in England and Wales before he decided—at John Glas's urging—to continue his missionary work in the American colonies.

Sandeman Emerges

Nathan Cole, a prosperous Connecticut farmer, was hard at work in one of his fields one chill October morning in 1741 when a neighbor hurried by to pass along word that the famous "Grand Itinerant," George Whitefield, was expected to preach at Middletown in less than two hours. The thirty-year-old Cole and his wife, Anne, lived in Kensington, at least two hours from Middletown by horseback. Nathan hastened to the house, pulled his wife from her chores, and they mounted their fastest horse to attempt the twelve-mile journey, hoping to arrive in time. Together they ran their horse to near exhaustion, Nathan occasionally hopping off to run until he "was *much* out of breath" before "mount[ing] my horse again." As they approached Middletown, Cole noticed "a Cloud or fogg rising ... and this Cloud was a Cloud of dust made by the Horses feet." Indeed a great crowd of people converged on Middletown, just as they had in every city and town Whitefield visited during his celebrated preaching tours of 1739–1741 to, again as Cole put it, "hear news from heaven." The Coles made it in the nick of time, and Nathan heard a sermon that changed his life, one that "gave [him] a heart wound."[2]

The 1730s and 1740s witnessed in Britain and its North American colonies a seemingly abrupt outpouring of emotionally intense religious sensibility, a "great and general awakening," as its greatest theologian, Jonathan Edwards (1703–1758), called it. A new generation of conservative Protestant clerics became sharply critical of the elder clergy for presiding over a thoroughly intellectualized Christianity, and favoring a faith that resided in the mind rather than in the heart. They deplored a growing Arminianism in the sermons and teachings of these ministers, and asserted a rigid Calvinism designed to rouse congregations out of their spiritual torpor. These critics accused the established clergy of being materialistic and careerist, more interested in political influence, monetary rewards, and social status than in their religious vocation. The established clergy, who in the American colonies became known as "Old Lights," defended themselves against these upstarts, the "New Lights," by hurling accusations of chicanery, doctrinal error, and of propagating "enthusiasm" among the religious.[3] They perceived in the New Lights the same materialism, ambition, and greed of which they were accused. The First Great Awakening produced a storm of theological and ecclesiological literature from all sides of the issue as churches and denominations split between the liberalism of the Old Lights and the conservatism of the New Lights. It also reinforced ties between dissenting Protestants in Britain and America, as evidenced by a heavy stream of letters that passed back and forth across the Atlantic Ocean.

Much of the character of American evangelicalism was a direct inheritance from Scottish and Scots-Irish revivalism, which derived from the seventeenth-century Covenanter "conventicles" that usually took place outdoors. By the eighteenth century, Scottish and Scots-Irish Presbyterians were able to celebrate their sacramental seasons unmolested, the legacy of the Covenanters vindicated in the massive annual revivals marked by marathon extemporaneous preaching and excessive popular enthusiasm. One acerbic Anglican critic rhetorically clucked his tongue at the *"strange Pomp"* of the proceedings and *"long Harangue[s]* ... supplied from the *stores* of the *Extemporary Spirit"* to be found in these sacramental seasons. Moderates were somewhat less disturbed by the conventicles, though they frequently criticized the radical clergy and laity for what they perceived to be the echoes of paganism in the festivities and a general disorderliness characteristic of these events. Robert Wodrow noted at Earlston in 1688 "there were one thousand Communicants, several thousands hearing, and twelve Ministers." This was by no means extraordinary, as Wodrow noted that one could count on encountering "vast confluences" of the faithful who traveled impressive distances to attend at every communion season. Apologists insisted that these were not raucous festivals, but overtly solemn occasions suffused with the spirit of God who, as "the great Master of Assemblies is pleased so far to countenance them with his presence and power," as George Wemyss averred in 1703. John Glas's negative opinion of the

Covenanters, and rationalist philosophic orientation, predisposed him to a revulsion against religious enthusiasm, which he passed down to Robert Sandeman.[4]

The Church of England was not immune to this climate of heightened religiosity, as "Methodists" emerged from a group of Oxford University clergy and theology students, some of whom formed what was somewhat derisively known as a "Holy Club" led by brothers John Wesley (1703–1791) and Charles Wesley (1707–1788), and George Whitefield (1714–1770). The latter gained notoriety for his evangelism and open-air revivals both in England and the American colonies, while John Wesley, under the influence of German Moravians in the newly founded colony of Georgia and Camisards[5] in England, instituted a type of primitive Christianity that gradually separated it from the Anglican Church in the 1750s.[6] One of the original members of the Holy Club, James Hervey (1714–1758), published a treatise titled *Theron and Aspasio: or, A series of Dialogues and Letters upon the most important and interesting Subjects* (1755), espousing his own interpretation of New Testament theology. The *Dialogues* elicited many responses, not the least of which came from John Glas's leading disciple, and whose name supplanted that of the sect's founder: Robert Sandeman. His criticism of Hervey launched him on a path that led to his becoming a tireless Glasite missionary, founding churches in England and the New England colonies in the 1750s and 1760s.

Sandeman was born in Perth on 29 April 1718 to David and Margaret Sandeman, members of the Glasite congregation there. David, a linen merchant and town magistrate, never exhibited a particular devotion to Glasite principles, as his service in government demonstrated, but young Robert's mother wielded great influence on her son, and her piety inspired him to prepare for a career in the ministry. Though unsure that service to God really lay in his future, Robert entered the University of Edinburgh and proved an able student of theology. While there he met John Glas and members of the latter's inner circle, who convinced him of the correctness of Glasite beliefs, and he joined Glas's Dundee congregation in 1735. That same year he left the University of Edinburgh to begin an apprenticeship in the weaving business, and two years later married Glas's daughter Catherine, thus deepening the mentor-protégé relationship. In 1740, he embarked on his own weaving business in partnership with his brother William, which he later gave up to assume greater responsibilities in the Glasite church. Catherine, whose health had been gradually failing, died in 1746, at which point the twenty-eight-year-old Sandeman alleviated his loneliness by throwing himself completely into Bible study and service to the church.[7]

Sandeman's first tentative foray into publication of a treatise in support of Glasitism was a short pamphlet, "Thoughts on Christianity in a Letter to a Friend," dated 4 February 1749. It is a simple affirmation of Glasite primitive Christianity, dependent primarily on the apostolic texts for support. In the forcefulness of his emerging style, Sandeman was careful to emphasize the Calvinist staple of the absolute helplessness of the individual before God, inverting a familiar biblical quotation that engenders spiritual confidence into one that generates abject despair for the sinner: "When he looks abroad upon the inflexible opposition of the Almighty to all sin, he must conclude, Seeing the Almighty is against me, who can be for me?" Only the power of God can rescue the sinner, who is otherwise bereft of hope, and that power is amply described in the New Testament, beginning with the Resurrection. The sinner's embracing of the divine truth, as evidenced by the Resurrection, is itself a spiritual resurrection, and Sandeman makes the symbolic connection. Divine truth cannot be grasped with the power of the mind, and no one can convert another. Sandeman, surveying the rationalist theological landscape, admits that this has led many to reject the gospels or even Christianity itself on account of so harsh a doctrine, but that only reinforces the fact that God—the author of Nature—may operate outside of natural laws for his purposes, and that the believer must accept with the spirit what cannot be understood with the mental faculties.[8]

Sandeman divided his time between Dundee and Edinburgh, acting as an elder in the Glasite churches there, and displaying an eagerness to utilize his abundant rhetorical skills to propagate Glasite doctrines in print. While Glas attracted controversy even as he tried to avoid it, Sandeman seemed to seek it out and to welcome it with fierce exuberance. He would not find it, however, until the publication of James Hervey's *Dialogues*. Hervey, a well-respected rector of Weston-Favel in Northamptonshire, had become fixated on the Calvinist doctrine of justification by faith alone, and published his famous treatise in defense of it. Renowned for his saintly character and keen intellect, Hervey enjoyed immense popularity from people across the social spectrum in northern England, and the *Dialogues* was an immediate bestseller in bookshops from Liverpool to London, selling out two editions between 1755 and 1757. It drew critical attention not just from Sandeman, but also from his former associates in the Holy Club.

In his youth, Hervey believed in the generally accepted Arminian conviction that faith is an active endeavor to emulate Christ as a means to approaching God, but quickly came to believe that this instead led to self-righteousness; of building faith on one's own efforts, and not on the gospels. Influenced by Independents in London, Hervey blended evangelicalism such as that propagated by George Whitefield with moderate Calvinism espoused by his new friend William Cudworth, and presented it in the *Dialogues*. Written as a series of fictional conversations and letters between "Theron" and "Aspasio," the three-volume *Dialogues* elaborately expounded upon the issues of righteousness—both Christ's and that of the believer—and justification. Rejecting means as an avenue to salvation, Hervey insisted that the sinner can only depend on Christ, and must have faith in God's willingness to offer salvation freely without any recommending qualification or preparatory conditions. This is not something that is applicable to all sinners in general, but only to particular sinners who are able to surrender themselves to divine mercy. It rests entirely on faith, which Hervey defined as a full personal acknowledgment of Christ's sacrifice for each sinner who receives the gospel, which confers righteousness on believers. "This righteousness," he declared, "as it was wrought out in the name and stead of the guilty, enemies and rebellious, was wrought out in *my name*, and in *my stead*; that is, in a name and character that undoubtedly belongs to *me*, and, according to the declaration of divine grace, sufficiently authorises *me* to draw near to God thereby."[9]

Hervey submitted the *Dialogues* to several friends and colleagues to solicit their comments, including his old friend John Wesley, who admittedly gave it only cursory attention. However, after a more thorough reading, Wesley composed an extremely lengthy reply that addressed what he believed were doctrinal errors in the work, to which Hervey neglected to respond. The *Dialogues* went to press virtually unaltered, and was received with generally laudatory acclamation. Wesley attempted to write another long letter to Hervey about the *Dialogues* in October 1756, which likewise elicited no reply, at which point Hervey published it and the previous missive in pamphlet form as *A Preservative against Unsettled Notions in Religion* (1758). Beginning with a criticism of its enormous length and elevated prose, Wesley rigorously attacked Hervey's insistence on justification by faith, seeing Calvinism as he did as the surest route to Antinomianism. In fact, Wesley found much in the *Dialogues* that was commendable and useful, but overall he believed that Hervey had confused the righteousness of God with the merits of Christ, which by logical extension implied that even notorious and unrepentant sinners had a sinless obedience to Christ.

Hervey, who had admitted that he was "what people would call a moderate Calvinist," had become in Wesley's estimation a "deep rooted Antinomian ... that is, a Calvinist consistent with himself." He saw the

Dialogues as a thoroughly Antinomian work, despite the fact that there is nothing in them to suggest that Hervey indeed harbored Antinomian inclinations. In fact, Hervey was careful to stress the primacy of moral law and the absolute necessity to obey the divine law. Wesley then learned that William Cudworth (1717–1763), now Hervey's close friend, had encouraged Hervey to respond negatively to Wesley's critique, and Wesley wrote to Hervey, firmly reminding him that "before I published anything concerning you, I sent it to you in a private letter; that I waited for an answer for several months, but was not favored with one line," and that nonetheless "when at length I published part of what I had sent to you, I did it in the most inoffensive manner possible." He asked Hervey to make his response in a private correspondence, and if no answer followed after several months, that he may publish such response as he saw fit. He sternly warned his friend to "give no countenance to that insolent, scurrilous, virulent libel which wears the name of William Cudworth. Indeed, how you can converse with a man of his spirit I cannot comprehend."[10]

The strongest criticism of Hervey came from Sandeman, who under the pseudonym "Palaemon" published the *Letters on Theron and Aspasio* in 1757. Intended merely to correct what Sandeman perceived to be Hervey's theological mistakes concerning the topic of salvation, the *Letters* became Sandeman's definitive statements on Christian belief and practice, and sent shockwaves throughout Scotland, England, and the North American colonies. In ways Glas had not, Sandeman elaborated on and further developed Glas's theological ideas in a forceful and engaging prose. It remains clear, however, as one reads the *Letters* that Glas's writings form the spine of the work, and that Sandeman's accomplishment lies in the distillation of his mentor's teachings. Both took the New Testament as their foundation, and labored to identify the purest practice of Christianity long lost under the accumulated layers of artifice and corruption. According to Sandeman, worldly rationalism had further obscured true Christianity, particularly in the steady growth of Arminianism, which encouraged the notion that merit had anything to do with salvation, and the *Letters* set out to destroy that notion once and for all. He went on to further elaborate upon his ideas in a later work, *Discourses on Passages of Scripture: With Essays and Letters*, written between 1765 and 1771, and published posthumously. The argument between Hervey, Wesley, and Sandeman played an integral role in the refinement of Methodist soteriology, with Sandeman's part being the most vital.

Sandeman began with that key "corruption of the gospel" that was Arminianism, which he alleged Hervey preached despite a superficial

Calvinism in the *Dialogues*. Sandeman opposed any preaching that advocated any duty or activity that could be construed as merits of salvation on the part of the individual. While this had long been considered a corruption of the Anglican Church, Sandeman accused the evangelical preachers of the Great Awakening of promising that one's deeds cultivate holiness. He quoted Hervey's *Dialogues* as suggesting that one's efforts can attract saving grace:

> Because you cannot by your own strength exercise faith, let not this occasion a tame resignation of yourself to infidelity. You must endeavor, diligently endeavor, to believe; and wait and pray for the Divine Spirit. Though it is his office to testify of Christ, *and bring near the Redeemer's righteousness*; yet his influences are not to supersede, but to encourage our own efforts.

In his reaction against such urgings to do works of righteousness, Sandeman saw in the popular concept of faith a kind of labor of the mind and will that proved to be no less offensive than other forms of works theology. He viewed any human effort not only in works, but in feelings and thoughts as well.[11]

Sandeman opposed any view or description of faith that left anything for the unbeliever to do. He opposed all preachers and teachers who presented salvation "not simply on *what Christ hath done*, but more or less on *the use we make of him*, the advance we make toward him ... or on something we feel or do concerning him." According to the popular theology propagated by evangelists of the Awakening, most descriptions of saving faith included "some good motion, disposition, or exercise of the human soul," which, Sandeman wrote, actually served "instead of clearing our way, to blindfold and decoy us." He wrote that when a soul attempts to believe, "a God of grace changes the attempt into a true genuine faith" before that soul becomes aware of what is happening, and thus is brought to belief in "a way it knows not how." In this way, Sandeman asserted, "justification comes by bare faith"; any action or disposition on the part of the believer is absent in true faith. In his opposition to those he called "popular preachers," Sandeman approached an opposite extreme. To avoid any suggestion of human effort in the salvation process, he defined faith as "the bare belief in the bare gospel." To think humanly of Christ is to rob him of all divine glory. "He gives his dearly beloved and only begotten Son. If we attempt to form any estimation of this gift, we are guilty of impiety by undervaluing the gift, but when we say that it was all that the Deity himself could give, bold as the expression is, we are no way chargeable with impiety." People cannot even think upon Christ, Sandeman insisted, because the depravity of their nature prevents them from giving proper value to Christ.[12]

Sandeman used several expressions to describe faith. The most frequent is "bare faith." He also referred to "the simple belief of the truth," "the simple Gospel," and the "bare persuasion of the truth." By these expressions, he was asserting that saving faith was the absence of human labor and the complete reliance on the truth of the gospel. He affirmed this view by pointing out that the apostles "never taught men to put forth any act, or to make one step of advance towards God." The faith of the apostles was what both Glas and Sandeman sought to emulate, for it was from Christ that the apostles learned about faith. Sandeman insisted that faith stands apart from any effort or merit, that "justification comes by faith and not by works, not by any thing we do in obedience to any law whatsoever." Faith did not come to believers because they sought it or prepared for it, in Sandeman's view. God gives faith in sovereign discretion, apart from any "willing or doing" on the part of the unbeliever. After salvation, the believer works together with God. To maintain a faith free from works, which merit God's response to a positive action, Sandeman contended that faith came to men who were worthless and destitute. Grace is thus enhanced and sovereignty maintained. Human effort nullified that scheme.[13]

By bare belief, Sandeman maintained, one obtains faith only when not engaged in seeking it. Only if one is not seeking faith can it be said to lack any effort or merit on the part of the individual. "The Spirit of truth," he wrote, "is at first found of them that seek him not, when men, in the course of their alienation from God, are surprised and overcome by the evidence of the truth." In fact, Sandeman claimed—paradoxically—that justification could only be achieved while "running away from the truth." God overtakes the sinner by grace and commands belief. That command "is a command of far different nature from any command in the law." The command is one that it is impossible to obey, but must come passively on the sinner by the work of the Holy Spirit. The truth imparted is the divine revelation of the Word of God, and only when accompanied by the agency of the Spirit. "The Holy Spirit [is] necessary to enable a man to make such a profession of the faith.... There is no separating the agency of the Holy Spirit from the knowledge of the truth." Sandeman maintained that there existed no difference between the work of the Spirit in bringing salvation and the comforting work of assurance in the heart of the believer:

> To have the Holy Spirit, as the Comforter, and earnest of the heavenly inheritance, is an attainment far beyond any influences of the Spirit that

are common to those who believe for a time, and those who believe to the saving of the soul; yea, beyond the regenerating work of the Spirit by which men are at first brought to the knowledge of the truth, and taught to love it.

The Spirit produces any affirmation of Christ, even one that does not result in salvation of the soul. Even a nominal belief in Christ is beyond the capabilities of human reason. Sandeman effectively removed any trace of human effects in the mind, will, and emotions of human beings.[14]

He repeatedly argued that the concept of faith used in scripture is no different from the "common" usage of the term. No distinction is made between "faith" and "belief" in Sandeman's thought. The terms are used interchangeably and regarded as identical, regardless of whether they are found in the Synoptic Gospels, John's writings, or the epistles of Paul:

> The apostles used the word *faith* or *belief* in the same sense we do to this day in common discourse. We are properly said to believe what any man says, when we are persuaded that what he says is true. There is no difference betwixt our believing any common testimony and our believing that of the gospel, but what arises from the very nature of the testimony.

Sandeman wrote that faith refers to the testimony or the report believed, and to the persuasion that the report is true. Faith is then dependent on the testimony brought by the Spirit, the testimony then becoming primary over the act of believing. Unless a report is accepted as truth, it has no value:

> The effect of a true report is the same as the effect of the persuasion of it; yea, we can have no idea of a true report but by the persuasion of it. Whatever, then, we say, of the persuasion, must equally be said of the report, and of the thing reported. So we find the word FAITH is used indifferently for either of these in Scripture.

Sandeman equated the testimony that comes by divine agency with the persuasion that is faith. "When once a man believes a testimony, he becomes possessed of a truth; and that truth may be said to be *his faith*. Yea, we have no idea of truth, but with reference to its being believed."[15]

There is little comforting assurance in Sandeman's theology. The assurance of salvation did not rest for him on the possession of the truth, but on the truth itself. Assurance is not in personal salvation, but only in the truth of the gospel of salvation; it is found in the fact of the gospel, and not in the faith of the believer. Sandeman addressed the issue of assurance, but with no confidence in a personal or subjective assurance. Assurance is based solely on the testimony that is given, or, more appropriately, in the truth that is believed. The believer is never certain about his or her part in eternal life, but can only gain assurance of the facts as revealed in scripture. Any assurance that comes is an effect of faith, rather than a mental or volitional affirmation, and that fearful doubt is an essential concomitant of faith:

> Now, a man may have some doubts about this, who is very firmly persuaded of the truth of the gospel; yea, Paul calls upon some whom he himself looked upon as believers, to examine themselves, whether they were in the faith ... intimating, that they could not warrantably be assured of their happy state by any exercise of the mind, without the fruits of faith, or the self-denied works of obedience.

Sandeman built on the distinction between the assurance of faith and the assurance of hope, the former given by the Holy Spirit without any endeavor on the believer's part, while the latter follows from the works of righteousness produced by that faith. The assurance of faith is "carried in the Divine testimony to the consciences of the ungodly; the assurance of hope arises from experience in the hearts of them that love God and keep his commandments."[16]

Sandeman argued that to question the truth of the gospel is the complete absence of faith. Assurance is not in the individual, but in the truth of the gospel, and doubts about one's assurance is a necessary concomitant: "No man can be assured that his sins are forgiven him, but in as far as he is freed from the service of sin, and led to work righteousness." Obedience to God in works of righteousness—the product of faith—is the mark of assurance. However, Sandeman never related how one is to distinguish between works of self-righteousness apart from faith and works that are the effect of faith. Thus, the assurance he sought apart from any works can never be guaranteed in his concept. He spoke against those who preached that human efforts could bring one to the point of believing the gospel, equating them with the Jews who taught the keeping of the law for righteousness. Whether it was called "law" or "gospel," he said that it was an effort of man to procure salvation, which opened him up to charges of having little regard or appreciation for the law; that he was an Antinomian. He held a high regard, however, for the keeping of the law, which was the duty of all to obey even if it did not itself lead to salvation. Everyone must conform to the law of God, lest the disobedient be "exposed to the awful and eternal wrath of God."

Christ never set the law aside, and "every thing in the gospel is calculated to enforce the law upon the human conscience, and to make men tremble at every breach of the law." It was in the keeping of the law in obedience to the command of Christ that the believer found some security, though such security was precarious at best, for the believer is subject to the same wrath for disobedience as is the unbeliever. The believer can delude himself or herself that their understanding of the way of salvation is in accord with that of the apostles, "yet some future trial of his faith may show, that what he spoke with his mouth, was not the persuasion of his heart." When one has the persuasion of the truth, or faith in one's heart, then a love for that truth is also present. That love is the activity that produces obedience. The threat of disobeying and giving evidence of a lack of faith is always present, which brings with it a fear that helps ensure obedience. "No man, then, by enjoying the Holy Spirit as the Comforter, can find any ground for being less afraid of sinning, or of its consequences, than he was before; for he no sooner indulges an evil affection, or any thought opposite to charity, than he loses that enjoyment." The believer must beware of the "neglect of the testimony of God" that is evidenced in sin.[17]

Although Sandeman did not assert that one could have faith and then lose it, his view of security came very close to that idea. He proposed, rather, that if one lost the persuasion of the testimony, it was because one never truly possessed it, like the mustard seed that fell on the stony ground in the parable. The doctrines, which should offer assurance and comfort to the believer, do just the opposite in Sandeman's concept. The simplicity of obtaining salvation by mental persuasion results in the equally simple disillusionment when sin gives evidence of a lack of faith. He never contended that believers are somehow free of sin; they will sin inevitably, and can theoretically lapse into apostasy without necessarily losing their salvation: "Christ's people do indeed very often go strange and awful lengths in apostasy and alienation from the truth, verging towards the sin of the wicked one, yet through the seed of God remaining in them they cannot go that length from which there is no return." Since an individual's faith is passive and has no volitional or emotional aspect, volition or the will has no part in offering any believer a sense of security. This logic led Sandeman also to reject repentance, which he considered another exertion of the mind and will, and has no place in procuring salvation. Repentance is an effect of faith "which always carries in it a sense of shame and regret at . . . former opposition to it. And he who knows the truth, so as to love it, will daily find occasion for repentance." Sandeman was aware of the narrowness of his views and of the broad objections that they would and did engender. He insisted, though, that he held to the truth and that all others had been deceived by cultural and historical prejudice, if not merely by theological error. If others accepted his views, he was certain that they would then know the truth and understand it perfectly as he did. This interpretation of faith was necessary for understanding God's revelation, and Sandeman asserted that every evil thought within a believer is the result of misappropriating this truth. Further, every error in doctrine and practice of the churches arises from the same fallacy—that is, applying some human merit to the cultivation of faith.[18]

Wesley, on reading Sandeman's stinging critique of Hervey, stepped in to defend his estranged friend in the form of a long pamphlet addressed to "Palaemon," whose identity he suspected was either John Glas or Robert Sandeman:

> Sir,
> It is not very material who you are. If Mr. Glass [sic] is still alive, I suppose you are he. If not, you are at last one of his humble admirers, and probably not very old; so your youth may in some measure plead your excuse for such a peculiar pertness, insolence, and self-sufficiency, with such an utter contempt of all mankind, as no other writer of the present age has shown. As you use no ceremony toward any man, so neither shall I use any toward you, but bluntly propose a few objections to your late performance, which stares man in the face as soon as he looks at it.

Wesley goes on to accuse Sandeman of slandering Hervey in what amounts to a load of nonsensical Calvinist gibberish, charging him with possessing a sort of religious fanaticism that is far more dangerous than that of which Sandeman marks as characteristic of evangelicals. In his deprecation of "popular preachers," Sandeman had, in Wesley's view, a penchant for persecution that would result in "more bonfires in Smithfield than Bonner and Gardiner put together." He was, however, a bit more charitable in the letter to Samuel Furly, wherein he described "Palaemon" as "a man of admirable sense and learning, but a Calvinist and Antinomian to the bone; as you may judge from his vehement anger at Mr. [Ebenezer] Erskine, [William] Cudworth, and Hervey for their legality." An anonymous threepenny pamphlet appeared at the close of 1757, *Remarks on the Revd John Wesley's Sufficient Answer to the author of the Letters on Theron and Aspasio by J. D.*, in which Wesley was accused of having "crowded more scandal, insolence, self-sufficiency, hatred, malevolence, rancour, bitterness and uncharitableness" into his penny tract than Hervey had put into his five-shilling book. Hervey's writing was at least "sarcastical, lively, volatile and pungent as the ether;

Wesley's was as dull as lead." James Hervey died in 1758 of a pulmonary ailment—most likely tuberculosis—and thus the controversy between him and his former friend ended.[19]

The *Letters on Theron and Aspasio* generated a great deal of interest and controversy, which initially took the form of correspondence between Sandeman and various Independent clergymen in England. Three of Sandeman's correspondents merit close examination: Samuel Pike, John Barnard, and William Cudworth. While the correspondence was collegial, Sandeman intimated to a friend that his purpose in discussing his theology was not so much to persuade any of them to convert to Sandemanianism, but to learn how to gauge reaction to his work and prepare for any criticism. "I will be content to hear of any motions in the congregations of my correspondents ... as also what my open or public opponents are doing. For, to borrow a military phrase, you know, as I have a wide controversy upon my hands, it is my business to reconnoitre the enemy."[20] However, he could not ignore the possibility that the strength of his rhetoric might effect a change in the dispositions of those he suspected might be opponents, and thus hoped that they might even come to embrace his doctrines.

Samuel Pike, pastor of an Independent church in London, heard about the *Letters* from members of his congregation, and wrote to Sandeman to express his mixed feelings on the book's theology. This series of letters were later collected and published in 1759. He began with the extension of his gratitude for Sandeman's "elaborate and ingenious performance" that confirmed many of his beliefs, but he sharply criticized the style and language of the book for its "peculiarly severe and satyrical [sic]" tone. In terms of Sandeman's theology, Pike approved of its Calvinistic focus, particularly the rejection of means as the route to salvation, but begged to differ on Sandeman's harsh critique of evangelicalism. The Word of God, particularly the gospels, offers a vehicle by which believers may approach God, and while "popular" preaching may have its hazards—not the least of which is enthusiasm—that which brings the sinner to his or her conversion is ultimately of secondary importance. Though Pike shared some reservations about evangelicalism, Sandeman's "injudicious" attacks on revivalism and revivalists went too far, and sounded too much like venomous grandstanding.[21]

Sandeman correctly surmised that Pike was half-converted to Glasite belief when he read Pike's first letter, and while Pike tried to discover the weaknesses of Sandeman's ideas, his inability to do so eventually led to an announcement in 1765 of his full conversion to Sandemanianism, as the movement had become known by this time. However, in this early period that was by no means a certainty. His congregation had divided between those who supported Pike's sympathy for Sandemanian ecclesiology and those who opposed it, and William Fuller, whose pamphlet "Reflections on an Epistolary Correspondence between S. P. and R. S." (London, 1759), represented the latter. Fuller deprecated Sandeman's growing influence in London, and Pike came to Sandeman's defense in a pamphlet, "Free Grace Indeed" (London, 1759), in which he fully explained his new principles. One of Pike's deacons, Thomas Uffington, weighed in against his pastor in "The Scripture Doctrine of Justifying Faith" (London, 1760), which elicited a spirited response from John Dove, a Pike supporter who, writing as a "Hebrew Tailor," published "Rational Religion distinguished from that which is Enthusiastic" (London, 1760). Matters came to a head when the church voted on whether to expel Pike from his pastorate, which came up even apart from Pike's deciding vote that he remain. Those who voted in the negative broke to form their own church, while Pike and his supporters joined the Sandemanian church that had formed in London.[22]

John Barnard, a convert of George Whitefield and a self-confessed "popular preacher," learned about the Glasite churches from their founder's son, George Glas, a merchant ship captain who had expressed interest in founding Glasite churches in London. Barnard wrote to Sandeman in July 1759, declaring his admiration and respect for Sandeman's devotion to the truth and the eloquence with which he defended it. After providing a brief account of his own religious history, Barnard mentioned having been approached by individuals who invited him to "join them in forming a little church on the Apostolic [i.e., Sandemanian] plan," and that he had been greatly influenced by the *Letters on Theron and Aspasio*. He also read the correspondence between Sandeman and Pike, and, while attracted to New Testament fundamentalism, remained somewhat skeptical on certain points, for which he requested clarification. Sandeman welcomed an opportunity to establish a foothold in the London metropol, and encouraged Barnard to embrace Glasite principles:

> If you can find but a dozen of the poorest and least esteemed in London, who appear to love the truth, and are frankly disposed to join you in obeying it, much better to set out with them, under care of the Chief Shepherd, than entangle yourself with others, however noted for piety and wealth, to the grief and vexation of your heart in the issue.... If you should need or desire any assistance from us in the business of forming yourselves into the Apostolic order, I have ground to assure you, that the Churches in this country [Scotland] would be willing at their own expense to send you some of their presbyters to assist you for some weeks.

He suggested that he himself might journey to London, being very interested in seeing the great city for the first time.[23]

Barnard's next letter proved greatly disappointing, for it intimated that his efforts at forming a Glasite church met with some resistance, as well as other practical difficulties. Sandeman could not hide his irritation in his reply, chastening Barnard that he had squandered a golden opportunity on account of his apparent irresolution. For this, he blamed the influence of Pike, who had continued to resist conversion. In a letter to George Glas, Sandeman vented his frustration and disappointment, noting with some mystification that if only they dared to form an apostolic church, "they would have had the assistance of members used to the Christian order." Sandeman was cognizant that Pike and Barnard experienced difficulties with their congregations and with their colleagues, but he could not understand how those who know the truth when they saw it could lack the courage to embrace and transmit it, for this was no idle matter. "If the Christian profession is indeed to take place in London," Sandeman predicted, "it will give a great grace and beauty to its beginning; and beginnings, you know, are always noticed, if it make its first appearance by the leaders showing themselves to be men of unreserved self-denial and confidence in the living God."[24]

William Cudworth proved to be the most challenging critic of Sandemanian theology at this point. He was a very close friend of Hervey, to whose defense he rose in December 1757 when he posted a letter to Sandeman that included a copy of his "Aphorisms on the Assurance of Faith." This pamphlet, a condensation of Hervey's works, convinced Sandeman that he had met a match, for which he summoned all his literary skill in penning responses. Cudworth likewise rose to the occasion, with neither able to breach the other's logical constructs. In his third letter to Cudworth, Sandeman admitted his fatigue with the contest, and complemented Cudworth on his courtesy: "Though I find nothing disobliging in your manner of correspondence, nothing to move personal pique or resentment, but the contrary, yet I have reason to be weary of the dispute, from the appearance it has of being fruitless." Sandeman believed that he had divested himself of an able opponent, but, after a while, Cudworth reopened the dispute in January 1760. Sandeman wrote in a letter to George Glas that "I received a long letter from Mr. Cudworth, of nearly 16 quarto pages, closely written, wherein he shows his disaffection to our creed in a more undisguised manner than formerly." It went on to inform Sandeman that he intended to publish his further thoughts on the subject as a defense of Hervey's *Theron and Aspasio*, which came out later that year.[25]

Sandemanian Growth in Britain

While he disputed and discussed his theology primarily with these three individuals, Sandeman never lost hope that a church would eventually be founded in London and other parts of England. George Glas was considering a return to London in order to accomplish this goal, but the impediments were formidable, and he hesitated. New hope, however, came in the form of a correspondence with George Hitchens of London, whom Sandeman encouraged to gather any and all who shared his beliefs into a core of a Christian society. He warned Hitchens to be aware that eminent "professors"—at this point probably Pike and Barnard, whose interest in the project he had cause to suspect—might step forward to become leaders in the "matter of union" who did not fully share Sandemanian theology. He had no evidence that even a dozen people in that great city demonstrated any inclination to take such steps, but it needed only a handful of committed believers to start a viable church, which would inevitably grow. He encouraged George Glas to go back to London and make contact with Hitchens and another promising prospect, Samuel Churchill, and that consequently he had every reason to expect "a church being erected there ere long."[26]

John Glas heartily encouraged his son to leave behind the seafaring life, and all of its attendant dangers, in preference to a life devoted to faith. He wrote to Sandeman that "If you can persuade him to stay at home and devote himself to the work of the ministry there, this would be very agreeable to all his friends, and ground of thankfulness to all our churches." Sounding very much like the anxious father he was, he concluded in March 1761: "For my part, I would rather see him a pastor of Christ's church in London than Lord Mayor of it, or Admiral of the British fleet." Sandeman followed George Glas to London the next month, accompanied by his brother William and two others to see about forming a church there. Barnard, Pike, along with other sympathizers, wished to meet John Glas and begged him to travel with Sandeman to London, but ailing health prevented the elder Glas from coming along. Barnard had already succeeded in forming a society at Glover's Hall on Beech Lane, in the Barbican district, which espoused some Sandemanian principles, but Barnard remained unable to cast his entire lot with the sect. George Glas, whom Sandeman hoped would buttress Barnard, began considering a commercial trip to West Africa that he eventually undertook, much to his father's dismay. To leave Sandeman in London in such precarious circumstances was to him "like Jonah's flying to Tarshish from the presence of the Lord." Angrily he confessed "that I cannot now pray or hope for success to him in that voyage."[27]

Whereas the church in London had been established in Butcher's Hall by April 1761, its leadership was uncertain. Sandeman considered the possibility that he should remain as elder in that congregation, but to this John Glas, who was at the time in Edinburgh, would not give his blessing. "You shall never have my consent, nor God-speed, to stay in London beyond the three Sabbaths at first proposed, and beyond that I will not stay here." There was some discussion of making Churchill an elder, but his lack of experience precluded this step, and by this time George Glas had determined to journey to Africa and would not submit to Sandeman's entreaties to remain in London. Reluctantly Sandeman made Churchill an elder, while George was named as a co-elder pending his safe return from his voyage. Sandeman left London for Scotland in May, quite worried about the unsteady situation of the tiny church, concerns reinforced by a letter from Churchill a few weeks later. Sandeman reassured Churchill that "if your small number continue stedfast in the faith and in works of love to one-another, there will be a better opportunity than at present, for chusing tried and proved men among yourselves for bearing office among you."[28]

Despite Sandeman's concerns, the London church managed to grow slowly but steadily, inspiring Sandeman to commend Churchill for his efforts. John Barnard accelerated the church's progress over the next five years by finally joining it as a full member in the spring of 1762, promising to bring with him his small congregation from Glover's Hall. In a letter dated March 1762, Barnard wrote apologetically to Sandeman for having been so long in coming around, for which he blamed his pride. "I know of nothing so desirable in this world as that I and my friends may now at last be one with you and yours," he confessed. This led Sandeman to take another trip to London, where he oversaw the inclusion of Barnard's congregation and Barnard's becoming an elder in the church. John Glas expressed his pleasure at this news, writing to Sandeman that Barnard's gifts would be of enormous benefit to the first Sandemanian church outside of Scotland. The expanded fledgling church held its meetings in Glover's Hall for the next three years until they relocated to an abandoned Quaker meetinghouse at the Bull-and-Mouth, in St. Martins-le-Grand. A number of ministers joined the church during this period, not the least of whom was Samuel Pike, who took it upon himself to chronicle the church's history and explain its practices in 1766.[29]

What brought Pike into the Sandemanians in full fellowship were the divisions that broke out in his own church over his adoption of certain Sandemanian principles. His publication in 1758 of *Saving Grace, Sovereign Grace*, a treatise that exhibits the high degree to which Pike was under Sandemanian influence, only exacerbated the situation. This sparked the aforementioned "Reflections on an Epistolary Correspondence between S. P. and R. S.," of William Fuller and the consequent dissolution of his Thames Street church. When he and his supporters joined the Sandemanian church at the Bull-and-Mouth, Pike's confession of faith in December 1765 ended without regret for the troubles he had undergone:

> What I have had access to observe among you within this fortnight has given me an idea of such faithfulness and zeal for the honour of God in connection with Christian tenderness, as has convinced me that God is among you of a truth; wherefore I desire fellowship with you, and am cheerfully willing to be ranked with the meanest brother of the church.

The incorporation of these talented ministers did much to strengthen the London church both in terms of the number of its adherents, as well as in its respectability. By this point Sandeman had become interested in spreading the Sandemanian faith to the American colonies, and while there he received a letter from John Barnard—by now an elder—written in June 1766 that confirmed Pike's ascension to an eldership, and that the church's membership stood at 106. The church grew to 149 members by 1768 despite frequent excommunications, and for the rest of the century became a prominent feature on the metropolitan religious landscape.[30]

Pike's defense of Sandemanian theology and church organization, *A Plain and Full Account of the Christian Practices Observed by the Church in St. Martin's-le-Grand* (London, 1766), is an epistolary treatise answering charges brought by critics against the peculiar sectarians. The bulk of the pamphlet is devoted to a basic description of Sandemanian church organization and practice as laid out by John Glas, liberally peppered with scriptural references from the New Testament. The final third of the work, however, addresses church discipline with particular regard to how violators are dealt with, which would appear to be the source of much of the criticism hurled at the Sandemanians, most likely by unredeemed excommunicants. This section begins with an emphatic statement that they

> dare not continue in our Fellowship any Railers, Drunkards, Extortioners, Unjust, Fornicators, or unclean Persons; any Sabbath-Breakers, profane Swearers, or Perjurers, Servants disobedient to their Masters, Subjects disaffected to their King or Government, any Smugglers, or such as refuse to give all their Dues; any covetous Persons, or such as are discontented with their Lot in Providence, &c. &c.

Pike went on to discuss in some detail the process of meting out discipline, especially as concerning excommunication, and the redemption of such who have been cast out upon the profession of repentance. As in all other matters concerning a specific church, the entire congregation must be involved, and all decisions agreed upon unanimously.[31]

A second issue Pike thought he had to address in the *Plain and Full Account* was the insular nature of Sandemanianism, for which he noted they were "reproached and hated." Sandemanians did not worship with other Christians, viewing them as apostates, and this Pike defended on the basis of liberty of conscience, "which we allow to others the same Liberty, without Grudging or Limitation." In keeping with their pacifist and apolitical beliefs Pike insisted that Sandemanians were prepared to turn the other cheek.

> If then we are reproached and hated, because we confine our Christian Charity within such seemingly narrow Limits, or for our following the Practices of the primitive Christians; we are willing to suffer it for Conscience Sake; without resisting Evil, but aiming to overcome Evil with Good; knowing it to be our Duty, "to love our Enemies, to bless them that curse us, to do Good to them that hate us, and pray for them that despitefully use us and persecute us."

Pike concluded this section with the somewhat combative assertion that "This reconciles us to Shame and Contempt, in Hope that our Reproach will be rolled away, when 'Christ shall come to take Vengeance upon them that know not God and obey not the Gospel.' "[32] Nothing brings a group together like the experience of shared suffering and persecution, and while this constituted a bond uniting the Sandemanian churches, divisions from within often threatened, as the many instances of excommunication prevented the churches from becoming very large.

London was not the only place where Sandemanianism took root in Britain outside of Scotland. Benjamin Ingham, an associate of John Wesley and George Whitefield, had formed a number of societies in Yorkshire modeled on Moravian-influenced Methodism in the 1750s and he read the works of John Glas and Robert Sandeman with great interest. Ingham sent two of his preachers, James Allen and Wiliam Batty, to Scotland in order to observe the Sandemanian churches in 1761. They traveled through Glasgow, Edinburgh, Perth, Dunkeld, and Dundee throughout the month of August, during which both Allen and Batty converted wholeheartedly to Sandemanian beliefs. Batty, in a letter to Ingham, wrote enthusiastically that "Upon every reflection of our journey ... I feel a love to the people, and my heart drawn after them.

Surely the journey was providential and seasonable. But the clear light shining among them, gives me to see things differently amongst us." At a conference of the Inghamite societies in October, Allen's and Batty's reports were formally presented, and it was decided to abandon the Methodist format in favor of the Sandemanian, but differences arose as to the mechanics of the process, and how far it was to go. The societies split into two factions, one that adhered to Allen and advocated union with the Sandemanians, and the other led by Ingham and a reluctant Batty who wished to maintain elements of Methodist practice. Allen returned to Scotland early in 1762, where he gained admission into fellowship and became an elder.[33]

James Allen became an active Sandemanian missionary, establishing his first church in his hometown of Gayle, in Wensleydale. A highly regarded public speaker whose "language and manner were peculiarly persuasive," Allen nonetheless had some difficulty convincing friends and colleagues of the superiority of Sandemanian theology and doctrine. He admitted that he and his fellow newly minted Sandemanians "made ... many enemies and stirred up opposition in every place." Many of those who joined Allen, Glas suspected, did so more out of friendship than out of religious conviction. The Inghamites placed a great deal of emphasis on preaching, and less on church order, and Glas predicted that this would cause problems in the future. By 1763, the church at Gayle counted eight members, the one in Kirkby-Stephen had thirty, the one in Newby had twenty-four members, and the one in Kirkby-Lonsdale counted sixteen adherents. Glas believed that these northern English churches maintained too much of Methodism despite Allen's Sandemanian convictions; the members were more interested in the sermons than in discipline, particularly with regard to the Lord's Supper, the importance of which seemed secondary among Allen's people. Glas put this down to their original connection to Ingham: "Till your people be cleared of this prejudice," he wrote to Allen, "they will make little of the ordinary officers, the elders or bishops of a church, nor will they make much of the Lord's Supper, nor of the work and labour of love amongst themselves, nor of the communion of churches."[34]

There was much confusion about church order and the authority of elders, as the English churches questioned the appropriateness of elders from one church asserting authority over members of another congregation. A lack of elders constituted an obstacle to church order, since at least two elders had to administer each church, and the English churches required elders from other churches to assist in the administration of the Lord's Supper, which necessarily took them away from their home congregations. Glas asked Allen in exasperation: "Will not your disciples at Newby, whom you are bringing into church order, when you visit them, receive you as an elder? Or will they not allow him they have chosen, when he visits Gayle, to be received there as an elder?" Glas instructed Edward Gorell, one of the elders of the Gayle church, that "when any members of your Newby church come there [Gayle] they are received and act as members of that sister church while there, by virtue of the communion of churches.... Thus our churches have from the first helped one another in this same necessity." Similarly, the Sandemanian interpretation of predestination proved a thorny issue for the former Inghamites, who inclined to free grace. Glas warned Allen not to entangle himself in "foolish questions and disputes" on this theological point lest his people be "driven toward free will in opposition to the scripture doctrine of grace." Better that the churches remain small rather than larger and divided by differences of opinion or doctrinal controversy, and indeed the English churches never grew large. Nonetheless, Glas was encouraged enough by the end of the year to write to Sandeman that "our sister church, with its presbytery in Newby gives us all great joy."[35]

One factor explaining the small size of the English churches was the unusually frequent cases of excommunication, most commonly on the matter of the marriage of believers with unbelievers, which the Inghamites prohibited, but not the Sandemanians. Though Glas preferred marriage within the Sandemanian communities, the New Testament placed no ban on such marriages, but even over minor concerns, the English churches too freely indulged in excommunication proceedings. John Barnard traveled from London to Newby to shore up church discipline in 1763, but his influence proved only temporary. Rifts began appearing in the other churches, with many withdrawing or suffering excommunication. The church at Kirkby-Lonsdale was reduced by half in this environment, and relations between Glas and Allen grew strained, though Allen eventually admitted that he had been in error. Attempts to compel greater discipline tended to exacerbate the situation rather than remedy it. Lacking an ultimate authority to which elders could look for guidance, internal tension usually prohibited church growth and cohesion.[36]

Despite these difficulties, the Sandemanian churches continued to spread, with congregations formed in York in 1763, in Norfolk in 1766, in Colne, Wethersfield, and Liverpool in 1767, and in Whitehaven, Trowbridge, and Nottingham in 1768. John Barnard, William Cudworth, and James Allen all were active in these endeavors. The churches were almost entirely composed of the poor and laboring classes, which rendered some of them unviable in Edward Gorell's opinion, who suggested that some of them be disbanded. A physical blow fell on the English churches with the departure of James Allen himself, who grew increasingly frustrated with John Glas's influence and dominance over the Sandemanian churches. He had left the Inghamites mainly because of Ingham's heavy-handedness, and from Glas encountered much the same attitude. Writing long after the fact, he surmised: "We have seen human authority superseding the authority of God, the fear of man taking the place of the fear of God, in subjecting one church to the control of certain individuals, or the members of a single church to the *ipse dixit* of a ruling elder." In the end, despite a professed doctrine of egalitarianism and decentralized authority, the Sandemanian "congregational-church principles have very visibly given way in practice to those of presbytery and prelacy." What precipitated his withdrawal was a conflict with Samuel Pike over the latter's conduct that resulted in Pike's temporary excommunication, but Allen's behavior drew fire from the London church, as well as many of the others, and Allen himself was excommunicated in 1769. Believing himself in the right, he refused to admit any error and remained outside the Sandemanian connection for the rest of his life.[37]

Glas's and Sandeman's writings were also distributed in Wales and produced keen interest, beginning with John Popkin, a Methodist who approached Sandemanianism indirectly through Hervey's *Dialogues between Theron and Aspasio*. He learned about Sandeman's critique of Hervey and duly read the *Letters on Theron and Aspasio*, which originally put him in a state of confusion. As he would later tell Glas, he thought Sandeman at some times "a bold and faithful friend of the truth; and other times I thought he was an enemy, a scoffer, a derider of all true religion." He turned uncertainly from Sandeman to Glas's four volumes of writings, and then to Sandeman's correspondence with Samuel Pike, as well as other Glasite-Sandemanian writings, some of which he translated into Welsh and printed at his own expense. Established preachers throughout Wales denounced Popkin and Sandemanianism from their pulpits, influenced by the evangelical labors of Howell Harris and Daniel Rowlands, the latter of whom was most vociferous in his opposition to this new theological importation. In a letter to Glas, Popkin bemoaned that these popular preachers "could [not] exert themselves with more zeal and vigour if they were endeavouring to prevent the plague from spreading through Wales; and the greatest fathers and most respected preachers were the foremost and most zealous in the opposition."[38]

Eventually concluding that he was no longer a Methodist, Popkin wrote to Sandemanian elders in London to request counsel and assistance in establishing a Sandemanian church in Wales. Barnard wrote to

Sandeman, who by now was in New England, in 1766 that Glas's and a few of Sandeman's treatises had been translated into Welsh,[39] and that plans were in formation to found a church with Popkin.[40] In preparation for their visit to Wales, they sent Popkin a copy of Pike's *A Plain and Full Account*, with Pike and Barnard arriving in Swansea later that autumn. Many of Popkin's supporters, and even Popkin himself, were reluctant to make such a drastic change in their practice of Christianity, and some did opt out, but Popkin believed that divine providence was at work with the visit of the London emissaries, and he became a Sandemanian along with a handful of others. Opposition continued to make its formidable presence known, but Popkin managed to distribute over seven hundred copies of the translated Sandemanian literature. He wrote to Glas expressing his expectation of publishing the *Letters on Theron and Aspasio* in Welsh, and his hope that "the hand of Providence, give a heavier stroke to the foundation of Babylon than it has yet felt in Wales."[41]

Barnard returned to Swansea in the summer of 1767 along with Thomas Vernor, a London elder, and another church member to check on the progress of Popkin in his absorption of Sandemanian doctrine, as well as to see if the establishment of a church was possible. Popkin was nominated for an eldership and unanimously approved, and William Powel became a deacon for the new church. The first Sandemanian service was well attended, with Barnard fulfilling the office of elder alongside Popkin, and later in nearby Carmarthen the number of interested attendees forced Barnard to address the assembly outdoors. Upon the completion of a love feast, the brethren approved the professions of two out of four candidates. Barnard and his company left behind a church with fourteen people, at which point Popkin followed Pike and Barnard to London to receive further instruction on church order and discipline. Edified by what he saw at St. Martin's-le-Grand, Popkin invited Pike to accompany him back to Swansea to ordain Powel as an elder. Popkin became an enthusiastic Sandemanian propagandist, as he traveled throughout Wales professing with all the zeal of a new convert. David Jones of Cardigan, a nephew of Rowlands who converted his uncle's daughter and son-in-law to the new faith, joined him for a while. So angry was Rowlands that he disowned his daughter and her husband. By 1770, Sandemanian churches had been founded in Carmarthen, Llangadock, and Llangyfelach, with sympathetic societies meeting in southern Wales. However, the strenuous efforts of Rowlands and William Williams of Pantycelyn successfully prevented the Sandemanians from spreading beyond northern Wales.[42]

Sandemanian Influence in Britain

Glasite-Sandemanian influence was not limited to conversions and the founding of Sandemanian churches in Britain. The impact of Glas's and Sandeman's writings can be discerned throughout British Protestantism, acting very much as stones cast into a pond, sending theological ripples radiating ever outward. Those who had come into contact either physically with, or through the reading of, Glas and particularly of Sandeman who failed to embrace wholeheartedly the Scots' brand of primitive Christianity, nevertheless went on to influence their own denominations, in some cases forming new sects closely related to the Sandemanians both in doctrine and in practice.

Archibald MacLean, a thirty-year-old Highland printer and fervent member of the Church of Scotland, began to question the propriety of church-state relationships in 1761 after reading Glas's *The Testimony of the King of Martyrs*, and wrote to Sandeman for clarification of Glasite doctrines. Receiving a series of voluminous replies that satisfied him of the correctness of Glasitism, MacLean became a member of the Glasite church in Glasgow at the end of the year. However, by late 1762, he had begun to turn away from the Glasites in protest of the harshness with which discipline was meted out in the churches, and receiving no satisfaction when he expressed his concerns to Glas, consequently resigned his membership. He perceived a political system operating in the church, with certain members deferred to in such a way as to upset the egalitarianism that was supposed to exist there, and since Glas did nothing to solve the problem, MacLean felt he had no choice but to withdraw. Robert Carmichael, who had joined the Glasgow church at the same time as MacLean, queried MacLean on the issue of infant baptism, who determined that there was no scriptural warrant for it, a conclusion with which Carmichael agreed and then consulted the church on the point. A small minority concurred with Carmichael, who felt compelled to leave the Glasite church along with his sympathizers in 1765. MacLean and Carmichael went on to become Baptists and establish the first Baptist church in Edinburgh later that year, with MacLean becoming co-pastor in 1768 and the acknowledged leader of the "Scotch Baptists."[43]

In terms of church organization and liturgy, the Scotch Baptists were essentially identical to the Sandemanians apart from the latter's rejection of infant baptism, in fact earning them the labels "Sandemanian Baptists" and "Baptist Sandemanians" by contemporaries and later chroniclers. The Scotch Baptists vigorously denied any connection to the Glasites and Sandemanians, even as they admitted to their admiration for

John Glas's and Robert Sandeman's published works. One early nineteenth-century historian, William Jones, insisted that "in so many and such important particulars ... there was very little congeniality; certainly no such similarity as should warrant the imputation of [MacLean's] belonging in that denomination." The connection had been made, according to Jones, by Andrew Fuller, an opponent of Sandemanianism in general and of MacLean in particular "to make [MacLean] amenable for his due proportion of the evil which, in his prejudiced judgment, attaches to it." MacLean made it clear that his break from the Sandemanians came as a result of individual members' self-righteousness and the frequent and uneven dispensation of discipline, even as they "countenance[d] theatre-going, merry-making, dancing, and other worldly diversions." "Take their word for it," he went on, "and they are the only true churches of Christ on earth." Nonetheless, a close examination of Scotch Baptist church discipline and doctrine reveals heavy Sandemanian influence, down to the particulars of Sunday worship. MacLean exerted a heavy influence on John Richard Jones, who founded Scotch Baptist churches in Wales during the 1790s.[44]

Sandeman's *Letters on Theron and Aspasio* also had a profound impact on other Church of Scotland ministers who founded churches loosely termed "Scots Independents." One of them, James Smith of Newburn, was inspired to write two short books, *A Compendious Account, taken from the Holy Scripture only, of the Form and Order of the Church of God* ... (Edinburgh, 1765), and *The Defence of National Covenanting, Non-Toleration and Sword of Steel, for Reformation under the New Testament* ... (Edinburgh, 1767), which indicate his conversion to Glasite-Sandemanian ecclesiology. Another, Robert Ferrier of Largo, was urged to read Glas's *Testimony of the King of Martyrs* by a ministerial colleague who lay on his deathbed, and upon doing so was converted as well. He sought out Smith, and the two concluded that they had to withdraw from the National Church, which they did in August 1768, publishing later that year a pamphlet to explain themselves. A later apology that Ferrier composed to clarify their withdrawal, published in a 1777 edition of Glas's *Testimony*, betrays that work's and Sandeman's *Theron and Aspasio* as influences, though Smith had some "rooted dislike" for the by-now deceased Glas that prevented Ferrier from directly attributing to Glas or Sandeman any direct influence.[45]

Smith and Ferrier established an Independent church at Balchristie in Newburn parish, while to the west in Glasgow a secession of two influential members of the Wynd Kirk congregation, David Dale and Archibald Paterson, over the issue of city council patronage in 1766 had led them to read the *Testimony*, and later Smith and Ferrier's *Case*. A tenuously founded church formed around them as they corresponded with Smith and Ferrier, leading to a merger of the Balchristie and Glasgow Independent congregations that closely resembled the Glasite-Sandemanian churches. Personality conflicts and arguments over church doctrine and discipline soon rent this crypto-Glasite congregation, resulting in Ferrier's resigning his connection to it in 1770 and joining the Glasite church in Glasgow. He justified his decision on the grounds that his associates refused to "practise some of the simplest commandments of the New Testament," which pushed him to become "more knit to the doctrine and order I beheld among them [the Glasites]." Other Scots Independent churches influenced by the reading of Glas's and Sandeman's works were founded at Maykirk, Perth, Methven, Kirkcaldy, Hamilton, Paisley, New Lanark, Dundee, Newburgh, and Sauchieburn over the remainder of the eighteenth century. While not formally Sandemanian churches, much of the church organization, order of worship, and emphasis on New Testament primitive Christianity show heavy Sandemanian influence among the Scotch Baptists, as well as among other groups arising later in the eighteenth and into the nineteenth centuries.[46]

ଓ

Sandeman's forceful personality and skill as a polemicist was the sole determinant of the spread of Glasite—by now more often called Sandemanian—theology in England, and the *Letters on Theron and Aspasio* did not just have an impact on Anglo-Scottish theologians and clergymen, but also generated interest in the American colonies. Pleased, though not satisfied, with the progress made, Sandeman turned his attention to the fringes of the British Empire in North America, from whence he had received letters of interest from a handful of Dissenters. The impact of "popular preachers" in New England, New Jersey, and Pennsylvania had been greater there than in the British Isles, and Sandeman perceived kindred spirits among the opponents of evangelical enthusiasm, and thus a potentially fertile ground for his theology. A voyage to America, though, would be a major undertaking, and John Glas was reluctant to part with his son-in-law and most capable disciple. Sandeman himself balked at the idea, reluctant to abandon the English churches that so greatly demanded his attention. Additionally, such a journey would be quite expensive. Yet the possibilities were undeniably compelling. Glas encouraged his son-in-law in this course of action, and thus Sandeman began planning his trip to America, deciding to go to New England, where the Great Awakening had aroused the utmost controversy. He had been receiving letters from curious New England ministers who read his *Letters on Theron and Aspasio*, and decided that he would seek these men out and attempt to replicate the success in New England that he had had in Old England.

෪ 4 ෪

"May God Preserve Our [Churches] Amidst All Attacks"

The Advent of Sandemanianism in New England

> He is of middling stature, dark Complexion, a good Eye, uses accurate Language, but not eloquent in utterance, has not a melodious voice, his expressions governed by Sentiment, his Dialect Scotch, not graceful in his Air and Address, yet has something which deforces attention ...
>
> —Ezra Stiles, *A Memoir of Robert Sandeman*

Robert Sandeman and his traveling companions entered the home of Ebenezer White of Danbury, Connecticut, shortly before Christmas Day, 1764, convinced that they were meeting the future elders and members of the first Sandemanian church in the New World. The *Letters on Theron and Aspasio* had generated no small amount of curiosity and interest in New England, particularly in Connecticut, which was going through a period of social realignment that made Sandemanian egalitarianism highly attractive to dissident elements in the Congregationalist churches. Sandeman had been frustrated in his attempts to attract disciples to form churches in Portsmouth, New Hampshire, Boston, Massachusetts, and Providence, Rhode Island, despite having recently been invited to preach in Newport by none other than Ezra Stiles, the eminent Connecticut divine. White and his lay and clerical supporters had written encouraging letters inviting Sandeman to elucidate his theological ideas, which gave Sandeman hope that here he would build his first American church. For over a month Sandeman and White, along with their respective followers, discussed and sometimes heatedly debated issues of Calvinist theology and church organization, with the result that no Sandemanian church would be formed in Danbury for the time being.

Although White and his supporters wholeheartedly agreed with Sandeman's theology, particularly the complete rejection of means as a path to salvation, the radicalism of Sandemanian church organization and governance repelled White and the majority of those who stood with him. He suffered expulsion from his pulpit for questioning the authority of the Congregational church leadership, which he had done under the influence of reading Sandeman's *Letters on Theron and Aspasio*, and his case exposed a groundswell of discontent among clergy and laity over the eminence given to members of prominent families. They held monopolies on positions of authority in the churches, sat in the choicest pews, and often refused to acknowledge the status of those who matched them in wealth, but did not have surnames traceable back to the founding generations. At the same time, Stiles, and those who upheld the established religio-social order that White and his friends attacked, saw in Sandemanianism a potential weapon against the shadow of an impending Anglican episcopate in the colonies that threatened the Dissenters' almost exclusive hold upon Protestantism in New England. Though temporarily disappointed in Danbury, Sandeman would be successful elsewhere, and his activities marked a significant change in New England society overshadowed only by British-American tensions that ultimately led to a revolution.[1]

The Great Awakening in New England

The New England colonies in the early eighteenth century were becoming secular societies; at least they were thought to be so according to conservative Calvinist critics who blamed this alarming development on the influence of Enlightenment rationalism, economic growth, policies of religious toleration, and—most alarming of all—the influx of Anglicanism under the auspices of the Society for the Propagation of the Gospel in Foreign Parts (S.P.G.), which since its founding in 1701 had steadily raised the profile of the Church of England in the northern colonies. The close relationship between secular and clerical authority grew strained as the New England governments' efforts to tax and otherwise constrain non-Congregationalists ran afoul of imperial authority that demanded adherence to the 1689 Act of Toleration. Gradually the general assemblies of Massachusetts and Connecticut bowed under pressure from the royal governors, while the majority of the clergy reluctantly abandoned the once central belief that one of government's roles is to enforce religious orthodoxy and individual piety. Popular anticlericalism also forced the Standing Order to accommodate the laity in ways that to a growing minority had come to jeopardize John Winthrop's cherished seventeenth-century hope for the "city on a hill." The criticism and ridiculing of ministers in the presses (at times in pornographic forms), the presence of prostitutes at the docks and even on Boston Common, and the disastrous smallpox epidemic of 1721–1722 in the city all elicited desperate jeremiad sermons. The defection of Yale College president Timothy Cutler and several tutors to the Anglican Church in 1722 convinced Cotton Mather that unless the purity and piety of the founding generation were revived, that covenant theology and strict Calvinism would not long survive in New England.[2]

Throughout the colonies, economic growth and diversity led to the rise of a middle class in the 1730s and 1740s. Artisans and craftsmen became increasingly common fixtures in colonial cities and towns in the eighteenth century, producing a widening variety of quality finished goods despite British restrictions on such production. This fed a booming merchant community and consumer culture in every Atlantic seaboard city and entrepôt that hastened a process of "Anglicization" in the more densely settled areas. Clergymen, physicians, lawyers, and college professors established greater uniformity of training, rapidly expanding what had been a very thin professional class. Advances in education and literacy expanded the market for books and pamphlets, which became less expensive and consequently more commonplace as a means of transmitting information and exchanging ideas throughout the British Atlantic world. Newspapers became an increasingly common feature in colonial cities, with the *Boston News-Letter* being the first American newspaper to appear in 1704, followed by Philadelphia's *American Weekly Mercury* and the *Boston Gazette* (1719), and the *New-England Courant* (1721). The eighteenth-century newspaper, as Charles E. Clark notes, was "intelligencer, gazette, propagandist, advertiser, and literary journal all in one." Colonial American politics, as Jon Butler characterizes it, "was often strangely 'popular,' sometimes ugly, [and] frequently exciting." The expansion and professionalization of the law after 1680 played an important role in the changing face of colonial politics characterized by the gathering power of the assemblies at the expense of the governors and their councils. Apart from Pennsylvania, the colonial legislatures became bicameral by the dawn of the eighteenth century, and just as the House of Commons in Britain wielded the most power, so gradually did the assemblies. If one wanted to find tumult, one need only look at local politics to discover something familiar, and in the eighteenth century the boisterousness of local politics gradually roiled colony-wide politics, as oligarchic factions headed by wealthy families and individuals wrangled and jockeyed for power—much as they did in the lay politics of the meetinghouses.[3]

Connecticut offers an ideal sampling of this shift away from seventeenth-century Congregational orthodoxy. The challenges to clerical authority and Puritan religious hegemony that occasionally rippled through Massachusetts did not reach Connecticut until the 1680s, when John Rogers and his small band of followers rejected infant baptism and Sunday worship, but even then Governor John Winthrop Jr. could state confidently that in the colony "there are 4 or 5 Seven-day men ... and about so many more Quakers." However, repressive laws against the heterodox were annulled by Crown policy in 1708, as they had been in neighboring Massachusetts in 1690, and denominations and sects critical of or downright hostile to the Congregationalist establishment began to make inroads almost immediately. The Anglican Church most worried the established clergy, as the S.P.G. sent missionaries and parsons into Connecticut and elsewhere in New England to raise the Church of England's profile there. Baptists were the next to take advantage, followed closely by the Society of Friends—the Quakers. They drew their adherents largely from among the disaffected who thought that Congregationalism made church order ultimately impossible to maintain despite attempts to shore up the clerical leadership's authority. Others were attracted to dissident denominations and sectarian groups out of frustration with the power wielded by prominent individuals in the churches, whose authority tended to outweigh that of the ministers. Much of the laity felt a sense of alienation from their clergymen, whose attention drifted into the more abstract, rarified realm of theological disputation at the turn of the eighteenth century. Yet the revivalists of the Great Awakening hurled another stone at the clay feet of the Standing Order.[4]

In the seventeenth century, the laity had a voice in the ordination of ministers, but by 1700 that voice had become muffled and eventually stifled, as decisions on ordination lay entirely with the professional clergy. By 1730, ordination sermons most often warned about—in Eliphalet Adams's venomous rhetoric—"*Cavillers* and *Opposers*" who, with "much Pride and Spirit and Self-Conceit ... can't relish such and such Doctrines, They can't approve of such and such Practices, They don't like such and such Orders or Methods of Discipline." Much of the eighteenth-century clergy had thus drifted away from those among whom they were bound to serve, and the laity had come to realize that a subtle undercurrent of mutual antagonism poisoned relations between what had become two discrete factions. But professionalization was only one aspect of this phenomenon. The clergy's mounting interest in theoretical theology was another. Calvinism's rigidity kept some New Englanders away from the churches or from seeking membership and the sacraments, while the clergy's theological contortionism put off the devoutly orthodox, sensitive as they were to even the slightest hints of

Arminianism or some other heterodoxy. There arose a controversy surrounding accusations of Arminianism among the New England clergy in the early 1700s, which exploded with the Yale College "apostasy" in 1722. It can be argued that late seventeenth- and early eighteenth-century Calvinism had not shifted to Arminian ground, and that Cotton Mather was not exaggerating New England's continued orthodoxy when he wrote in 1726 that "every one knows, That they [the churches in New England] perfectly adhere to the CONFESSION OF FAITH, published by the Assembly of Divines at Westminster." New England Calvinism may not have become completely Arminian, but it had conceded some theological ground, albeit subtly.[5]

The waves of Protestant revivalism that began in New England in the 1730s had already been taking place in New Jersey, Delaware, and Pennsylvania, where Presbyterians recognized a similar need for conservative reform to combat doctrinal and liturgical laxity. Fundamentalists such as William Tennent Sr. and his sons William Jr., Gilbert, and John complained of the same ills afflicting colonial American societies that their Congregationalist neighbors to the north perceived: Antinomianism, Arianism, Arminianism, Deism, Pelagianism, and Socinianism.[6] They detected corrosion in the underpinnings of American Calvinism, and decried the reluctance of the clerical leadership to correct the problem despite the evidence that surrounded them in the form of apostates, false prophets, and the irreligious. William Sr., an Irishman from Ulster who had been ordained by the Church of England there after his education at the universities in Glasgow and Edinburgh, established a crude seminary at Neshaminy, in Bucks County, Pennsylvania, in 1726 that became known as the "Log College." There he trained like-minded clerical aspirants to challenge the elder clergy and laity to move immediately against this process of degradation that threatened Presbyterianism. Such radicals failed to receive licenses to preach from the Presbyterian authorities, who declared in 1738 that no minister be licensed to preach without a degree from an officially recognized seminary. Log College graduates, thus forced into itinerancy, had already made themselves well known for their boisterous sermonizing in outdoor, sometimes impromptu gatherings, and the rising tide of evangelicalism threatened Presbyterian orthodoxy both in America and in Scotland.

William Tennent Sr. intended for the Log College to inculcate a particularly Scottish brand of Presbyterianism and, while in Scotland, he had come into contact with Covenanters and Seceders, befriending Ebenezar Erskine, from whom he imbibed a strong sense of cultural conservatism leading him to leave the Church of England and convert to Presbyterianism. When Tennent moved his family to New Jersey in 1718, William

Sr. explained to the Synod of Philadelphia his reasons for renouncing episcopacy and received a license to preach shortly thereafter. He and his sons circulated among New Jersey's and the Delaware Valley's Scottish and Scots-Irish communities, reinforcing Scottish identity through highly conservative Presbyterianism. The multiethnic, multicultural, and religiously pluralistic character of the Middle Colonies dismayed the Tennents, who blamed this dynamic for the growing influence of Enlightenment rationalism in religion, as well as other errors reflecting those that degraded the Church of Scotland at the same time. William Sr. established the Log College as an alternative to the liberal education that, as he and his sons interpreted it, had led many Presbyterian clergy into doctrinal error and laxity. Tennent drilled his students in the Westminster Catechism and the Scottish Shorter Catechism, the latter of which they were required to memorize and recite, in part in or whole, verbatim on command. John, just graduated from the Log College in 1730, came under the influence of Walter Ker, a recent Scottish immigrant and former Covenanter, who encouraged the young itinerant to assume the pastorate in Freehold, New Jersey. He was an immediate success with his ecstatic, evangelical preaching style, but his untimely death in 1732 led to his being replaced by his elder brother William Jr., who presided over a dramatic increase in the church's membership roll. The heady emotionalism of the Freehold revival came as a similar revivalist energy began making its presence known in New England, noted initially by Jonathan Edwards among his flock in his Congregationalist church in Northampton in western Massachusetts in 1729 and 1735, and spread rapidly throughout the region.[7]

New England, which had no primary ecclesiastical structure over which to wrangle, experienced dozens of local church divisions as congregations split between those wishing to maintain the status quo and those who determined that their ministers indeed lacked the spiritual vitality indicative of true conversion. These schismatics—the Separates—repudiated absolute clerical authority and ministerial taxes, declaring these to be magnets attracting candidates enticed more by the promise of a comfortable living and the high social status usually accorded to clerics than by any general sense of spiritual vocation. Separates recruited New Lights to settle ministers in new churches, while others managed to expel established ministers and replace them with men they deemed more suitable. The Separates worked to rediscover a purer, simpler Christianity devoid of formalism and aesthetic embellishment where they could absorb the unadulterated word of God instead of dry exegesis full of rhetorical flourishes. They deplored the blending of civil and ecclesiastical authority that left churches vulnerable to governmental interference, thus championing the cause of separating church from state. This proved to be a boon to the smaller denominations that had struggled in the past, such as the Baptists, who saw their numbers increase exponentially in the 1740s and 1750s. Methodists, led variously by English expatriates George Whitefield and John Wesley, had by 1770 established a number of small meetings and larger societies from New York to Maryland, and soon spread further southward.[8]

The accumulated result, a "great and general Awakening," was not just an American phenomenon, but also a transatlantic one. The Awakening, as it unfolded in New Jersey, maintained a distinctly Scottish flavor carefully directed by Log College graduates. The Presbyterian churches in New Jersey began cutting ties of association and cooperation they had forged with the Dutch Reformed churches, and consciously brought non-Presbyterian Scots into their fold. They formed the Trustees of the Presbyterian Church in Monmouth County, which raised funds for new meetinghouses, and oversaw the replication of the religious landscape of southwestern Scotland in central New Jersey. When Whitefield, the former member of the Holy Club and Anglican evangelist, toured the Middle Colonies in 1739, the Awakening had been well under way, and it was at this point that the Tennents and Jersey–Pennsylvania Presbyterians became aware of the intercolonial and indeed transatlantic nature of the revivals. The Presbyterian revivalists began running into criticism and opposition to the revivals from the Synod of Philadelphia, which expressed its concerns over the Tennent's mysticism, as well as the enthusiasm they inspired among their auditors.[9]

A similar dynamic is evident in the revivals begun by Church of Scotland ministers concerned about the influence of schismatic movements such as the Glasites and the Seceders. Prayer societies, which had declined in the seventeenth century, began to experience new life in the first years of the eighteenth century, following consolidated rules for membership and procedure, which inspired outdoor revivals. These spontaneous conventicles happening throughout southern Scotland caught the attention of George Whitefield, who visited there after his first preaching tour in the American colonies, where he found "a constant levee of wounded souls" to save. The town of Cambuslang emerged as the center of the Scottish revivals, with a secondary locus being the town of Kilsyth in 1740. William McCulloch and John Erskine, who corresponded with New Lights in New England and New Side Presbyterians in the middle colonies, led the revivals. This inspired Thomas Prince to begin reporting news of the revivals in America and Britain in *The Christian History*, published between 1743 and 1745, which interpreted the transatlantic revivals as a promising sign of the oncoming Millennium.[10]

Jonathan Edwards, who took the earliest note of revivalism in New England, received reports from correspondents in Britain of similar waves of evangelical energy generated in the cities and the countryside. Although in comparative terms much less prevalent than those taking place in New England, Edwards nonetheless thrilled to the news of the British revivals, in which he also perceived signs of the Millennium. The news of thousands in America returning to a piety reminiscent of that of the Separatists and Puritans who founded New England a century before indicated a momentous change confirming America's identity as the New Canaan. This outlook Edwards shared with Prince, who in *The Christian History* speculated that Christ's millennial kingdom would soon be established in British America. Edwards, vigilantly searching for signs of the imminent Judgment Day, had been chronicling events conforming to the prophecies of the apostle John, since 1723, as well as his own interpretations of the Book of Revelation titled "Notes on the Apocalypse." Influenced by the English biblical exegete Moses Lowman, who devoted the bulk of his work to interpretations of apocalyptic prophecies, Edwards believed that the revivals heralded an effusion of God's spirit upon the world, perhaps even the pouring out of the sixth vial described in Chapter 16 of the Revelation: "[A]n extraordinary outpouring of the Spirit of God is to accompany this sixth vial; so the beginning of a work of extraordinary awakening has already attended the probably [sic] beginning of this vial." The sixth vial, to be poured out onto the Euphrates River and drying it up, Edwards asserted in "An Account of Events Probably Fulfilling the Sixth Vial on the River Euphrates," meant the flow of money and power into the Catholic Church, which would pave the way for the triumph of Protestantism at the Latter Day.[11]

The Awakening was more than a revival; among the clergy it involved bitter disputes over theology, standards of professionalism, and centralized authority. James Davenport's temporary insanity aside, the New Side and New Light factions never approved of disorder—in fact, Jonathan Edwards stoutly insisted that people's religious instruction and ministration be conducted by properly trained and ordained clergy— but the rifts created by the Great Awakening were not confined to the ecclesiastical arena, but bled over into the political arena as well. Arguments over lay participation and clerical leadership in the churches were continuations of long-standing political disputes. In Connecticut, political conservatives were branded by their opponents as "Old Lights" while the democratic radicals became the "New Lights" in the sociopolitical upheavals that attended and followed the height of the revival period. A similar dynamic played out in Pennsylvania, where the Quakers allied themselves with German Pietists against the Scots-Irish

Presbyterians, German Lutherans, and Anglicans in squabbles over frontier defense and the future of proprietary government. Both sides created elaborate networks of local, regional, and colony-wide meetings—in imitation of the Quaker ecclesiological organization. In Virginia, the dominant Anglican political establishment was challenged by the Presbyterians and the Baptists, with the latter arguing throughout the colonies for religious liberty and the separation of church and state.[12]

By 1745, however, the once-rampant flames of revivalism began to sputter and die in the northern colonies. Spontaneous "awakenings" declined precipitously, forcing Prince to halt publication of *The Christian History*, and New Light ministers throughout the colonies wondered what had happened. Even Edwards, who knew that popular piety has its tidal seasons, expressed bafflement at the suddenness with which the revivals petered out, proclaiming it "a day of the Enemy's triumph." A renewed conflict with France in 1743 constituted one source of the decline in revivalism, at least in New England, which caught the fever of patriotism suffusing King George's War and the campaign to capture the French fortress of Louisbourg on Cape Breton Island. A simultaneous tour by George Whitefield in New England went hardly noticed, and Edwards could only conclude that America might not be the stage for the Millennium he had thought it to be—at least not yet. Developments in Scotland held his attention by then, and there he sought fresh signs of a true revival of religion. These signs proved chimerical, however, thus inspiring his son-in-law, Aaron Burr Sr., to posit that the sudden advance of irreligion confirmed Cotton Mather's much earlier contention that (Protestant) Christianity would continue to decline until God saw fit to intervene. Worried that Anglo-American Protestantism might indeed be destroyed from within and without, Burr predicted that the "sorest Calamity and Distress" lay ahead.[13]

The Great Awakening, regardless of differences of historiographical opinion about its existence and dynamics, did bring about a splintering of Protestant congregations and entire denominations in the decades preceding the Revolution. The Separates broke from the Congregational Church, the Presbyterian Church split in two, Methodists emerged from within evangelical wings of the Anglican Church, the Baptists broke into two main and a few more very small groups, and an internal reformist movement opened a rift within the Society of Friends. Only the Dutch Reformed Church managed to maintain its integrity, weathering the evangelical storm with only some minor cracks caused by arguments over the Classis of Amsterdam's authority in the colonies. The divisions within these denominations ran roughly along similar lines: a conservative reformist wing emerged with goals of reviving a simpler, more streamlined ecclesiology dedicated to removing the doctrinal clutter that separated the faithful from God. The "conservatives"—to borrow Alan Heimert's terminology—deplored the accretion of worldliness onto a Christianity that now valued intellectualism over emotion, social status over vocation, and materialism over spirituality. The same contagion had apparently ruined the Catholic Church, corrupted the Church of England, and threatened to pollute the American churches as leaders stepped forward to confront the danger, while "liberals" in the clerical establishments, attracted by Arminian theology, fought to maintain their authority and to fend off the conservatives' charges.[14]

The Great Awakening in New England faded at last with the outbreak of the Seven Years' War in 1755, when reasserted French territorial claims along the Mississippi and Ohio rivers threatened to restrict the British American colonies to the east side of the Appalachian Mountains. Though seemingly yet another round in the long series of diplomatic and military conflicts between Britain and France, it was also another round in the much bloodier collision between Catholicism and Protestantism, and Americans took this aspect of the war very seriously. Apart from the smattering of Catholics in Maryland, Pennsylvania, and New York, and tiny Jewish enclaves in the largest seaport cities, the colonial American population was Protestant, and they feared that French encroachment could destroy a fundamental American religious identity. The opening of hostilities in July 1755 at Fort Duquesne began a war that took on an apocalyptic flavor in America, as Protestantism once again engaged Catholicism—this time for dominion in the New World. However, political exigencies tended to override the demands of spirituality in this new time of crisis, though the cosmic implications of the war occasionally took center stage. However, just as the Awakening divided Americans more than uniting them, so war likewise caught the colonies at cross purposes, even as Protestants managed to set aside their differences when facing Catholic armies on the horizon. Anti-Catholicism had long been a familiar aspect of colonial American culture. It had provided the English with much of their identity since the reign of Mary Tudor in the mid-sixteenth century, fueled by the reprinting of John Foxe's *Actes and Monuments of . . . Great Persecutions against the True Martyrs of Christ . . .* (1563) into the seventeenth and eighteenth centuries. Celebrations of Guy Fawkes Day—known in New England and New York as "Pope's Day," the anniversary of Queen Elizabeth I's accession—English military victories over Spain and France were thus rife with popular expressions of anti-Catholicism.[15]

The war with France and its Indian allies went far in repairing the fissures that had developed during the Great Awakening. The shadow of

French Catholicism brought the Protestant denominations together in ways that promised an eventual Protestant union for which Cotton Mather and Jonathan Edwards had longed. The Presbyterian Church reconciled with its New Side brethren in 1758, and many of the New England Separates found their ways back into mainstream Congregationalist churches. The Society of Friends heeded the demands of its reform-minded members, who gradually instigated the Quaker withdrawal from government and redefined the Society's doctrines into ones of strict quietism and pacifism. Dissenting denominations joined with Anglicans in propagating a patriotic anti-Catholicism that galvanized the otherwise heterogeneous American societies. The Presbyterian itinerant Samuel Davies of Virginia made patriotism an integral element of Christian faith and practice, as did the Congregationalists John Ballantine and James Cogswell in Boston. The turning of the tide in 1759 with the capture of Quebec, and the rapid collapse of the French-Canadian war effort that followed, intensified apocalyptic expectation among New Englanders especially. The succession of victories coming so quickly after years of anxiety and dread seemed nothing less than miraculous. The humiliating defeats of the early war years became a period of purifying trial, and the more recent victories a demonstration of providential American exceptionalism. Samuel Cooper exulted that "We have received a Salvation from Heaven, greater perhaps than any since the Foundation of the Country," and Samuel Langdon assured a New Hampshire audience that "God has thus prov'd and humbled and convinc'd us that *the race is not to the swift.*"[16]

Another concern was the rumored establishment of an Anglican bishop over the colonies, a project that deeply interested Thomas Secker, Archbishop of Canterbury, as well as S.P.G. missionaries in the northern colonies. American Dissenters were convinced that this would be a first step toward undermining Dissenter strength in America and establishing the Church of England in every British American colony. Given the atmosphere of suspicion in New England especially, Secker cautioned that "pushing [the scheme] openly at present would certainly prove both fruitless and detrimental." So convinced was Connecticut's Ezra Stiles that this was going to happen that in April 1760 he called for the union of the Congregational churches with other dissenting denominations to resist this supposed threat. In prescient language, he connected religious liberty to political liberty:

> The right of conscience and private judgment is unalienable; and it is truly the interest of all mankind to unite themselves into one body, for the liberty, free exercise, and unmolested enjoyment of this right, especially

in religion.... And being possessed of the precious jewel of religious liberty, a jewel of inestimable worth, let us prize it highly, and esteem it too dear to be parted with on any terms; lest we be again entangled with that yoke of bondage which our fathers could not, would not, and God grant we may never submit to bear.... You are very sensible that there is a formal attempt on the chastity and order of our churches, which is vigilantly to be guarded against, at present, till our churches grow into one ... large, pure, defensible body.

While Secker was keen to establish an American episcopate, matters of practicality certainly militated against it, of which he was well aware. Northern S.P.G. missionaries may have been enthusiastic about the prospect, but their southern counterparts were not, which further doomed the plan. Nevertheless, Stiles's argument for a union of the dissenting churches met with an animated response, and came to some fruition with the onset of later events. Stiles, however, was not just worried about Anglican bishops and missionaries, but about other external threats to Congregationalist orthodoxy and influence.[17]

"Some Disaffected and Uneasy Spirits"

The Rev. Alexander Cumming of Boston heard from English friends about a much-read and debated book, the *Letters on Theron and Aspasio*, and arranged to have a copy sent to him. At the same time, a Danbury, Connecticut, merchant learned about the book from friends with whom he corresponded in Edinburgh, and he gave a copy to Ebenezer White, pastor of the Congregational church in Danbury. From White the book circulated among other Connecticut ministers: David Judson of Newtown, Noah Wetmore of Bethel, James Taylor of New Fairfield, James Beebe of North Stratford, Thomas Brooks of Newbury, and Elnathan Gregory of Philippi. Sandeman's forceful refutation of "popular preaching" deeply impressed them, and they wrote him admiring letters soliciting his further thoughts on that and other theological subjects. There followed a reinvigoration of the controversy between Old Lights and New Lights originally started by the Awakening, but in Connecticut especially the dispute took a less traditional turn as antirevivalists under Sandemanian influence would attack a conservatism that preserved social hierarchy in the churches. Tensions deep beneath the surface of seemingly placid New England communities, rooted as they were in economic and social dynamics, provided a language with which western Connecticut residents expressed their discontent. It enabled people to reconceive of their communities in ways that appeared more satisfying than the older forms of cohesion. Sandemanianism provided one outlet for expressing dissident frustration.

Danbury, Connecticut, in the early eighteenth century retained all the characteristics of the church-centered, oligarchical New England community of the previous century. So entrenched was the social and political structure of the town that the tremors of the Awakening failed to shake it to nearly the extent it did other parts of New England or the British-American colonies. The First Congregational Church of Danbury remained the town's only house of worship until 1763, when the very few Anglicans who lived there were forced to travel to nearby Newtown to attend their Sunday services until they constructed their own church. The lay-controlled Ecclesiastical Society, whose membership overlapped with the residents of the town, conducted all Congregational church business, such as the collection of the minister's salary, the support of the town schools, and the maintenance of the church building. All decisions required the majority vote of the entire Society. Although the final stage of the process was technically democratic, the most prominent members of the Society controlled the direction and tenor of the meetings. Much as in most other New England towns, Danbury was dominated by a set of powerful families whose roots extended to the founding of Connecticut. The Benedicts, Gregorys, Starrs, and Taylors supplied mayors and councilmen to the town government, and they were also moderators, clerks, and administrators of the church. This became visually evident at Sunday church services, as people took pews assigned to them because of their social rank. In the administration of the town, the Ecclesiastical Society, and in the physical arrangement of the church service, Danbury's oligarchical social order was repeatedly articulated and reinforced.[18]

During the 1750s, however, rapid demographic, economic, and social changes resulted in the exponential growth of the town, thus placing a great deal of stress on this firmly established institutional town structure. Between 1756 and 1774, Danbury's population nearly doubled, expanding by close to sixty new residents every year. This growth forced ever increasing numbers of residents to find homes farther and farther from the town center, which led townspeople to reconsider Danbury's cohesiveness as a physical and social unit. Those living beyond the set town limits were not isolated, however, due to a surge in road-building in the 1750s that connected the towns of western Connecticut to one another. These "outlivers" established their own schools and churches to supply their needs independent of town centers, the latter subsequently suffering from the lack of increasing municipal revenue that they would otherwise have received. Amid these physical and demographic transformations, people's personal, political, and ecclesiastical allegiances became more complicated, multi-layered, and sharply contested as they forged social connections that extended beyond their immediate localities.[19]

While more residents engaged in activities outside the purview of Danbury's ruling Ecclesiastical Society, those who remained resisted these changes and became less able to agree on the structure of authority within the Society. The January 1755 meeting witnessed a heated battle over the appropriate method of seating the most prominent members of the Society in the church. The meeting opened with a long list of specific seating assignments, which were to be agreed upon by a vote. Someone made a successful motion to revise the seating arrangement, during which "the Society by vote ma[de] Null ... all the Votes past at This meeting Respecting Seatting [in] sd. meeting house." A similar meeting held in March 1756 resulted in a bitterly divided Society revising the seating assignments and then voting against it. They tried to settle the seating problem again in December, this time deciding that every person should give his or her age to the committee in charge of seating. A few other new criteria were established in order to aid the committee members in their work. This seemingly petty squabbling over seating reveals a community unable to agree on the proper basis of social authority. The old arrangements worked as long as there was consensus within the community about who the leaders were, but the changes of the post-Awakening years rendered social status a highly controversial subject. The Society's resort to age as a criterion for church seating involved a recognition that one's social status was no longer obvious, and that the old bases of authority were no longer relevant to the present social circumstances.[20]

It was in this contentious environment that a group of western Connecticut divines, led by Ebenezer White, had begun a correspondence with Robert Sandeman, in whose work they found theological support to specific concerns they had about the unchallenged authority of "our modern divines, as they are constantly styled." Their scorn is indicative of the overall antipathy they had for those traditionally regarded as clerical authorities, yet were unable to articulate a theology that could provide a persuasive explanation and solution for the changes that their communities had been undergoing. White commented on the great amount of "opposition we have met with, both from ministers and people" who were justifiably alarmed by the radical implications of Sandeman's doctrines. Resistance was not just local, for White was convinced that "these books ... [were] carefully kept out of the country; for they say, 'We shall be overrun with heterodoxy.'" Frustrated and disenchanted, White had abandoned hope for a godly reformation through traditional means, and Sandeman's works struck a chord with his sense of dissatisfaction. Influenced by Sandemanian theology, White, who had held the pulpit in Danbury for twenty-four years, began to challenge the norms that had governed the community for decades. In December 1762, a significant number of Danbury's residents decided that the situation demanded address. They called the Ecclesiastical Society for a meeting where they resolved, "the Society was Dissatisfyed with Mr. White's preaching," and several of the "Doctrinal points or matters he hath Delivered in Some Time past."[21]

The process that White was forced to endure was merely a magnified extension of similar procedures utilized against wayward church members, which brought immediate and awful consequences for those against whom judgment was rendered. In Connecticut especially church discipline tended to be rigorously enforced, and given the zeal with which church members were tried for lapses in behavior—whether public or private—or doctrinal heterodoxy, that ministers were even more carefully watched comes as no surprise. Adherence to the Cambridge Platform[22] was of particular concern to both the membership and the laity, and clergy were brought before ecclesiastical councils as often as anyone else. Ministers often warned the newly ordained about this obnoxious tendency in their ordination sermons. Thomas Clap complained in 1732 that "some disaffected and uneasy Spirits ... seem to envy the tranquile State of the Church; and are ready to take all Opportunities and Advantages, to stir up Opposition and Contention." Societies tended to pay ministers meager salaries, in any case, and sometimes used discipline cases against clergymen to excuse pay cuts or to remove ministers who complained about low pay or the lack of cost-of-living increases. In this way, the church membership and the laity maintained a greater share of church authority than that ordinarily granted to ministers, and rifts within communities further complicated church affairs.[23]

Before White was scheduled to appear before a council of his peers to answer for his actions, his accusers presented him with seventeen questions to which he was to respond in writing. Though purely theological in nature, the questions reveal the extent to which the controversy within the church was about much more than the fine points of Calvinist doctrine. Every theological query implied a certain set of concrete behaviors. The combatants certainly took their theology very seriously, but to reduce the conflict to a mere intellectual endeavor would be to ignore the profound social implications of White's "new doctrines." White's reading of Sandeman had led him into a root and branch denunciation of many of the key theological pillars that had supported the Standing Order. Many of the respectable members of the Danbury church could no longer "feel easy" because they believed that White's ideas "encouraged licentiousness" and "had no tendency to convince people of the necessity of soul-concern." White's adoption of Sandemanian theology threatened to subvert the church's role as an instrument of community order. From White's perspective, however, he was undertaking an effort to reconstruct Danbury's society along more godly lines, and the opposition he encountered from the "heretick hunters" only strengthened his resolve.[24]

The first pillar of the traditional order that White attacked was the assumption that the church was responsible for encouraging godly behavior among all members of the community, from the elect down to the most degenerate sinners. The last question that White's accusers asked him to answer dealt with the minister's fundamental responsibility to "set before christless sinners ... the dangers of an utterly careless, vicious, and profane life ... and ... the encouragements of the gospel, attending the sinner's painful endeavours, ... in the diligent use of all appointed means." White's accusers wanted him to tell his charges that their behavior was inextricably linked to their salvation. If this was not so, then what encouragement was there to listen to the behavioral prescriptions of one's superiors? Indeed, White's Sandemanian dismissal of means had caused many worshippers "pain, lest our children should believe some of his doctrines." White recognized that his doctrines would profoundly disturb some of his respectable auditors. "I know ... it will be like death, to tell some of you, that there is no connection between your doings, and eternal happiness," he admitted, so far had Arminian Calvinism progressed.[25]

After reading Sandeman, however, White became convinced that any sinner's attempt to gain salvation served only to glorify the sinner and profane the omnipotence of God. He acknowledged that "there is an absolute connection betwixt the *believers* doings and eternal happiness," but this doctrine served little function as a mechanism of social order, since it only applied to the behavior of those who had already been recognized for their godliness. By reducing God's law to a mere "rule of life and action" for the unconverted, rather than a means of salvation, White limited the church's ability to monitor and enforce moral behavior in the entire community. For White, this doctrine was probably a relief, since the minister's control over his flock had been steadily diminishing anyway. Sandeman's writings merely legitimized and made concrete the actual experiences that White had had over the past decades. In the eyes of his opponents, however, such a limitation of the church's power, regardless of how minimal it had become, would only make the problem worse and lead to increased "licentiousness."[26]

White's doctrines also undermined the traditional methods of designating and preserving authority among the church members. A cardinal principle of Calvinism was the perseverance of the saints; the tenet that once the community acknowledged someone to be a member of God's elect, that state was a permanent one because God never revoked salvation once it is bestowed. White, however, held that it was possible for a saint to "finally and totally fall from grace." Permanent grace, when translated into daily practice, entailed a body of incorruptible church leaders whose salvation and godliness were unquestionable. To intimate that grace itself could be lost was to subvert the stability of the church lay hierarchy. The men who had been administering the business of the church and the community for decades on the basis of their sanctified position in the church would be more accountable for their actions than they otherwise had been. White emphasized the equal fallibility of all men, and this served only to weaken the respect that people had for their social superiors. White's notion of salvation implied a fluid and more egalitarian social order, which threatened those who had prospered under the older, oligarchic pattern of church organization.[27]

White's attack on the existing power structure through his repudiation of means was so powerful because he was exploiting a fundamental tension within eighteenth-century Congregationalist doctrine. Not even the most conservative Congregationalist would have agreed that human actions—works—could gain salvation. This idea was associated with Arminianism, and, even worse, with Catholicism. On the other hand, the idea that one's actions had nothing to do with one's salvation was thought to lead unavoidably to anarchy. The Congregationalists of the 1750s and 1760s fell uncomfortably between the two poles of Arminianism and Antinomianism. This uncertainty about the connection between means and salvation runs throughout the proceedings against White. For example, White's accusers admitted that sinners could "hope" for grace "only in a way of sovereign mercy" and could never use God's means "in a right manner," yet they steadfastly believed that "neglecting" the use of means made a person "more sinful and displeasing to God." Simply put, godly behavior could guarantee nothing, yet it made God less angry if one followed his laws. Later the accusers corrected an error that they had made when they had acknowledged that there was "no connection" between behavior and salvation. What they had meant to say was that there was no "*absolute certain* connection." Sandeman's doctrines exploited the ambiguity of this position, espousing what White's son Ebenezer Russell White called "Calvinism in its true Extent" and attacking the absurdity of "Ministers telling Men how many good Convictions they must have in Order to prepare & qualify them for Mercy." Within the context of Calvinist doctrine, White's accusers had little grounds for their arguments against him and their exasperation shows in their appeal to the reader of the pamphlet explaining their actions: "Surely the sovereignty of God may be defended without having recourse to such doctrines as these."[28]

The final component of the traditional order that came under White's attack was the Saybrook Platform. It allowed councils of ministers to mediate and pass judgment on conflicts within the churches that belonged to its county associations. Ebenezer White and his followers had little use for the plan of church government, which they referred to garishly as "a Rag of the whore of Babylon." They believed that the Saybrook Platform gave "absolute authority" to people who had no spiritual right to exercise it. According to White, the gospels gave "free liberty of conscience." Asking people to submit to a decision made by those outside of one's church, therefore, was tantamount to "requiring an absolute blind obedience and an implicit faith." Indeed, immediately after White was dismissed from his pulpit, his adherents declared that "no authority on Earth could do [so] with out our consent" and warned the Society of Danbury not to "Trye to Impose a nother [sic] minister upon us." White's opponents never tried, in writing, to defend the Saybrook Platform in the abstract, pinning their argument instead on an appeal to "our Fathers (of whom the world was not worthy) who first settled this country [and] were strictly Congregational. . . . Yet the most eminent of them . . . were deeply sensible of the absolute necessity of the consociation of churches." The platform served to unify the churches, thereby hedging against the spread of heterodoxy and the threat of sectarianism. Conflicts that could not be settled within a community posed an enormous threat to the maintenance of order and cast the standing authorities in a negative light. The platform's councils of ministers served as the last bastion of orthodoxy, their decisions binding and serving to shore up the position of the town's ruling elite. White's refusal to recognize their jurisdiction implied a repudiation of the traditional patterns of church administration.[29]

White's assault on the Saybrook Platform was especially ominous because it merged with a preexisting frustration with this instrument of church government. White's accusers freely admitted that "there are a number in the country that are at enmity with the platform," and this was reflected in the highly contested vote to dismiss White, which saw five ministers dissent from the decision. One account of the case reported that "some were remarkably strenuous" both against and for White's

"May God Preserve Our [Churches] Amidst All Attacks"   111

ouster. To at least one participant, the future of Connecticut's churches rode on this case, for if White was allowed to continue preaching, "they will flock from all Parts, to hear [him], and he will have the largest Congregation in the Government." Within eight years of White's dismissal, three other established ministers in East Fairfield County, the aforementioned James Taylor and David Judson, as well as James Beebe of North Stratford, renounced the Saybrook Platform. These churches were let go without the same proceedings that occasioned White's dismissal, for afterwards, the East Fairfield Association no longer had the power to enforce its edicts. In December 1764, in New Fairfield, for example, James Taylor, who suffered dismissal along with White, continued to preach in the town meetinghouse. Criticism of and resistance to the Saybrook Platform continued to mount until one-by-one Connecticut's towns abandoned its practice, preferring to maintain community harmony as Americans generally grew weary of living in a hierarchical, class-conscious society.[30]

White's ordeal ended in April 1764, a few months before Robert Sandeman arrived in the colonies, when the ministers of East and West Fairfield counties voted by a narrow margin to dismiss White from his ministry in Danbury. Approximately half of his former congregants followed him out of the church, worshipping three times a week in White's house because their attempts to gain recognition as Danbury's First Church were unsuccessful. White's detractors maintained control of their church because they had the force of traditional authority on their side. The committee of five that pursued the case was composed of the town doctor, a militia captain, and the town's representative to the General Court. Most of these men had served at some time as the justice of the peace or town clerk. Although Danbury's most prominent citizens led the movement against White, the battle over Danbury's church was not a class war, but a cultural one between two different conceptions of how intrachurch and intracommunity dynamics should operate. Indeed, White's adherents, like most Sandemanians throughout the colonies, were generally respected residents of the town, predominantly merchants and artisans. By 1763, however, many of these people no longer regarded the Congregational church as a legitimate, godly community. Robert Sandeman's ideas were not solely responsible for the division within the Danbury church and the disintegration of the Saybrook Platform in East Fairfield County, but constituted both a cause and a consequence of the fragmentation of western Connecticut's communities.

It must be emphasized that the realignment of the sociopolitical landscape was not the only force assailing the established churches in New

England. While Anglicans regularly attacked the system of ecclesiastical taxation, which to men like Ezra Stiles indicated the Church of England's desire to usurp the Congregationalist Church in New England, the more troubling were the New Light Separatists, whom Stiles estimated as matching the Anglicans in number.[31] The Great Awakening might have seemed over, but there was no end to the disputes between Old Lights and New Lights and the splitting up of churches, particularly in Connecticut. The Separates demanded religious liberty even as they and others were demanding civil liberties as a result of the disturbing changes to imperial trade regulation and revenue policies. In pamphlets and newspapers the Separates—or "Strict" Congregationalists—made dark comparisons between the colonial governments' support for the established churches and the unjust policies of the British parliament,[32] while others kept to scripture and history to justify the logic of their complaints and demands. It was in this milieu that the Sandemanians made their inauspicious debut in New England, and found themselves swept up in the controversies.

Sandeman in New England

Robert Sandeman, encouraged by the letters from Connecticut, considered visiting New England and confided his interest in doing so to John Glas, who immediately gave his wholehearted approval:

> I cannot help thinking that your motion toward New England is from the Lord calling you by what they wrote, and by inclining your heart toward the writers. Your being disposed to go knits my heart to you more than ever; and you may be sure of all the blessing whereof I am capable to go with you; nor do I question your being attended with the blessing of the churches, who I hope will readily recommend you to the grace of God, and cheerfully contribute to the bearing of your charges.

Sandeman dithered, held back by his sense of responsibility to the fledgling English churches. George Glas believed that the London church needed Sandeman, and in a letter to his father asked "would it not be better to abandon his design of going to New England and come up here where he will be so much wanted?" George's attitude dismayed John, who detected a desire to leave that city, and to relegate the work of propagating true Christianity to others. James Allen of Gayle offered to go to London to take up George's duties as elder, while James Cargill agreed to accompany Sandeman to America. They, along with two of Sandeman's nephews boarded the *George*, which sailed for Boston on 10 August 1764.[33]

The *George* arrived at the port of Boston on 18 October 1764, and after spending a week in the city recuperating from the voyage, Sandeman and his companions traveled to Portsmouth, New Hampshire, where they spent a disappointing fortnight before resolving to go to Danbury and meet the ministers who had encouraged him to make the trip in the first place. While lodging in Providence, Rhode Island, they were joined by Andrew Oliphant, a Glasite from Scotland. On 28 November, they passed through Newport, where Ezra Stiles was then the minister of the Congregational church, and Sandeman accepted Stiles's offer to preach. Stiles found Sandeman's theology intriguing, but Sandeman did not stay long enough to acquaint Stiles more fully with his ecclesiological ideas. The company arrived in Danbury just before Christmas, where Ebenezer White and his followers warmly greeted them. Throughout the month that Sandeman's party stayed in Danbury the divines condoled the long winter evenings with animated discussions on issues of theology and church governance, but Sandeman could not convince the Americans that his system of church order was the correct one. They agreed on the doctrine of saving faith, but on virtually nothing else, particularly with regard to church organization. The extreme egalitarianism of Sandemanianism, and the complete lack of ministerial authority of any kind, proved too radical even for White and his adherents, who thought it more like Quakerism than apostolic Christianity.

Sandeman took his leave of them and departed at the end of January 1765, expressing deep appreciation for the courtesy and kindness he and his companions received, even as he admitted his disappointment "that it happens not to be in our power to return you suitable services as we hoped and intended." The visit was not without apparent impact, however, as James Dana of Wallingford informed Ezra Stiles that the man himself had converted a few to Sandemanianism. Sandeman traveled from Danbury to New York, then on to Philadelphia, and from there to New London, then to Providence, and finally back to Portsmouth by 20 April 1765. On this second trip to that city, he founded the first Sandemanian church in North America on 4 May 1765, which was composed mainly of himself, Cargill, Oliphant, and his nephews. Sandeman's brother George and David Mitchelson, an elder from the London church, soon after joined them. Making contacts among Portsmouth's merchant community, the church members welcomed brothers Nathanael and Colburn Barrell, as well as John Marstes, a physician. The Barrells donated much of their wealth to the building of a meetinghouse, which held its first Sandemanian services barely three months after the foundation of the Portsmouth church.[34]

Sandeman had not rested on his laurels, though. He returned to Boston within a month of establishing the Portsmouth church to found a church there in the home of Edward Foster, proprietor of a prosperous blacksmithing and carpentering business. According to Sandeman, the Boston church also included several "persons of high social and political standing." From there Sandeman revisited Danbury, where he gathered many of Ebenezer White's followers into a formal Sandemanian church, with Sandeman and Joseph Moss White serving as elders. Relations between Sandeman and Ebenezer White could not have been too comfortable, for it was reported that Sandeman called the new Danbury church the only true church of Christ in the town, since White's church practiced Sandemanian theology without adopting Sandemanian ecclesiology. For the next year, Sandeman shuttled between Danbury and Portsmouth before establishing a permanent residence in Danbury in the autumn of 1766. James Cargill returned to Scotland that year, bearing a letter from the Portsmouth church to the church in Dunkeld, which praised the efforts of the Scots who brought them the light of true Christianity, and in which they expressed their fervent hope that Robert and George Sandeman, and David Mitchelson may yet remain in America longer: "We love them much for the truth's sake, God knows; but we do not know what we should do without them."[35]

From the moment Robert Sandeman arrived in New England, he was the subject of much curiosity and discussion among the leading Congregationalist clergy. After meeting Sandeman in Newport, Ezra Stiles composed an eighty-page, deprecatory *Memoir of Robert Sandeman on his First Coming to America 1764*, and circulated this treatise among nine of his colleagues, who pledged to report back with "speedy intelligence" on Sandeman's activities. This work is neatly summarized in a letter Stiles wrote to Benjamin Stevens, when he dismissed Sandeman as "a haughty domineering man, who mistakes his natural, national arbitrariness for gospel zeal." The Congregationalists' interest in Sandemanianism initially had little to do with the nuances of theology. At this moment in New England ecclesiastical history, Dissenters had been feverishly observing the rising prominence of the Anglican Church and the supposed plan to establish a resident bishop who would ordain American novitiates. Sandeman's apparent anticlericalism signaled a greater threat than episcopacy to orthodox Yankee Calvinists, and they believed that should his doctrines gain popularity, this might lead all of New England into apostasy and anarchy. Sandeman's converts, "jovial Debauchers," in Stiles's phraseology, reveled in the repudiation of means as "the shortest Cutt to heaven." However, even more disruptive than theological differences were Sandeman's outright critiques of Congregationalist elitism that threatened to undermine the traditional social order. Almost immediately, Sandemanians came into conflict with their neighbors over theology and ecclesiology. Throughout these episodes, Sandeman showed himself to be a poor sectarian leader, refusing to exert any disciplinary authority, and through his inaction encouraging others in the sect to behave in a confrontational manner. Sandemanians conceived of themselves as a special community of believers that superseded geographical or family ties, and thus dissolved the bonds of local identity necessary to maintain a hierarchical social cohesion. Within a year of their introduction to New England, the Sandemanians' thinning connections to their local communities put the sect in grave jeopardy.[36]

The reports that Stiles's ministerial colleagues sent greatly concerned him as more information surfaced about Sandeman's ecclesiological doctrines, and the letters reveal the worry that Sandemanianism was gaining traction. James Dana's letter of January 1765 reported on seven divines in his area of Connecticut concerning their attitude toward Sandeman. He found that some "suspend judgment," others "counter-preach" Sandeman, while a few "appear to be in his scheme," in this case a likely reference to Joseph Moss White and David Judson. Charles Chauncy, minister of Boston's First Church, had already formed a negative opinion of Sandeman, having seen the effect of his doctrines on Alexander Cumming, who ended up repudiating Sandemanianism on his deathbed, confessing "that he was very sorry he had so fallen in with Sandeman, [since] his motive of faith had no moral goodness in it." Much to Chauncy's delight, Cumming eventually came to realize that Sandeman's rejection of the utility of means "was dangerous to the souls of man." Stiles concluded in a letter to Chauncy Whittlesey that the Sandemanians constituted a grave threat to New England orthodoxy through their rejection of means, ending the letter with a prayer: "May God preserve our [Churches] amidst all Attacks."[37]

Stiles's greatest fear was that Sandeman's egalitarianism and disdain for ministerial authority would encourage antisocial, even anarchic, behavior. Samuel Langdon, Stiles's colleague in Portsmouth, found Sandeman's ideas tended to appeal mainly to those who had always found "religion ... galling to their consciences," and Charles Chauncy described the Sandemanians and their sympathizers as "those who despise ... superiority and importance." In the eyes of these three men, Sandeman's theological inconsistencies were far less important than the fact that his ideas were "pleasing to the licentious." The Sandemanians, of course, did not think of themselves in this manner, and in fact the churches enforced a rigid standard of proper behavior within their communities. Stiles's hyperbolic fear of the Sandemanians reveals little about the sectarians, and much about his own skeptical attitude toward the viability of small, self-regulating, and consensual communities of pious Christians. As Stiles put it, Sandeman's rejection of means eliminated all distinctions between men concerning religious feelings and therefore "demolished all the Encouragements and foundations of Morals." Spiritual and social equality, along with the maintenance of morality, were incompatible for Stiles and his colleagues, and this further set them at odds with the Sandemanians, who drew some strength from this opposition.[38]

The source of the contention lay in the different constituencies that these two mutually opposite views addressed. Stiles saw religion as the means of instilling moral behavior in all of the colonies' residents. Although few are saved, Stiles believed that all people are bound to follow the gospels' dictates. Sandeman was concerned only with those within his own, pure church. Sinners were sinners and therefore had no place worshipping with God's elect. If one was suddenly infused with God's grace—and it was necessarily a sudden occurrence—he or she was joyfully welcomed into the church and made subject to the strict moral rules that all church members enforced collectively. Those who remained unsanctified, however, were left to work out their salvation on their own. In this way, Sandeman chose religious purity over the maintenance of a universal social order. From the Sandemanian perspective, ministers like Stiles who viewed themselves as the moral arbiters for their entire communities were, as White acerbically characterized them, "domineering Worms of the Dust," the agents of a "magisterial, Ministerial Despotism" whose behavior was "tyrannical & arbitrary." In Stiles's eyes, such an attitude was merely an abrogation of the minister's responsibility for his entire flock and a sure path to anarchy.[39]

Although Stiles and his correspondents saw anarchy looming in Sandeman's ideas about salvation, they thought his plan of church governance overly oppressive and strict. Since every decision in Sandeman's churches had to be unanimous, Stiles believed that this would form "the basis of a Spiritual Tyranny & Dominion, instead of charity[,] Freedom & Benevolence." One correspondent observed scornfully that if a Sandemanian was "as they say out of line, any one perceiving it stops him, & sets him right," citing the excommunication of a member "for not dancing" as evidence of this point. Stiles, for whom order and hierarchy were inseparable, thought that every community must have gradations of power in order to function properly. Sandeman's community of equal brethren would only "tend to internal division" since no single authority existed. Stiles and his correspondents also attacked Sandeman's style of ministerial leadership, casting him in the role of the self-serving demagogue. Sandeman was not the genteel, Enlightenment preacher that had become the cosmopolitan ideal in the port cities of the American colonies. His "high national spirit" and stubborn righteousness intimated that he was more concerned with "immortalizing his name" than spreading the truth. They found Sandeman's charismatic, and often domineering, style to be contrary to the proper exercise of ministerial influence. Sandeman's strong sentiments may have "startle[d] weak minds," but they left his auditors with "no rational aptitude to rectifie their mistakes." This denunciation rested on the fact that Sandeman did not appeal to people "as reasonable creatures," thus making him and his fellow elders the tyrants, exerting authority over people who had not willingly joined the community of the truly saved.[40]

Rooted in these mutual accusations of ministerial tyranny were two very different conceptions of how power should be exercised within a community. Sandeman thought power emanated solely from God and expressed itself through the unanimous decisions of small communities of true believers. Unanimity was essential since the truth was indivisible. One incorrect opinion constituted evidence that a church member did not possess God's light, which could lead directly to expulsion. Stiles and his friends, however, imagined power as exercised by God's select few over the entire community. Although Sandeman imposed a much stricter code of behavior, he thought that godly behavior was a result and not a precipitant of salvation. Stiles, on the other hand, imagined a less restrictive God, but one who demanded correct behavior from all humans irrespective of the state of their souls. He believed that ministers had to teach all of their followers to behave as God intended. Sandeman insisted that all a sinner could do was wait and hope for God's overwhelming grace, and thus he conceived of a social regeneration that would work outward from small congregations of the elect. In this way, he explicitly limited his audience by renouncing his responsibility for those outside the fold. Stiles, by contrast, wanted to broaden the minister's influence and marshal the gospels in a top-down effort to restore universal harmony.

Opposition came not only from the Old Light tradition, but from those with New Light roots as well. Andrew Croswell, who rose to prominence in 1740 with his spirited defense of George Whitefield's evangelicalism against Church of England commissary Alexander Garden's severe criticism, accused the latter of being "a *Meritmonger*" who championed a covenant of works in a way that made him an ally of "that Mother of Abominations the *Church of Rome*." Croswell considered it his mission in the ministry to root out Arminianism in all its forms, and did so with such vehemence that many suspected him of Antinomianism throughout his career. His attacks on the clergy of the Standing Order were not limited to Old Lights, but also to moderate supporters of the revivals, thus earning him many enemies among the clerical establishment. Croswell reveled in opposition, believing that true Christianity can only be propagated amid controversy and "Confusions[,] blessed Confusions." While he agreed with Sandeman about the futility of means, Croswell detected Arminianism in Sandeman, and launched invectives against the Scottish newcomer almost as soon as he had arrived. Croswell seems not to have taken any notice of the Sandemanians until one recent Sandemanian convert, a "Mr. F——r," dared to comment on Croswell's 1765 sermon, *Free Justification thro' Christ's Redemption*, that the divine lied in a marginal note asserting that the man of faith believes that his justification means he should be saved. Croswell responded by publishing an open letter to Sandeman wherein he accused him of saying that justification only means that the man of faith may be saved, and used this to run down Sandemanian doctrine by noting that all their hopes are hung upon the uncertainty of a "may be." Croswell went on to charge the Sandemanians with exclusionism, and reminded Sandeman that he had apparently upbraided this "F——r" for similar behavior in the past, but now did nothing to rebuke him or abjure his calumny.[41]

Another New Light critic was the Baptist itinerant Isaac Backus of Middleborough, Massachusetts, who sharply confronted Sandemanianism in *True Faith will produce good Works: A Discourse ... with some Remarks on the Writings of Mr. Sandeman* (1767). Backus stringently attacked the rationalist element in Sandemanianism, as well as its explicit hostility to evangelicalism that emphasized legalism over spirituality. Responding essentially to Pike's *Plain and Full Account*, yet occasionally referring to Sandeman's *Theron and Aspasio*, Backus's treatise was most critical of Sandemanian particularism with regard to primitive Christian practice. One by one, Backus took on the love-feasts, the kiss of charity, and foot-washing described in the New Testament as ancient customs rooted in the pragmatic concerns of that bygone era, and without specific scriptural warrant binding on modern Christians. Next, he excoriated the Sandemanians for their rigid discipline that forced unanimous conformity. While claiming "that *nothing* is decided by the *vote of a majority*," nevertheless among Sandemanians "the *church rejects* a person that *dissents*," which in Backus's eyes constituted an assumption "*of the prerogative of the most high*."[42]

Although Backus took some reassurance from the fact that in New England "few have received his [Sandeman's] model of church affairs," he remained deeply alarmed by the fact that "many are pleased with his crafty rants upon our most awakening [sic] preachers and writers." Determined to see to it that Sandemanianism's appeal be reduced, he dismissed the movement as indirectly elitist and superficially Christian:

> And what does all Mr. S's religion come to at last, more than speculative *notions* about the *truth*, and some outward *doings*, without *thinking* he is posses'd of any *good principle* by which he stands *more nearly related to God than other men*; and without being *conscious* of having experienced any inward *change*, so as to act from *right motives*, or *desiring so to do!*

It is impossible to judge exactly how successful Backus was in his detraction of Sandemanianism, but it would seem that it was not as effective as he had hoped, for he noted that the Baptist churches at Stratfield, Connecticut, and Chelmsford, Massachusetts, had become "infected" with Sandemanian ideas. Five or six members of the Stratfield church converted to Sandemanianism while an elder in the Chelmsford church became "somewhat entangled with Sandeman's notion of exalting the atonement in such a manner as to pay little or no regard to a divine work *within* us, of conviction by the law, and relief by the Gospel."[43]

Sandemanianism involved an alteration of the individual convert's mental boundaries—solidifying some and making others more permeable. Within the church, the boundaries between members' private property were to a high degree porous; one was obligated to give an extra coat or surplus food to those among the brethren in need. He or she was, however, under no such charitable obligation with regard to those who existed outside the Sandemanian community. The Sandemanians readily and frequently censured one another for improper behavior, but they did not proselytize or pay heed to those who chose not to join their fellowship, in keeping with John Glas's injunction against fellowship with outsiders. This redrawing of boundaries extended to almost every realm of a Sandemanian convert's world, from his conception of moral authority to his sense of geography. Becoming a Sandemanian involved breaking free from older patterns of social interaction and learning a new language of community and human solidarity. This new religious culture provided one with a new identity that superseded all other connections and allegiances. It was this aspect that, apart from the theological and ecclesiological deviations, so alarmed Ezra Stiles,

Andrew Crosswell, Issac Backus, and the established New England clergy. However, aspects of Sandemanian ecclesiology and doctrine rendered the tiny churches prone to internal tensions. As the Reverend Doctor Samuel Langdon noted in a letter to Stiles in 1766: "I am persuaded [that] if they are not drove firm together by some kind of persecution, they will soon grow lax & disjointed by jealousies & quarrels among themselves."[44]

☙

Robert Sandeman was busy founding churches and consolidating them just as the imperial crisis dawned in the mid-1760s, and the newly converted Sandemanians found themselves coping with these changes in mind-set and community even as colonial Americans began making the far more difficult transition in *Weltanschauung* from provincialism to nationalism. The controversies over British oversight of the colonies that eventually precipitated the American Revolution tested the integrity of the Sandemanian communities at the worst possible moment, and their insistence on doing without individual ministers vested with authority to enforce doctrine and conformity constituted a near-fatal weakness. A few recent converts, some of whom had been designated as elders, responded to criticism of their apolitical tenets and adherence to the Pauline exhortation to obey constituted authority—even if tyrannical—with all the rash zeal of the newly converted, which put the Sandemanians under a glaring spotlight of the harshest scrutiny from their neighbors. They would not be able to bring themselves to see George III as a tyrant, however, perceiving only a benign constitutional monarch surrounded by poor ministers and advisors. They would exhibit a clear antipathy for the despotic character of imperial measures to raise revenue, but would not endorse protests that bordered on rebellion, nor certainly armed resistance that led to national independence in 1776. Their refusal to do so would result in disruption and, for many, exile.

☙ 5 ☙

"Spirited Conduct"

Sandemanians in the Crosshairs of Revolution

> We think every Christian must be a loyal Subject, submitting himself in civil Concerns to every Ordinance of Man for the Lord's sake, punctually regarding the Rules laid down [in] Rom. xiii. 1–7, 1 Peter ii. 13–17. This was required of the Disciples and Churches, when they were under a tyrannical and persecuting Government; and it cannot be less a Duty, under the present mild and peaceable one.
>
> —Samuel Pike, *A plain and full account of the Christian practices of the Church in St. Martin's-le-Grand*

> ... we hold our Selves bound in Conscience to yield Obedience to the Commands of his Majesty King George 3^d ...
>
> —Statement of New Haven Sandemanians to the Committee of Inspection, October 1777

A curious pamphlet hit the shelves of Boston printshops in the final months of 1774. *The Wonderful Appearance of an Angel, Devil & Ghost*, according to "S. W.," purports to be the true relation of a series of supernatural encounters experienced by an unidentified "gentleman" who at the time had been active in the military government of Boston in the wake of the Boston Tea Party. He imparted his story to "three credible Persons" designated only by their initials, who subscribed to a solemn attestation to the veracity of their interview, and agreed with the man that others would be edified by learning from his harrowing experience. In a city beleaguered by the execution of the Boston Port Act, Massachusetts Government Act, and the Impartial Administration of Justice Act, all passed in 1774 by Parliament as components of the Coercive Acts, the citizens divided along Patriot and Tory lines. Differences of opinion on both sides, not to mention the added difficulty of the presence of neutrals—regardless of their being of strong conviction or simply indifferent—

generated an atmosphere of tension demanding that people declare themselves openly and thereby know their friends from their enemies. Aimed at a popular audience, *The Wonderful Appearance* was just one of many pamphlets and treatises addressing the exigencies of living in a city that increasingly saw itself as the besieged seat of the defense of colonial American rights, and appealed to religious sensibilities in case the political and philosophical arguments fail to hit their mark.

The anonymous protagonist of *The Wonderful Appearance* undergoes an even more dramatic transformation that prefigures that of Ebenezer Scrooge in *A Christmas Carol*. Similar to Scrooge, the unknown gentleman is confronted by three supernatural visitors on three successive nights. The first is an angel who stays only long enough to warn the man that he is going to be visited by the Devil, and though he is far too lofty to associate with "such hell-deserving wretches" and "miscreants" as this man, he must warn him lest the poor man be frightened to death at the sight of the Prince of Hell. Dismissing this initial encounter as the product of a long night of drinking and carousing with some British army officers of his acquaintance, the man nonetheless prepares himself to meet with "Belzebub," whom he encounters on the second night. In a much more lengthy interview, the Devil informs the man that, though it is against his infernal inclinations, he is genuinely concerned about the man's spiritual welfare, and that unless he mend his loyalist ways he will suffer eternal damnation and punishment in hell for oppressing his fellow Bostonians. Understandably shaken by this more awesome encounter, the protagonist begins to form the conviction to change, and then he is visited on the third night by the ghost of one of his esteemed ancestors, an original founder of Massachusetts. Appealing to a fellow Calvinist New Englander's sense of guilt and Puritan filial piety, the ghost expresses his deep disappointment with his descendant, and curses him for the shame he has cast upon the family name. It had always been associated with resistance to tyranny, and now it will be associated with tyranny itself, the ghost sadly predicts, and this seals the protagonist's conversion.[1]

What is most interesting about the piece is that the author believes that Boston's troubles are serious enough to warrant supernatural intervention. New England already had a long tradition of reporting and analyzing such portentous phenomena as earthquakes, comets, storms, and other providential wonders. By the early eighteenth century, published accounts of monstrous births, visions, necromancy, witchcraft, sexual deviancy, and gory violence enjoyed a wide popularity that resonated with the highly literate public of New England. It is in this milieu that *The Wonderful Appearance* can best be understood. By placing the growing conflict between colonial Americans and British authority in a grand cosmic context, the author or authors underscored the seriousness of the situation in Boston and the necessity for freedom-loving New Englanders, and Americans more generally, to declare themselves on the side of righteousness. So despicable is the protagonist that even the Devil expresses disgust at the man's politics, and promises that should he ever get his hands on the man he will administer the most horrific tortures upon him personally. It would at first seem curious that the Devil should be depicted as a friend of American liberty, particularly since he appears carrying a halter, an unmistakable symbol of subjugation and mastery. However, as any reader of Dante's *Inferno* is aware, the lowest circle of hell is reserved for Satan and all traitors, and this work is designed to remind wayward Bostonians, especially those who wavered between their loyalty to Great Britain and loyalty to New England, that their duty is to their forebears and the city they built.[2]

Wars of words also raged in the newspapers, as Whigs and Tories traded rhetorical blows over the nature of government and liberty, economics and taxation, colonial representation, and the demands of loyalty. One such battle involved a recently arrived Sandemanian elder and merchant from New Hampshire, Colburn Barrell, against the bulk of Boston's merchant community that subscribed to the boycotts in protest of British policies. A voice from that community, the "Protestant," took up his pen and severely criticized Barrell for wavering in his support of the boycotts and for eventually withdrawing it altogether. Barrell undertook his self-defense based on pragmatic and religious principles, which the Protestant in his replies ridiculed as emanating from doctrinal error and outright heresy. Though an elder in the Sandemanian church in Boston, Barrell's religious authority was not respected by the Protestant, whose pseudonym was certainly intended to cast the Sandemanians as crypto-Christians at best. Barrell's behavior over this matter, and Robert Sandeman's reaction to it, highlight some very important aspects of Sandemanianism as it developed in the colonies as they stepped at first cautiously, and then boldly, into rebellion. The actions and reactions of a handful of Sandemanians were decidedly atypical and stand in contrast to the behavior of Sandemanians throughout the rest of New England. They underscore the serious tensions within the sect, and in a larger sense reflect the complicated pattern of clefts in American society, which made the Revolutionary War a bitter colonial civil war. As the imperial crisis reached its breaking point in 1775, events forced other Sandemanians to declare their position. Taking their cues from the gospels, they espoused their loyalty to Britain as a ruling authority to which all Christians owed obeisance, for which they paid a terrible price.

"Wicked and Unreasonable Men"

The *Newport Mercury* proclaimed in 1765 that the Stamp Act threatened to "deprive us of all our invaluable charter rights and privileges, drain us suddenly of our cash, occasion an entire stagnation of trade, discourage every kind of industry, and involve us in the most abject slavery," while the *Pennsylvania Journal* called it "a wedge ... this *Trojan Horse*[,] *this Engine big with exorbitant Mischiefs*." Such inflammatory rhetoric inspired people to form mobs that unceremoniously greeted the stamp distributors upon arrival at their offices. Loosely dubbed the "Sons of Liberty," they gathered under oak trees renamed "Liberty Trees" and carried out acts of vandalism, intimidation, and violence against the stamp distributors and anyone else who dared to defend them, their property, or the legitimacy of the Stamp Act. Mobs throughout the colonies paraded effigies in cities and towns, destroyed the stamp-men's offices, ransacked their houses, terrorized their families, and otherwise indulged in the mayhem that tended to accompany their destructive outbursts. Aside from their anger over the economic impact this broad sort of direct taxation would have, those who organized or joined the mobs protesting the Stamp Act interpreted it in religious terms, and expressed their outrage in a traditional fashion closely tied to religious symbolism. In New England, the Stamp Act riots borrowed from Pope's Day celebrations common throughout the eighteenth century.[3]

In Portsmouth, New Hampshire, Congregationalist opposition to the Sandemanian presence there met its match in Nathaniel Barrell, an elder of the church, who rashly predicted that "Christ will come in flaming fire to take Vengeance on all who know not God and Obey not the Gospel." This outspokenness made the Sandemanian church on Divinity Street an easy target for rioters protesting the Stamp Act on 1 November 1765. According to a petition to Gov. Benning Wentworth, Barrell and five other subscribers to the petition reported that "a number of people ... assembled together in a Riotous manner ... did damage, break & spoil a house built at our expense for the purpose of Worshipping God." That the Portsmouth crowds never bothered to damage the Anglican Church—which had been built in 1732—at any point during the Stamp Act tumult serves to underscore the ire that the Sandemanians elicited from their "orthodox" neighbors, an ire that occasionally was returned with equal vigor, even if the response did not take the form of acts of violence or vandalism. Subjected to scorn and open hostility for their unusual manners and heterodoxy, some Sandemanians' responses to opposition exacerbated an already menacing situation.[4]

American Dissenters found a disturbing connection between the Stamp Act and the designs for an American bishop, as the act implied that those taking college degrees or accepting ordination from any denomination required royal approval, which automatically meant the Church of England's approval as well. They saw in this a double-edged sword with which the Grenville ministry and Archbishop Secker might revoke the colonial charters and quash dissent, thus helping to fuel the ensuing unrest and riots. While some clerics worried over the connection between bishops and stamps, apocalyptic interpretations of the Stamp Act came mainly from the laity, who found in biblical imagery a potent device for raising colonial indignation. The Sons of Liberty in New London characterized Connecticut's stamp distributor, Jared Ingersoll, in effigies and in print as a devil, while King George III's friend and closest advisor, John Stuart, Earl of Bute, became a scapegoat for originally concocting the Stamp Act. An orator speaking ex tempore on the "gallows" from which the effigy was hanged, compared William Pitt to Moses, and Ingersoll to "the Beast that Lord Bute set up in this Colony to be worshipped," conjuring up an image of the Antichrist. John Adams likewise depicted America as Joseph, "the King, Lords, and Commons, Joseph's father and brethren. Our forefathers sold into Egypt, that is, persecuted into America, &c." Paul Revere captured the millenarian flavor of the time in an engraving, "A View of the Year 1765," that features a demoniacal beast tearing the "Magna Charta" and crushing two hapless victims underfoot while ten figures heroically prepare to fight the monster, in emulation of Saint George.[5]

Americans received the news of the Stamp Act's repeal with much rejoicing, and there followed a flurry of thanksgiving sermons extolling the benevolence of the king, the wisdom of Parliament, and the superiority of the British constitution. They were not devoid of criticism, however, for suspicions about what originally lay behind the presentation and passage of the bill lingered. The ominous possibility that French influence in London dictated British colonial policy sounded notes of fear and paranoia in those sermons. William Patten of Massachusetts accused the sponsors of the Stamp Act of being "perhaps no Enemies to France, and not very friendly to Christian liberty," while Stephen Johnson of Rhode Island believed in the existence of "a corrupt, Frenchified party in the [British] nation." Reinforcement of these fears came in 1774 with the passage of the Quebec Act, but more immediate disturbances followed in the wake of the passage of new fiscal measures designed to generate revenue in 1767. As with the Stamp Act protests, resistance to the Townshend Revenue Acts was most palpably visible, as mobs became extralegal "committees" that forced observance to countermeasures such as boycotts, nonimportation, nonexportation, and nonconsumption of English manufactures.[6]

The Sandemanians, already subjects of scrutiny and scorn from their neighbors for their peculiar religious orientation, fell under greater surveillance for not joining in the popular protests against British policies that appeared to violate Americans' rights under the British constitution. Sandemanians found that the wary curiosity about them turned swiftly to hostility on account of their pietistic insistence upon abstaining from political affairs. That they stressed the Christian's duty to obey the magistrate, even if a tyrant, likewise did not win them any friends among those of a Whiggish inclination. The vast majority had only recently converted to Sandemanianism, and having had so little experience in the sect rendered many of them incapable of practicing what their elders preached, as a few—one of them an elder himself—ventured to defend themselves from criticism and outright attack. In Boston, Benjamin Davis Sr. operated a merchant trading business with his brother, Edward, until Edward's refusal to sign the 1768 Non-Importation Agreement precipitated a political argument leading to Benjamin's dissolving their partnership. Edward Foster, a Boston blacksmith and host to the first Sandemanian meetings, made no secret of his loyalism, and when a Patriot mob seriously damaged Boston Light on the night of 20 July 1775, he volunteered his and his employees' assistance to the British army to repair the lighthouse. The majority of Sandemanians, however, maintained a prudent silence during these unstable times, preferring to practice their faith discreetly without attracting attention. Among the prominent exceptions to this rule stood Nathaniel Barrell and his brother Colburn, a Portsmouth merchant-trader who had recently been named an elder of the Sandemanian congregation in Boston. Colburn Barrell was more demonstrative in his loyalism, as were several others in the city.[7]

Nathaniel became embroiled with Whigs who attacked the Sandemanians for their refusal to join in the protests against the Stamp Act. In several letters written in 1766 and 1767, Robert Sandeman encouraged Nathaniel to remain strong in the faith. "[W]hen I think of the grand cause that has exposed you so much to the hatred of wicked and unreasonable men I am rather disposed to congratulate you on the post of honour the Captain of Salvation hath assigned you." Sandeman reminded Nathaniel of the privations and persecutions suffered by the apostles and first Christians at the hands of both Jews and Romans. In a postscript he noted that "Neither you nor Colb[urn] have yet been confin'd to your lodgings two whole years as Paul was, & none of you has yet been honour'd to wear a chain by way of bracelet round his arm.

Have patience[,] you know not what further degrees of promotion are yet awaiting you." At the same time, Nathaniel came into conflict with one of the church members over the procurement of firewood. From Boston the following month, Sandeman wrote to Nathaniel that "my ears have been pester'd with accusations against you" for the latter's outspokenness, and though Sandeman assured Nathaniel that his behavior in the face of his Congregationalist enemies was beyond reproach, "I cannot help beseeching you by the meekness & gentleness of Christ ... that you would arm yourself with the same mind."[8]

A subsequent letter written shortly after New Year's Day, 1767, goes into great length on Nathaniel's conduct and Sandeman's advice on proper Christian deportment during controversies, to the point of dictating his next response to the firewood imbroglio:

Sir;
On reflection I am now sensible that what I formerly wrote you did not flow from the christian temper but from selfish resentment occasioned by unexpected reflections on my conduct, therefore I take this opportunity to retract the bitterness of that letter & to beg you will settle with me, setting aside both the wood given you [in] 1765 & 1766. For I am now sensible that I ought to pay more regard to the intention I expressed at the respective times of bestowing the wood as a free gift, than to any occurrences that have since occasioned altercation between us.

While certainly this was a trifling matter, and Sandeman generally had only complimentary things to write about Nathaniel's handling of the situation, the former's impatience with the whole affair leaks out in glancing references to honor, generosity, and forbearance. On Nathaniel's development as a church leader, Sandeman obviously thought that the man had much still to learn. "I wish too you would first convince some of our modern pharisees [sic] that they are no better than those we read of in the N. T. before you bring general charges against them as being a great deal worse. For this at best bears the air of exaggeration & a delight in reproaching." Abrasiveness seems to have been a family trait, for Colburn Barrell, a merchant, likewise threw himself into a controversy of his own with the merchant community of his newly adopted hometown of Boston.[9]

Colburn Barrell originally signed the Nonimportation Agreement, but later regretted and publicly abjured his subscription to it, after which he was attacked in the popular Whig press. Barrell published a letter of 13 November 1769 in the December issue of the *Boston Chronicle*, in which he described a calculated scheme by Boston's Patriot merchants to ruin his business on account of his renunciation of the Agreement. Publishing alongside it an earlier one of 6 October, Barrell explained that while he shared in principle the grievances that inspired the Agreement, he could no longer ignore the second thoughts troubling him after he initially joined the "Well Disposed Merchants." Citing practical matters concerning the payment of duties on the goods, the risks of seizure and detention in the Customs House for failure to pay those duties, and the inevitable spoilage of perishables left unsold and in storage should he maintain his end of the boycotts, Barrell respectfully excused himself from adherence to the Agreement. He pledged, however, not to sell any of the enumerated items until the new year. This failed to satisfy the majority of Boston's merchants who had entered into the "Solemn Agreement," and they apparently threatened Barrell with a general boycott of his business and the maligning of his character lest he acquiesce. He angrily responded by accusing his colleagues of having coerced him into the joining them in the first place. This, as the Whigs well knew, was not Barrell's first public appearance as a Tory. In New Hampshire, Portsmouth's Sandemanian community sought redress from the governor for Patriot vandalism of one of their houses, presenting him with a petition signed by six men, two of whom were Colburn and Nathaniel Barrell. Though clearly smarting from various Patriot abuses, most Sandemanians characteristically opted to trust in the law to render them justice. Colburn Barrell, however, had begun to abandon all hope of winning earthly justice for his inconveniences, and invoked higher powers to his cause.[10]

Barrell continued to argue his case in the press, to justify his conduct and thereby mend his reputation in Boston, where anti-British sentiment was coalescing. In a lengthy letter of 26 October 1769, Barrell declared his obedience to God and King George III, which he regretted having allowed to lapse when he signed the Nonimportation Agreement. He also published with it an anonymously written letter sent to him by "A Protestant" as further proof of the determined effort to ruin his reputation and business. Following a long section in which he reiterated the practical reasons for delaying his participation in the boycott, Barrell launched into a bitter invective against those who extolled the virtues of liberty while practicing extortion:

> Upon the whole, Gentlemen, I would be far from having any dispute with you on a point of my own interest, tho' I must say it is extreme hard, that in a land where *LIBERTY* is the cry, and where Patrons for it abound, a poor man shall not be suffered quietly to enjoy the benefit of an honest and fair trade, which the very constitution of the nation is admirably

adapted to secure to him, thro' the very influence of those who stile [sic] themselves *"The Friends to that most excellent Constitution."*

Barrell refused to back down in the face of impending misfortune at the hands of those he was beginning to think of as hypocrites and criminals, but his waging a public battle is inconsistent with quietistic Christianity in general, and Sandemanian doctrine in particular.[11]

The letter to Barrell from the Protestant opens a window into the minds of the Boston merchants who, to Barrell's mind, singled him out for retribution for withdrawing from the Agreement. The Protestant implied that at least a part of the merchant community's rancor originated from Barrell's eldership in a minority Christian sect. However, most of the letter is concerned with the issues of loyalty to God and country, his argument being that Barrell should not presume to judge either his fellow Bostonians to be "asses or idiots." He also reprimanded a supposedly pious "Christian" to return to spiritual contemplation rather than embroil himself in what is obviously a worldly matter, thus impugning Barrell's credibility as a Sandemanian. The Protestant deprecated Barrell's seemingly unquestioning loyalty to Britain, explaining how such willfully blind loyalty encourages "tyrants and traytors." He asserted that the word of a few fringe-element "schismatics" was insufficient to guide a distraught people and betrayed a design for advancing despotism. He listed the various injustices already passed over the colonies by Parliament and warned of greater abuses to come "while such subverters of the liberties of mankind as [Barrell] and [his] accomplices" preach "the most damnable and treasonable doctrines of unlimited submission and passive obedience." He concluded his polemic by inquiring, "are you, Mr. Barrell, apprehensive of no evil consequences from a total overthrow of all public faith and mutual confidence, so indispensably necessary to the very being of society, especially in large communities?"[12]

In response, Barrell published a short thesis on the subject of political and civil liberty. Starting with Montesquieu's dictum that liberty cannot be limitless, as that would be anarchy, Barrell protested that he had been made to suffer on account of his religious and political convictions, particularly his audacity in defending them. He then revealed that he was under a grand jury indictment "for publicly speaking against the country and the clergy," and denied the charge's validity on the basis that he had spoken against neither Parliament nor the king, but rather against an extralegal body's violations of his liberties. As for his criticism of the clergy, he was speaking only of those ministers who, he insisted, fomented a sedition that flew in the face of the gospels' exhortations to obey magistrates. He concluded by asserting that Parliament's fiscal measures, specifically the taxes on tea, paper, glass, and oil, among others, were never the onerous financial burdens that the merchants alleged, and remained duties on trade rather than direct taxes like the Stamp Act. Barrell argued that in fact the markup colonial merchants attached to necessities from Britain that were not subject to the Nonimportation Agreement, such as woolens, constituted a far greater injustice to the average consumer being denied access to many other goods without their consent, not to mention the potential for putting many American tradesmen and merchants (such as himself) out of business. He ended this final public offering with a standard appeal that both Whigs and Tories could agree on: a wish for a return to the former status quo.[13]

"I find by the *Boston Chronicle* that you are very closely beset by wicked and unreasonable men," Robert Sandeman wrote to Colburn Barrell, having inevitably heard about the frank exchange of views between a Sandemanian elder and the greater part of Boston's merchant community, "I see you need to be reminded of your hazard of forgetting the attention due to *Him* who, when he was reviled, reviled not again." Sandeman was trying to warn Barrell against getting knotted in hopeless controversy. Barrell was too focused on worldly affairs, Sandeman opined, and he counseled Barrell not to allow himself or other Sandemanians to be identified as Tories, which would bring more unwelcome attention and lead to greater troubles. Instead, he should remember "*the patience and meekness of Christ*" and "live *as quietly as possible*, especially while you are encompassed on every side by wicked men." He reminded Barrell of the changeable nature of government, and that he must remain flexible on the subject in order that he may adapt should a new situation arise. "In such times it is not our part to rebuke our neighbors for their disloyalty," he wrote, "but as quietly as possible to preserve our own loyalty till God either strengthen the hands of those in authority or give us new masters."[14]

In a subsequent letter, Sandeman admonished Barrell to consider the virtues of perseverance achieved through patient and, most of all, silent endurance, and repeated his warning that carrying on a rancorous public debate could not only lead him to grief, but also and more ominously, adversely affect all Sandemanians. Barrell could not be content with such passivity, though, and continued to express his opinions, this time using his authority as an elder to do so. At this point Sandeman's thoughts on the matter take an interesting turn. Rather than insisting on Barrell's silence in more forceful tones appropriate to the authority of a sectarian leader, Sandeman began to incline toward an agreement in principle with some of Barrell's actions, though he nursed his fear that such actions would ultimately be misconstrued:

> Your first printed paper exposing the unlawful and oppressive conduct of the cabal seemed in some sort necessary ... and as I was far from thinking that you said any thing of them beyond what was true, or that you was [sic] any way deficient in point of due respect to them, and as *I have a general bias in favour of spirited conduct*, I was not disposed to find fault with you, but was rather sorry to see you meet with any discouragement from among the brethren.... [But] surely it would be a wild project at present to think of persuading the people of Boston to admit the Scripture doctrine about subjection to Government.... From all I have said you will see I must have the greater satisfaction among my friends in Boston, the more they study to keep quiet even about their loyalty, and must have the more entire sympathy in their sufferings[,] the more confident I am that they suffer only for righteousness sake.

By November 1770, Barrell clearly refused to hide his light under a bushel, and began pronouncing acerbic condemnations of the Patriot leadership and the Congregationalist clergy allied with them. He declared that the people of Boston "were disaffected to the Laws of the Land" and were in a state of "open Rebellion, Disobedience, & Disloyalty," and that the clergy were principal figures "oppugning the Authority of the Laws of the Land." For this Barrell was himself finally indicted and fined for delivering sermons fomenting loyalist resistance, as he had suspected would happen nearly a year before.[15]

Distiller and rum merchant Isaac Winslow Jr., like some other Boston Sandemanians, believed that he had to demonstrate his loyalty publicly by signing petitions to Governors Hutchinson and Gage, for which he and those identified or suspected as Tories suffered threats and indignities at the hands of the Sons of Liberty. William Hutchinson wrote to Winslow from New Providence Island in 1770, assuring him that "I can most sensibly conceive the uneasiness you feel under the present posture of publick Affairs, and most cordially wish, that all the tumults and animosities occasioned by them were at an end, & that perfect Harmony was restored by measures, the most salutary for America and honourable for Government." Winslow, like most Tories who endured the surveillance and tender mercies of the Patriots, managed to keep a low profile and endure the gathering storm of rebellion, which by 1774 was becoming inevitable. Simon Pease, one of Winslow's business associates, wrote from Newport, Rhode Island, to express his wish for some sort of resolution that would bring an end to the troubles, as the increasingly likely prospect of the colonies combining together in militant opposition to the Mother Country would bring about an interruption of trade that would have "terrible consequences": "I can most sensibly conceive the uneasiness you feel under the present posture of publick Affairs, and most cordially wish, that all the tumults and animosities occasioned by them were at an end, & that perfect Harmony was restored by measures, the most salutary for America and honourable for Government." Such pressures may have prompted Winslow to take a more active role as a Loyalist, if only briefly.[16]

Winslow petitioned for and won appointment as a Mandamus Councillor, granted by royal appointment through a provision in the 1774 Massachusetts Government Act, but only a few days after accepting it he resigned on 29 August—much as had "S.W.," protagonist of the Patriot ghost story. His behavior in this matter is typical of the sociopolitical conflict sundering Boston at the time, and underscores the fissures that weakened the Sandemanian churches throughout New England. The 5 September issue of the *Boston Gazette* reported that Winslow "waited on Governor Gage last Monday, when he made an absolute and full Resignation of his Place at the Board," after which "several of the most respectable Gentlemen, who have appeared foremost in the Cause of their Country's Liberties have paid their compliments to him on account of his Resignation." Responding to some apparent confusion in the city regarding his actions, Winslow published a clarification in the 8 September issue of the *Massachusetts Spy* "that such resignation was made by him on Monday the 29th of August inst., that he has not since attended at council and that he is determined not to give any further attendance." Clearly, Winslow resigned under pressure from the Sons of Liberty or other local Patriots, as did many others who accepted royal commissions at the time. A letter from John Andrews to William Barrell written the day after Winslow's resignation states that at a Roxbury town meeting, Winslow, with regard to his initial acceptance of the appointment, "made an apology for [it], and said that it was more owing to the perswasion [sic] of others than to his own inclinations." Winslow certainly felt conflicted. He sought and accepted the post to demonstrate his loyalty in a city whose citizens generally verged on open revolt, but immediately relinquished it for fear of Patriot wrath. Despite this capitulation, an unforgiving mob burned his Roxbury house to the ground in 1776.[17]

Winslow violated the tenets of his sect by seeking an office in the civil government. In the uncertain atmosphere of Boston politics on the eve of the Revolution, it is evident that Winslow gravitated toward one pole by his loyalism and then back toward the center by the threat of violence to his person and reputation. As both Tories and Patriots vied for devotees, and the Sons of Liberty were actively harassing known and suspected Tories as well as vandalizing their homes and businesses, Winslow was surely not alone in being conflicted and apprehensive. Colburn Barrell had advocated active loyalism, condemning all resistors to British authority as traitors, and his brash example was persuasive if the evidence from the actions of other Boston Sandemanians is any indication. That Winslow backpedaled is understandable, as is the fact that this relatively new sect would have members who feared for their lives as much as for their souls. Even Sandeman was confused as to where he stood on the issue of Winslow's political activities. Whether or not Winslow remained a Loyalist was immaterial. The fact that he was a Sandemanian had placed a permanent stamp of loyalism on him that no act of civic contrition could eradicate, and the same applied to all Sandemanians.

While Sandeman was exhorting Colburn Barrell to circumspection in his conflict with Boston's merchant community, he himself clashed with the Danbury authorities on account of his religious activities. The town's selectmen, combining their disgust with Sandeman's politics and heterodoxy, began in 1770 to apply measures designed to force the undesirable and his associates out of town. For lodging Sandeman and his nephew in their home, Asa Church was fined £40 on 28 February, at which time Church's guests were warned to leave. Three weeks later Thomas Benedict, Danbury's Justice of the Peace, hauled Sandeman and Theophilus Chamberlain up before his bench and charged them as strangers and vagrants who had ignored the eviction warning, an offense that carried a mandatory £40 fine for both men. Sandeman forcefully countered that the law against transients "was intended not against harmless strangers but against persons of ungoverned and dishonest conversations," and that any reasonable person could plainly see that he and his nephew—and by extension the rest of the Sandemanians—posed no threat to the community. Benedict nonetheless found both men guilty as charged, though he unofficially commuted the fine and execution of the eviction order. Then, Robert Sandeman died suddenly of an undisclosed ailment on 2 April 1771 in Theophilus Chamberlain's house in Danbury, and the members of the Danbury church arranged for his burial in the Old Wooster Street cemetery, in spite of the brief objections of a group of citizens.[18]

The New Haven church, composed only of ten families, most of which had moved to New Haven from Danbury after Sandeman's death, prudently avoided any involvement in the tumult of protest against British policy. In that city, the newly formed Friends of Constitutional Liberty focused their attention on the Sandemanians in the early fall of 1774. Their silence was interpreted by this ad hoc body as loyalist cowardice, and their refusal to subscribe to the Solemn League and Covenant was met with violence. In September, according to Rev. Samuel Andrew Peters, Joseph Pynchon and some other Sandemanians were "barbarously insulted by three Mobs" and the crowds "cried along the streets, *that the Sandemanians had proved themselves to be guilty of the Damnable Sin of Loyalty to the King of England by not signing the Covenant.*" In November of the next year, the selectmen of New Haven passed an edict that anyone who defended George III or Parliament would be warned out of town, and the members assumed the offices of a Committee of Inspection to expose all Loyalists and expel them. The Sandemanians constituted one of their initial targets.[19]

"Impiety, Bigotry, Persecution"

By 1774, the various branches of the Sons of Liberty throughout the colonies that organized and coordinated the protests against British policies reformed into committees of correspondence, inspection, and safety. The tactics they used were the same ones used to varying effect in the previous economic embargo measures of 1764–1765 and 1768–1770: intimidation, coercion, and violence. Those who criticized the members of the associations or refused to join in the boycotts suffered public insults as enemies to liberty, had their names published in the newspapers, and faced ostracism at the very least. More often, they found themselves faced with hostile crowds led by Sons of Liberty who promised to tear down their houses, destroy their places of business, and even to inflict bodily harm through beatings or tarring and feathering. They faced arrest and imprisonment for being foes of American liberty, and thus recourse to the law did little or nothing to remedy the situation, for the majority of the colonial assemblies endorsed the boycotts and commended those who signed the agreements. Some the authorities treated as criminals, subjecting them to punishments ordinarily meted out to convicted thieves and witches. As American resistance to British policy and authority deepened in the 1770s, these extralegal bodies gradually assumed many of the functions of local and provincial government in the absence of colonial governors and their allies in the assemblies and town governments. It became the committees' task to bring the American people together in the revolutionary cause by appealing to their unique "Americanness," and obliterate—if not eradicate—their allegiance to Great Britain. In some cases, this was easily achieved, but in most instances support for the Revolution had to be forcibly garnered through tactics that had served the Sons of Liberty so well during the 1760s. However, the campaign to forge an American identity among a largely indifferent or politically ignorant people displayed a sharper, more sinister edge than it had before.[20]

The passage of the Quebec Act in 1774 alarmed Protestant Americans because of its abrogation of the Toleration Act of 1689, which extended toleration only to Protestant Dissenters outside the Church of England, and upon which colonial American voting rights and office-holding criteria were based. To those most alarmed by it, the Quebec Act could only mean that Roman Catholicism had once again resurfaced at the Court of St. James. The First Continental Congress, in an address to the British people, alerted its target audience to Parliament's aim of establishing in Canada "a religion that has long deluged your island in blood, and dispersed impiety, bigotry, persecution, murder, and rebellion through every part of the world." John Adams, in his famous pamphlet debate with Daniel Leonard, argued that anti-Catholicism elevated New England to a higher moral plane, since the Catholic Church fostered ignorance and superstition among its adherents, while Protestant nations repeatedly defended civil liberties throughout its history. Not only did Americans fear papist machinations in George III's court, but also the Church of England's perceived drift back into Rome's orbit, adding still more ominous tones to the possibility of an Anglican episcopate. Paul Revere again utilized vivid demonic imagery in a famous engraving called "The Mitred Minuet," in which four bishops dance over a copy of the Quebec Act while Lord Bute, King George III, and the Devil look on approvingly. Samuel Sherwood of New York counted the Quebec Act a part of "the flood of the dragon that has poured forth ... for the establishment of popery," linking the Act to the campaign for an Anglican bishop. Thus, biblical prophecies of the growing power of the Antichrist were being fulfilled, and Sherwood concluded that "it need not appear strange or shocking to us, to find that our own nation [Britain] has been, in some degree, infected and corrupted therewith."[21]

When the imperial crisis turned into a revolutionary war, the committees of inspection became committees of safety, which both openly and covertly observed the townspeople's behavior, looking for those who dared to disparage the Continental Congress or the newly devised provincial governments, if not publicly to proclaim loyalism. Known violators appeared in newspaper advertisements and on broadsides demanding their ostracism, and members took note of any who deliberately or inadvertently spoke or socialized with them. In some cases, the committees went so far as to threaten the lives of offenders, but preferred more indirect social pressures to compel a suspect's disjunction from British society. "These committees," wrote John Adams in

February 1775, "are admirably calculated to diffuse knowledge, to communicate intelligence, and *promote unanimity*." However, even he had to admit that, in some cases, individuals took advantage of their newfound power as members of the revolutionary committees to settle old political scores or simply to indulge in acts of vandalism and terror. The elites among the revolutionaries usually thus found themselves in the uncomfortable position of watching the incipient Revolution hurtling out of their control as mechanics, artisans, laborers, and farmers vented their class antagonism at anyone who stood in their way.[22]

Among those whose loyalties wavered, the revolutionary committees just as often acted as divisive forces sullying the principles the Patriots claimed to be defending. The revolutionaries, in the manner of idealists passionately devoted to a cause they believed to be right, drew no distinction between Loyalists and Neutrals, declaring both to be of a piece in their refusal to support independence or the war effort against Britain. Both groups were presumed to be Loyalists in need either of "correction" or banishment. Usually Neutrals came in for harsher treatment, perceived as "trimmers" watching the contest from the sidelines in order to join the victors once it became clear who that would be. Those pacifists who espoused a political agreement with the Patriots, while their religious beliefs precluded their participating in the Revolutionary War, came under fire as cowards who wanted the blessings of liberty without sacrificing their safety in order to attain them. A case in point is Westchester County, New York, where the majority of the population hesitated to declare their loyalties, and thus suffered terrible abuse from New England militia who, during the collapse of the American defense of New York City, declared them "not worth defending." Any inclination toward the cause of independence among the uncommitted was thus nipped in the bud by the rash behavior of Patriot leaders, and a process of depoliticization steadily took place there and elsewhere.[23]

Unlike the passing of sectarian leaders such as Mother Ann Lee among the Shakers, or Joseph Smith among the Mormons, which tended to strengthen the movements they started, Sandeman's death actually had the opposite effect. It is, therefore, tempting to conclude that if Sandeman had continued to live, he may have been able to exert a guiding influence during the turbulent years of the Revolution that would witness the Sandemanians undergo so much stress and persecution. However, Sandemanian theology and ecclesiology effectively prevented him from acting as a proper sectarian leader, and even if it had allowed him to play such a role, his penchant for controversy and disputation would most likely have led him to encourage "spirited conduct" rather than mere "sober dissent." However, it is noteworthy that Sandeman worked hard to discourage combativeness from his newly ordained church elders, when he was better known as a controversialist in Britain. The Sandemanians, already the subjects of discussion and harassment for their refusal to join their neighbors in criticism of and resistance to British authority in the decade preceding the Revolution, attracted still more attention to themselves as the war broke out in their midst. What confronts one in following the Sandemanians into the Revolutionary War years is their comparative silence and, after 1777, their absence. So effective had the Whigs been in squelching the Loyalists and Neutrals, that the majority of Sandemanians preferred to leave New England for Nova Scotia in the early years of the war, while the remainder virtually disappeared from contemporary view.

This is not to say that certain individuals did not attract uncomfortable attention from the revolutionary authorities or their popular adjuncts at the beginning of the war. In fact, the attention the Sandemanians drew to themselves as they attempted to stand by their principles of pacifism and apoliticism led to a systematic harassment that disrupted their churches. As they sought shelter from the revolutionary tempest, those who opted against Canadian exile found little cohesion or mutual support. A few of the New England churches eventually disbanded apart from the one in Danbury, which had always had the strongest congregation. Most of the societies struggled to stay together, but in most cases each church's numbers—which had never been great to begin with—dropped severely. The Danbury church's endurance is attributable to Sandeman's presence until his passing in 1771, and it is his marked absence that permeates this bleak period of Sandemanian history in North America. Similarly, one notices an almost complete lack of surviving communication between adherents in Britain and those in America once both Sandeman and Glas had both died. The attempts by relatively inexperienced converts to maintain Sandemanian discipline show no coordination or even adequate contact among the remaining churches. The Revolution essentially doomed the Sandemanians from becoming more than a minute denomination, notable more for their eccentricities than anything else. Anything else, that is, except for a dogmatic loyalism that elicited a disproportionate persecution from professed lovers of liberty.

"Check'd by the Command of God"

Hopestill Capen languished in a Boston jail cell through the night of 6 August 1776, contemplating his dilemma as a prisoner of conscience. He believed it had been his duty to admonish his fellow Bostonians that resistance to Parliament's measures were impolitic at best, and at worst treasonous. He joined other Boston Loyalists in signing petitions condemning the more violent actions of the Sons of Liberty and the raising of local militias to oppose the British army, as well as subscribing to several petitions to Governor Thomas Hutchinson and his successor, General Thomas Gage, declaring loyalty and a willingness to take up arms to preserve civic order. Capen, a merchant and member of this Boston Association of Loyalists, became a target for the Patriot authorities assuming the functions of government in the wake of the British evacuation, who promptly arrested and imprisoned him. In a mollifying petition to the Court of Inquiry for release, Capen affirmed that

> ... had I not been check'd by the command of God ... to be subject to the Higher Powers ... I should have been one of the foremost in opposing the measure of the British Parliament ... neither do I think myself in any ways bound in conscience to become an informer against my country ... but to be subject to all the laws that are made that are not contrary to the laws of my Maker.

Capen's attitude is typical of the Sandemanians' uncomfortable—indeed impossible—position before and during the American Revolution.[24]

Encouraged by Robert Sandeman to embrace pacifist quietism, the American Sandemanians found themselves—depending on personal disposition or circumstances—either unwilling to hold their peace or unable to do so. As a new and still minute feature on the American religious landscape in 1775, and thus still in the process of mastering Sandemanian doctrine, they became caught up in an economic and political whirlwind in a place that found them at the very least an irksome curiosity, and at worst an incipient threat to New England orthodoxy. At a point when colonial Americans had awakened to their political, economic, and cultural maturity, a sectarian group that espoused doctrines of political noninvolvement and pacifism happened to live in a region where such a combination would not be tolerated. Already a source of some controversy and suspicion, their attitudes toward the Revolution worsened their situation. Revolutionary American society had already deviated significantly from what it had been in previous decades, and the Sandemanians are representative of a native American inability to accept those changes. New Englanders' religious bigotry played no small part in the persecution heaped upon them, and underscores the role religion played in the Revolution, which was far from marginal.[25]

In October 1775, while preparing for their ill-fated invasion of Canada, New England militia officers under the command of Benedict

"Spirited Conduct" 139

Arnold broke into the Newburyport, Massachusetts, crypt wherein lay the body of George Whitefield, and proceeded to snip off bits of the collar and wristbands for distribution to the soldiers as tokens of divine favor for their expedition. This bizarre incidence of relic-hunting among nominal and devout Protestants highlights a significant aspect of the American Revolution: its overtly religious character. Just as the storm of protest that erupted over sweeping changes in British imperial and colonial administration was often interpreted through the lens of religious conviction and spiritual sensibility, so also was the much more disturbing War for American Independence and the formation of an independent United States of America. While there are certainly those who see only indirect religious concern in the swirl of events from 1775 to 1783, one has little trouble discovering abundant evidence of a blending of religious and political subject matter during the war, and the utilization of religious language—often of an eschatological variety—even from none other than some of the "Founding Fathers." The Sandemanians, albeit from the loyalist perspective, were not alone in casting the War for Independence as a war over religious principles.[26]

For Pietist denominations and sects, the Revolutionary War was the regrettable outcome of civil strife born of an overall inattention to Christian duty. The German Reformed Coetus of Pennsylvania implored its congregations in 1775 to stay away from active involvement in the conflict, citing that they lived in "precarious times." Indeed they did, for German Pietist neutrals came under attack from Patriot neighbors for their refusal to support the Revolution, which they equated with loyalism. Mennonites suffered the greatest measure of Patriot abuse, while Moravians in North Carolina maneuvered with greater agility, offering humanitarian aid to rebel and Redcoat alike. Quakers likewise endured mistreatment for their pacifism and resistance to military conscription. The disruptions caused by this "sad war," in the words of the Coetus, resulted in grievous neglect of "the keeping of the Sabbath Day and Christian exercises in the families at home." The socially fractious nature of the conflict led John Murray of Massachusetts to warn against satanic "*selfishness* and *extortion*" threatening American unity in 1779.[27]

On the civilian front, Herman Husband, a Pennsylvania farmer and evangelical preacher originally from North Carolina (where he supported the Regulator uprising), urged heightened vigilance against corruption, idleness, and luxury in a pamphlet anonymously published in 1782. It outlined a reformation of the American government, with his text heavily borrowed from passages in the books of Ezekiel, Daniel, the gospels, and the Book of Revelation. In keeping with the egalitarian rhetoric of the Declaration of Independence, Husband saw direct taxation as leading to vice on account of its antilibertarian nature. He pointed out that the Israelites in the Old Testament maintained their society through voluntary tithing, and the New Testament deplored Roman taxation and its system of collection as a sin, even though it is incumbent on Christians to "render unto Caesar what is Caesar's." The colonists rebelled against direct taxation, and Husband noted that Congress's tax schemes were being evaded and resisted, thus encouraging the vice of avoiding one's civic and Christian duties. Governments should subsist on the voluntary payment of a proportional share of one's profits or surplus, with the rest coming out of what amounts to a national sales tax. This, he predicted, would ultimately lead to a truly equal society envisioned by Ezekiel and Daniel, and only when the American government implemented his or some other similar scheme would the biblical prophecies come to pass.[28]

George Duffield of Philadelphia, in his thanksgiving sermon delivered at the Third Presbyterian Church, though effusive in his praises of the Revolution, its leaders, and the selflessness of patriotic Americans, still issued a stern warning that those few who chose to exploit the hardships of their fellows imperiled the new nation's millennial potential. Millenarian themes permeated texts appealing for a reformatory overhaul of an American society at war. Isaac Backus and Elisha Rich of Massachusetts, and John Leland of Virginia, all Baptists, targeted religious establishments in New England and the South as being synonymous with the despised and satanic papacy, which in their turn must fall before Christ's millennial reign. Rich, in the first year of the war, was especially clear about identifying the Beast as not merely Roman Catholic theocracy, but Protestant establishmentarianism as well. All in all, Stiles, Duffield, Backus, and Rich, among other exegetes, believed that only through a total reformation of American society— through a national rejection of and repentance for a smorgasbord of sins—could the true promise of the United States be accomplished. But the so-called Black Regiment reserved for themselves the prerogative to define the nature of that promise, and they allowed precious little room for dissent or debate, whether it be of the political or theological variety.[29]

Loyalist interpretations of the ongoing Revolution in religious terms ultimately do not effectively counterbalance the religio-political expression of the Patriots, but cannot be ignored. In New England, where Anglicans scraped against the established Congregationalist hierarchy, the predominance of High Church principles and the overwhelming support for the Revolution among the Dissenters amplified Anglican loyalism. According to data compiled by Nancy L. Rhoden, of the forty-seven clerics resident in New England during the war, all but eight were avowed Loyalists, and of those eight remaining, six professed neutrality. Only two Massachusetts ministers supported the Revolution. The rest pointed to the popular tumults as evidence of the vulgarity of this particular revolt and that they most definitely had nothing to do with legitimate resistance against tyranny such as had precipitated the Glorious Revolution in England. To them it was a vital issue of whether the God of Abraham was a God of chaos and violence, or one of peace and order, and they saw nothing in the Revolution that could convince them that God had sanctioned this rebellion. William Clark in Massachusetts saw men's minds infatuated with rampant licentiousness, and Samuel Andrews of Connecticut contended that the Whigs' abundant use of the word "liberty" disguised wanton violence and destruction under a "Cloak of Maliciousness."[30]

New York's Anglican leadership agreed with Lord North's ministry that the rebellion had begun among New England Congregationalists, and they harnessed the long-standing rivalry between New York and Massachusetts to paint the Boston Patriots as being of the same ilk who practiced religious oppression over non-Congregationalists. Thomas Bradbury Chandler, in *A Friendly Address to All Reasonable Americans* (1774), portrayed the protests against British authority as originating solely among New Englanders, whom he compared to the fanatical Münsterites, and most directly to Oliver Cromwell's rebellious Roundheads of the English Civil War. Chandler concluded with a short catalogue of the persecution that awaited Quakers, Baptists, and those Germans and Dutch of the Reformed and pietistic persuasions under an intercolonial government dominated by New England. Chandler's predictions were borne out by incidents of violence against loyalist Christians. German pietistic sects such as the Mennonites, Dunkers, and Schwenkfelders in Pennsylvania endured sporadic official and popular reprisals for their refusal to swear loyalty to the Continental Congress after the passage of the Test Act of 1777. They and the Moravians in Pennsylvania and North Carolina likewise faced fines and imprisonment for their refusals to answer military draft notices. Baptists throughout the rebelling colonies and Methodists in the South were harassed for espousing their pacifist, neutralist, or loyalist inclinations, and the handful of Presbyterians and Congregationalists who questioned the wisdom of the Revolution and independence suffered abuse at the hands of the revolutionary authorities and the mobs.[31]

News of the Battle of Lexington and Concord, where Boston area militia clashed with British Regulars on the morning of 19 April, electrified

New England as no other developments had since the military occupation of Boston the year before. Patriot militia from Massachusetts, Connecticut, and Rhode Island converged on the hills surrounding Boston, seething with, as Thomas Jefferson had commented with regard to the Virginians, a "phrenzy of revenge" among "all ranks of people" to besiege the city. The First Continental Congress's optimism in the ultimate rationality of the British government had all but evaporated as the Second Congress convened in May, and John Adams captured the martial spirit of the majority of the colonists when he grimly opined, "Every Body must and will, and shall be a soldier." Despite the pyrrhic British victory at Bunker Hill, Gen. Thomas Gage preferred caution to decisive action, precipitating his replacement by Gen. William Howe, who had no choice but to pause when the guns of recently taken Fort Ticonderoga appeared atop the Dorchester Heights and the hills northeast of Cambridge in late February. The British evacuated the city between 17 and 27 March 1776.[32]

Throughout the British occupation of Boston, resident Loyalists eagerly participated in city government as well as formed a provincial militia unit, the Loyal American Associators under the command of Timothy Ruggles, to augment Howe's Regulars. The Associators drafted a declaration to Gen. Gage pledging that

> We the subscribers considering the present Alarming situation of the Town being now invested by a large body of the people of the Country, and at all times ready to do all in our power for the support of Government and good order and to resist all Lawless Violence, Have voluntarily assembled together and do mutually engage each with the other by this subscription, That in Case the town should be attacked or assaulted or things brought to such emergencies as that our Aid may be thought necessary by the General that we will upon proper notice Assemble together and being supplied with proper Arms and Ammunition will contribute all in our power for the Common safety in Defence of the Town.

Among the subscribers were at least ten known Sandemanians, four of whom are especially noteworthy: Benjamin Davis Sr., Edward Foster, Isaac Winslow Jr., and Hopestill Capen. Though clearly a violation of their pacifist quietism, these Sandemanians most likely agreed to join the Associators only for the purpose of defending Boston from Patriot attack. By the time the city was evacuated, 10,000 Redcoats had mustered there and consequently the likelihood of their being called up appeared remote at best, given the British military's low opinion of provincials in arms. Indeed, Gage did not call for their services, thus saving the Sandemanians from further compromising their religious principles.[33]

"Wo unto you, for you make it your dayly Practis to distress and Parsicute those who are conscientious in being Lige Subjects" complained Stephen Gorham of Fairfield, Connecticut. Matters in that colony for Loyalists had been no better than in Massachusetts, and for the Sandemanians a higher degree of persecution prevailed. Loyalism cut across the socioeconomic spectrum, as it did in the other rebelling colonies, but Connecticut could claim the distinction of having one of the highest proportions of well-placed and politically powerful Loyalists. Many of them were militia officers, such as Col. Eleazer Fitch, Governor Jonathan Trumbull's business partner, and this prevalence among both the militias and constabularies prompted Titus Hosmer of Middletown to move in the General Assembly "to turn every known Tory out of the Commission of the Peace" in May 1775. A group of Windham County Whigs likewise complained to the Assembly in September 1776 that their sheriff was a Loyalist. As widespread as this phenomenon was, western Connecticut harbored the greater proportion of Loyalists, with Fairfield County being most notable on this account, its proximity to New York City—occupied by the British in September 1776—was a key factor.[34]

Hopestill Capen, who signed his name to the Nonimportation Agreement, further distinguished himself—like Colburn Barrell—by later retracting his assent to the Agreement and proclaiming his pietistic necessity to remain loyal, as well as by refusing to flee the city with other Loyalists when the British evacuated. He and his family remained in Boston, hoping to ride out the Patriot storm in anonymity, just as Sandeman had implored Colburn Barrell to do and Isaac Winslow Jr. had tried to do. He managed to avoid detection until the summer of 1776, when the new Patriot government of Boston discovered and imprisoned him as "an Enemy to the Country." Attempting to persuade the Court of Inquiry that his loyalty to the king was based simply on the dictates of his faith, he acknowledged that he was just as angry about British colonial policy as any other in his position—hence his initial subscription to the Nonimportation Agreement—and that should the Americans win their independence, he would be a loyal citizen in accordance with his beliefs. His petition was obviously unconvincing and summarily denied, as the Patriots tended to look upon even the vaguest hints of neutrality or loyalism as a threat to their authority. As far as Capen's persecutors were concerned, he and all other Sandemanians were no different. He was held for over two years, and finally released in October 1778, when he decided that emigration to Nova Scotia would be the only option if he wished to live in peace.[35]

While Boston's Sandemanians are especially noteworthy for their outspoken and unabashed loyalism, others likewise distinguished themselves, though on a much smaller scale. Late in 1775, western Connecticut was aflame with rumors that the Loyalists of that region awaited a British invasion in order to join the Redcoats in despoiling their neighbors and seizing confiscated property. The residents of Fairfield believed that combined Loyalist and British forces would soon be "coming down in the night, and setting fire to the houses and barns and destroying all before them." The Patriots of eastern Connecticut organized a dragnet and, joined by furloughed Continental Army soldiers, swept through Newtown, Redding, Danbury, Ridgefield, and Woodbury, disarming all known and suspected Loyalists. Ensnared were Ebenezer White and John Sparhawk, a prominent member of the Portsmouth church who had just relocated to Danbury. As Sparhawk was returning home from a visit to New Haven, he was shocked to discover

> several hundreds of armed men [in?] the Town on the Sea Coast, who had taken prisoners about 30 Tories (as they are called) & among them 8 or 9 of our Brethren ... I did not think it expedient to fly—the next morning Mr. White & I were taken from our homes by [illeg.] men, & were conducted to the place where the other prisoners were, [some] of our Brethren had been already two days prisoner—we continued in [this] situation [until] about twelve where all of us who were distinguished by the name of "Glasites" were carried before a kind of Court Martial, composed of many of the Militia Officers of the County & some of the Committee of this Town, here we were examined in an [inquisitorial] way for they had nothing to charge us with, we were first ask'd whether we would take up arms against the Country, to this we answd [sic] we were bound to be subject to any ordinance of man etc.... We were then asked if we would discover all plots & conspiracies against the Country—I answered that they were equivocal times & a direct answer could not be given without they were explained—I added, however, we might be class'd with Tories—It was with us a point of Conscience, a religious test—that we could in no sense join with them without giving up a Commandment of the Lords—than which it would be far better for us not only to suffer imprisonment but Death itself.—This contrary to my expectations exasperated them beyond measure—I was called a Scoundrell not fit to live in this world.

The drumhead trial lasted until three o'clock the next morning, at which point Sparhawk charged that "however a persecution may look at a distance, at a closer view the heart shrinks—at least my heart did."

Sparhawk's release on £200 bond was secured finally by a "Lt. St[even]s," a former Sandemanian "whose conscience was somewhat touched," while the others were let go on a total bond of £1,000.³⁶

Following his release in December 1775, Sparhawk visited the New Haven church, which he found in a deplorable condition. The congregants were "scattered, the body of inhabitants having insisted upon all our [leaving] town—in consequence of which T[itus] & B[enjamin] Smith have gone to Newtown—Mr. Pynchon to Guilford—Mr. Humphreys to Derby." The town selectmen learned of his presence and brought him in for examination, to, as Sparhawk phrased it, "give them my principal [view] of government, etc. etc." No action was taken against Sparhawk at the time, and, in fact, no official action against the Sandemanians as a body was taken until April 1777, after the British attack on Danbury. Sparhawk, White, and Munson Gregory were arrested and detained after the British withdrawal. According to Daniel Humphreys, Sparhawk

> had been a prisoner above 30 days, sometimes out for a day and sometimes for a night on some person's word. He has been greatly threatened & to appearance in eminent hazard of life—Men loading their Pieces in his Sight, before or when he was taken, and swearing by their Maker that he should die, threatened to be shot when carried along the street by the Guard.... The most that was alledged against him was that he was in the Streets while the Troops were there.

Significantly, it was Humphreys's assessment that Sparhawk's horrendous treatment stemmed primarily from the fact of his being a Sandemanian and nothing more: "his being a Leader among the Brethren there, was what made him so obnoxious."³⁷

While Sparhawk's jailers and guards only threatened to shoot him, it is clear that the Patriot authorities condoned any violence that furthered their cause. In the same letter, Humphreys detailed Munson Gregory's travails at the hands of the Patriots:

> Sabbath Morng. just as the King's Troops were leaving the Town—a certain Capt. belonging to the town came to [Gregory] & gave him to understand that there would be the utmost hazard to any man's tarrying who was a friend of government, that such were shot at by ye people, that he had been shot at, & his son shot dead by his side (it appeared afterward that this was not so, he was only wounded). This alarmed bror. Gregory to such a degree, that he packed up a few things, and went down to Mr. Sparhawk to ask his advice respecting going off. He advised him to return

home & not to go. He was accordingly returning to his own house with a view to tarry; but taken up, carried over to ye Province of New York, treated with great severity, finally brot back, & released on bond.

The individual who had been shot at, and whose son wounded, was another Sandemanian, Hezekiah Benedict. The dangerous atmosphere prevailing in Danbury in those days is further confirmed by Samuel Hoyt, a Sandemanian church member who fled the town because "he was informed and really believed that the justly incensed multitude of the people threatened to put to death all those people who had remained at their homes while the enemy was there, and that they had so far carried their threats into execution as to fire upon one Hezh. Benedict and his sons of sd Danbury and had shot one of sd Benedicts sons thro' the thigh." While certainly other known and suspected Loyalists were similarly treated, and that some of them were Sandemanians does not mean they were specially singled out for that reason alone, it can nevertheless be certain that the Sandemanians were already identified by their neighbors before the troubles began. They were among the first to be harassed in any town or city where they lived. As for Ebenezer White, his Sandemanianism was not the only factor incriminating him. The British officers used White's home for their headquarters, preferring as they did to lodge in the houses of known friends of the king, and for this an angry mob likely torched the Sandemanian church in retaliation.[38]

The Committee of Inspection detained Theophilus Chamberlain, elder of the New Haven Sandemanians who remained behind, and demanded a statement defining the nature and degree of the sect's loyalism. While eloquently, albeit circuitously, professing their duty to God and concomitant loyalty to the king, the statement expressed a desire to be left in peace:

> We hold ourselves equally obliged ... to live peacefully with all men; to do good to all men as we have Opportunity; to be inoffensive among our Neighbours, to love & pray for our Enemies; never to avenge ourselves, nor to bear ill-will to any men; to be no busybodies in other men's matters ...
>
> If we are to be deprived of that Liberty, which we have in no wise forfeited, happy shall we be if it be given to us from above to suffer with patience. We are able to get a subsistence in this place in our lawful Callings without being a burden to our Neighbours. If we are removed or confined, this is taken from us. We would be glad therefore to be permitted to continue here if we may live in quiet & unmolested.

The petitioners finished this lengthy statement by requesting the release of Oliver Burr from jail. Daniel Humphreys, Titus Smith, Richard Woodhull, Thomas Gold, Joseph Pynchon, Theophilus Chamberalin, Benjamin Smith, and William Richmond signed it. This statement, forwarded to Governor Trumbull, bore an annotation that the Sandemanian perspective was "Diametrically opposite to the Recent System of Politicks adopted by the American States for Their Preservation and Safety ... & by the Late Conduct of some of their Number we believe them to be Enemies to our Common Cause." The committee further insisted that Gov. Trumbull "adopt some method regarding them whereby the Publick ... may be rid of Their Fears." Still more infuriating, according to the committee, was the Sandemanians' refusal "to advance a Shilling ... in Support of the Resent Dispute as They say their [Consciences] will not allow them to support this Warr."[39]

When the committee insisted on a more concise answer, the Sandemanians responded through Richard Woodhull, emphasizing that they had no intention of acting on behalf of the British beyond the limits of the law, and resolutely affirming that they would not take up arms against their neighbors or any of the Patriot forces:

> I do not feel myself bound either from Conscience or Choice to give Intelligence to his Majesty's Officers or troops nor do I feel my self bound either from Conscience or Choice to take an active part, or to take up arms against this town or the united Colonies.... I also feel my self bound in Conscience to seek the Peace of this town.

There soon followed in October 1777 another significant statement, in which the Sandemanians candidly admitted that they had been equivocating in an effort to ensure their safety: "We were not in giving the above Answer acting in the Fear of God ... but of Man." The committee's response was to clap all of the Sandemanian men in jail, forwarding their statement to Danbury's delegate to the General Assembly, along with a commentary explaining their actions and a recommendation for further measures leading to their forced removal from the town. Though the brethren were imprisoned for a brief period, the New Haven authorities ultimately decided that they may "continue in this state upon giving their Parole ... [and] will not do any thing injurious to this state or the united States of America, or give any intelligence, or Assistance to the British offices or forces at war with this and the other united States." Convinced that their freedom might be ephemeral, most of Danbury's Sandemanians opted to leave the colony. According to Ezra

Stiles, they made for Loyalist strongholds on Long Island. Only Richard Woodhull remained in the town.[40]

John Howe, since 1774 the co-owner and printer of the venerable *Massachusetts Gazette and Boston News Letter*, was a Loyalist not simply out of his Sandemanian religious principles, but also by general political inclination. The twenty-one-year-old Howe could not deny the giddy excitement of the first year of the American War for Independence, which he believed Britain would easily win, based on his personally witnessing the Battle of Bunker Hill and the influx of redcoated troops that subsequently poured into Boston. That brash confidence turned to disillusionment when Gen. Howe ordered the military and Loyalist civilian evacuation of the city in March 1776. John Howe and his fiancée joined the majority of Sandemanians who fled to Halifax. Still, eager to serve his king and country, he accompanied British forces that sailed from Halifax to New York City later that year, eventually joining the occupying garrison in Newport, Rhode Island, where he began printing the Loyalist *Newport Gazette* in January 1777. Howe and his family were forced by American advances to return to New York City in 1779, and conceding the eventual erasure of British government over its rebellious colonies, returned to Halifax in 1780, reluctantly "abandon[ing] his prospects and property." Other members of Howe's immediate family emigrated to Halifax, helping to form the core of the Sandemanian exile community there. He also resumed his printing enterprises yet again, founding *The Halifax Journal* in December 1780, which became the voice of the American Loyalist communities in Nova Scotia. Howe's experience is unique in that apparently there is no record of his ever suffering from any Patriot abuses, due most likely to his close attachment to the British army, but, like other Boston Sandemanians, he took little or no care to conceal his political opinions.[41]

Military conscription flushed out still more Sandemanians. A petition signed by nineteen members of Danbury's Sandemanian community in March 1778 requested exemption from the draft because "they have at all times behaved peaceably among their Neighbours & Countrymen, and most of them have payed fines without murmuring for not going into the war which they look upon as unjust." They insisted that their hope was simply to be left to enjoy the "liberty of Conscience" they had previously enjoyed, and "which is enjoyed in all protestant Countries." One of the signatories, Comfort Benedict, fled to Long Island when he received a draft notice the previous year, but was arrested upon his return and confined for three years. His petitions for release echo the objections of the Danbury declaration to military service and to rebellion against the king, citing the Continental Congress's exemption of conscientious objectors. Nonetheless, he remained in custody until transferred to Hartford, where he worked off the remainder of his sentence before his eventual release by the Connecticut General Assembly. However, while the sheriff allowed him to trade confinement for a work detail, "the people with whom he ... labored ... tho't generally that twas [wrong for] ... such a Malefactor to be allowed his Victuals for his Labor." Just what made him so detestable to his coworkers—loyalism, Sandemanianism, or both—is unclear. Nevertheless, Benedict's Christian piety and obvious harmlessness to the Patriot cause eventually won him his freedom.[42]

Colburn Barrell, who had been so vocal in his opposition to resistance to British colonial policy, vanished from public view in 1771, living apparently undisturbed until the outbreak of the war, when circumstances forced him to flee Boston. His property damaged and his family threatened, he determined to remove to Philadelphia, where there existed a substantial Loyalist community and a place where he might revive his business. According to the text of his petition for compensation from the Loyalist Claims Commission:

> to avoid the fury of the Sons of violence, he was constrained to send his wife, tho' in an ill state of health, from Boston to Philadelphia with a Servant, not daring himself to travel openly, and when he did leave Boston it was at Midnight, and he went thro' the Country in the most private manner, in constant terror lest he should be discovered and insulted.

Matters failed to improve in Philadelphia, however, so Barrell decided to move his family to Charleston, South Carolina, "where thro' the industry of the same Sons of violence, pointing him out as an addresser of Gov. Hutchinson and Gov. Gage, he was repeatedly on the point of being publickly insulted." He finally fled to England where he lived in poverty until he managed to regain enough of his fortune to return to America at the end of the war. To his grief, he learned that all of his property in Boston had been confiscated and auctioned off, as well as some land in Connecticut, a small portion of the latter of which he successfully regained through litigation and then sold. He traveled to New York to petition for land in Nova Scotia from Sir Guy Carleton, who refused the request. He promptly left America for England, never to return. Interestingly, Barrell was one of fifty-five other Boston petitioners who argued that their previous high social status accorded them special consideration in terms of royal compensation, and that they should receive land in Nova Scotia proportional to their rank, free of quitrents or any other stipulations. None of the fifty-five had their petitions granted.[43] This highlights yet another aspect of the New England Sandemanians' behavior that was out of character for avowed Pietist Christians—the maintenance of a class consciousness. John Glas and Robert Sandeman had made themselves clear that social distinctions did not exist within the church—indeed this was why many were attracted to the sect in the first place—and without either Glas or Sandeman to ground them, it would become increasingly difficult to maintain discipline and doctrine.

The contrasts in reaction to persecution and adversity exhibited by the Barrell brothers, Hopestill Capen, John Sparhawk, and Comfort Benedict are striking. The Barrells—especially Colburn—started out in the late 1760s as fiery zealots, insisting on their religious principles as they informed their political stance in favor of loyalism, despite Sandeman's intermittent pleas for restraint and meekness. Capen, Sparhawk, and Benedict much more closely conformed to the Sandemanian ideal of the unobtrusive Christian enduring constraint, mistreatment, and coercion without complaint. Petitions notwithstanding, their overall attitude is one of quiet determination to be left alone and unmolested for their principles, seeking redress for wrongs committed against them by the revolutionary authorities and the mobs that enjoyed official sanction. The privations and abuses inflicted upon the Sandemanians during the Revolutionary War were a physical extension of the criticism and hostility directed at them in the prewar period, which had an extensive history in New England with regard to those sects and movements determined to be heterodox.

The Sandemanians of Boston stood out due to their deviation from the doctrine of pacifism and avoidance of political office. For the most part, the Sandemanians tried to be a quiet part of their various New England communities, but the internal rifts that Samuel Langdon identified contributed directly to the public behavior of members of the Boston congregation, as opposed to those in New Hampshire and Connecticut. The latter generally did not garner attention until some event forced them to reveal themselves. Despite Robert Sandeman's fervent admonitions, the Boston Sandemanians did not at first set themselves apart from other Tories who adhered to Britain for various political or social reasons, and this is a key to understanding the harassment and persecutions they experienced, which were as severe as any endured by adherents of other Pietist sects. Nevertheless, for all their rhetoric of pious loyalism the Sandemanians never took up arms to defend their civil rights, or even to restore order in their hometowns, despite formulaic pledges to do so. They neither served as soldiers in Loyalist regiments nor attempted to undermine the Revolution. In their determination not to offend their Patriot neighbors, the Connecticut and

New Hampshire Sandemanians distinguished themselves from those of Boston, who participated—enthusiastically, in Colburn Barrell's case—in the activities of the Loyalist community there. The combativeness of the Boston Sandemanians rained scorn and suspicion hard upon all of the Sandemanian churches, which barely survived the revolutionary storm.

෴

The responsibility for the Sandemanians' inability to cope with the crisis in American society before and during the Revolutionary War rests on the fundamental doctrines of the sect. The Reformation dilemma of how to maintain religious authority within the priesthood of all believers informed John Glas's basically eliminating the office of minister in favor of elders, but offered no other effective means of enforcing doctrinal discipline. Each church was left essentially alone to face rapidly changing situations, and Robert Sandeman's failure to temper Colburn Barrell's activities is indicative of how fatal a flaw that constituted for a sect newly arrived on America's troubled shores. The pacifism of the Sandemanians may be admirable, but their loyalty to George III, though motivated by genuine Christian faith, ultimately splintered the sect beyond any hope of full recovery, due to the politically charged environment in which they existed. Their behavior generated suspicious questions, and their public professions, ranging from silence to declared loyalism, left them vulnerable to criticism and attack from the Whigs. The death of Sandeman in 1771 robbed them of an anchoring force that may have made a difference as the Revolution exploded four years later, but, in the end, a reverse of Samuel Langdon's prophecy came true. Assailed from within and without, a dogmatic minority brought suspicion and persecution to all Sandemanians. They had merely wanted to be left alone to live their lives, practice their trades, and worship God in their own way without interference. However, a combination of circumstances, some beyond their control, prevented that, and for their well-intentioned attempts to avoid the American Revolution, many Sandemanians suffered the loss of their homes and livelihoods, and the near-destruction of the sect. Rather than driven closer together by adversity, they fell almost completely apart.

∞ 6 ∞

"Mine Eyes Must Flow with Rivers of Tears"

Concluding Assessment of Eighteenth-Century Sandemanianism

> The mystic body of Christ—that catholic and heavenly assembly, the true Israel—is most frequently called the church in the New Testament. This is that "general assembly and church of the first-born," written in heaven; Christ's church, built upon him the rock, so that the gates of hell cannot prevail against it.
>
> —John Glas, *A Commentary on a part of Acts XV.1–11*

> A Glassite church is a machine; all the wheels, and pins, and movements of which are as nicely adjusted as the posts and pegs of the tabernacle; and considered to be as clearly specified in scripture as the atonement.... This system ... preserves something of the external form of primitive christianity. But it is such a resemblance as a skeleton bears to a human being. It wants the flesh, the loveliness, and the animating principle.
>
> —[William Orme], *Historical Sketch of the Rise, Progress ... of Independency in Scotland*

The term "sect" has occasionally been utilized here to describe the Glasite-Sandemanian movement, but, in view of the term's definition it is somewhat inaccurate.[1] A sect is a religious phenomenon whereby disciples follow a spiritual leader, and while one can refer to John Glas and Robert Sandeman as spiritual leaders on the basis of much of their behavior, in other aspects they patently refused to act in the role of religious authorities. This is directly attributable to the fundamental doctrines of the movement, with its grave distrust of authority born of Glas's unpleasant experience with the Church of Scotland. In his zeal to resurrect New Testament Christianity, Glas blinded himself to inherent contradictions that endangered the cohesiveness of his churches, seeming at some points to be a sectarian leader while rejecting the role at others.

Sandeman took this allergy to the exercise of authority one step further with the churches in America, leaving them somewhat isolated and vulnerable to internal stressors. His death in 1771 compounded the problem, as elders in the various American churches, still neophytes to primitive Christianity, found themselves unable to cope with the oncoming Revolution that decimated the fledgling congregations.

At the height of the Glasite-Sandemanian movement in the 1760s, with two exceptions individual churches never exceeded forty members or the aggregate membership boast more than a thousand people.[2] Yet for all their seeming insignificance, the breadth and depth of their impact on the eighteenth-century theological landscape were entirely out of all proportion to their size. During the greater part of the 1700s, and for a time in the early nineteenth century, the works of John Glas and Robert Sandeman, as well as others such as Samuel Pike, were widely disseminated and read. Among those who identified themselves with the movement were people of education and social standing, including ministers of the Presbyterian, Congregationalist, Baptist, and Methodist denominations. Many who never joined the membership, or only did so briefly, imbibed Glasite tenets that they introduced into their own religious groups. During its history, the movement has had associated with it, either directly or indirectly, many distinguished people in the realms of literature and science.[3] By way of conclusion, stock must be taken of the movement, and the reasons for its ultimate decline more closely examined.

The movement arose in Scotland during the turbulent period following the arduous struggle of Presbyterianism to secure its position as the national faith. The Revolution Settlement, however, did not usher in an era of peace and unity. The history of Christianity in Scotland in the eighteenth century is one of theological controversy and ecclesiastical division. Presbyterianism had once presented a solid front to both episcopacy and independency, but this century saw several secessions that resulted in the rise of new denominations, both Presbyterian and Independent. The Revolution Settlement led not only to the exclusion of those Episcopalians who refused to conform, but also to the isolation of the Cameronians, or extreme Presbyterians, who remained outside the Church that they regarded as "uncovenanted," for in the new compact between church and state the old Covenants had been ignored. But there were also within the National Church many who held the binding obligation of the Covenants and hoped for their renewal. Opposed to these Evangelicals were the Moderates who cared little for the Covenants and disliked a narrow, dogmatic, and enthusiastic form of Christianity, and they became the dominant force in the Church of Scotland for nearly a hundred years.

John Glas had something in common with both Evangelicals and Moderates. He denied with the latter the binding character of the Covenants, but with the former he emphasized the importance of spiritual Christianity as distinguished from conventional morality, but he could not bring himself to ally with either party. He objected to the Establishment principle so stoutly maintained by the Moderates, some of whom were distinctly Erastian;[4] he also disliked their indifference to theology and their cold respectability. On the other hand, he strongly disapproved of the importance attached by the Evangelicals to the Westminster Confession of Faith, which to him was merely a human document unwarranted by the New Testament. Consequently, Glas stood outside the two principal parties in the National Church. His attitude and principles incurred the scorn of the two sides, though it was from the Evangelicals rather than from the Moderates that the chief opposition came, though it must be said that most of his criticism was of the Evangelicals. He had defenders in both camps, though, but they were unable to prevent his deposition from the ministry of the Church in 1728. Though expelled from his pulpit, it can be argued that Glas led the first secession from the Church of Scotland. Unlike later leaders of secession movements such as Ebenezer Erskine (1680–1754) and Thomas Gillespie (1708–74), Glas's movement, like that of Robert Haldane (1764–1842) and his brother James Alexander Haldane (1768–1851) at the end of the century, was developed along strictly Independent lines.

Glas's break from Presbyterianism was final, but then his conception of the nature and constitution of the Christian Church was undeniably Independent, and perhaps always had been. However, though rarely acknowledged, the Glasite movement was not without repercussions on Scottish Presbyterianism during the period extending from the Secession to the Disruption. The increasing emphasis by the Secession and Relief Fathers on the essentially spiritual nature of Christ's kingdom reflects the position definitively espoused by John Glas. As early as 1726, before Glas's separation from the Church of Scotland, Ebenezer Erskine, at that time a minister of the National Church, wrote to Glas approving of his "exaltation of the Mighty God and the Prince of Peace, on whose shoulders the government of his Church is laid, and the levelling of everything that would usurp his Throne or jostle him out of his room, as the alone foundation God hath laid in Zion." Erskine went on to say that he also had thought that the Civil Constitution was too much blended with the affairs of Christ's Kingdom which is not of this world, in these public engagements; as also that the way of forcing people to subscribe was not the way to make proselytes to Christ, the weapons of whose Kingdom are not carnal but spiritual,—suited to the soul and spirit, where his Kingdom is principally established.

At a later point, strong antipathy developed between Glas's followers and those of Erskine's, so that the latter were loath to acknowledge any indebtedness to Glas, but the debt was nonetheless real.[5]

It is true that the Secession Fathers differed from Glas on the questions of the Covenants and the polity of the church, yet they were at one with him in his antagonism to the invasion of Christ's prerogative by the secular power. Evangelical in their outlook, they viewed with deep concern the Erastian and latitudinarian tendencies of the Moderate party that was gradually acquiring the ascendancy in the church. It only required the passing of the act on the election of ministers by the Assembly of 1732 to bring matters to a head. Erskine and others regarded this act as a violation of the inherent rights of the church, as well as an encroachment on the privileges of the Christian people in their choice of pastors. Ebenezer Erskine's words to his parishioners at this time might have been uttered by Glas himself, so identical are they to his sentiments:

> Is it so that the government is laid upon His shoulders? Then see the nullity of all acts, laws and constitutions, that do not bear the stamp of Christ, and that are not consistent with the laws and orders He has left for the government of His Church. They cannot miss to be null, because Zion's King never touched them with His scepter, and there is no church authority but what is derived from Him.

These words are almost a paraphrase of those already quoted from Erskine's letter to Glas of six years before. At the outset, the Seceders had no intention of abandoning the Establishment principle, but in course of time the logic of fact and event forced them in the direction of voluntarism, similar to that which originated with Glas.[6]

The Relief Church also owed something to the pioneering work of John Glas. It cannot be argued that their principles came directly from him, but before Thomas Gillespie entered the Church of Scotland he held views similar in some respects to those of Glas. Trained and ordained by the English Independents, his thought was naturally influenced by their conceptions of the spirituality and independence of the Church. He would only sign the Confession of Faith with reservations concerning the article on the power of the civil magistrate in the sphere of religion. Later, when ecclesiastical requirements conflicted with his principles, he refused to compromise on this vital issue and, as a result, he was deposed by the assembly. Several years later brought the constitution of the first Relief Presbytery in 1761, and after that a number of congregations came together. The constitutional basis of the new body was much broader than that of the Seceders, and shared points in common with Glasite church constitution, taking, according to historian Gavin Struthers, "the outlines of his [Glas's] system, but not his crochets." The opponents of the Relief Church charged them with plagiarizing Glas, specifically Patrick Hutcheson's *Messiah's Kingdom*, which follows Glas's *Testimony of the King of Martyrs* very closely. The Relief Church's strong stance on the relationship between church and state, the National Covenants, and the Voluntary Principle originated with John Glas, whose influence on the Relief Church's early apologists is clear.[7]

Glas's greatest influence, however, is not to be sought in the later evolution of Scottish Presbyterianism, but in the number of religious denominations that took their rise either toward the end of his lifetime or during the half-century that followed. While the Secession and Relief churches followed Glas in his views of the nature of Christ's kingdom, they maintained their allegiance to the recognized Presbyterian doctrine and polity. The other bodies that came under Glasite influence were mainly Independents in church order. Passing by such truly minuscule groups like the Bereans and the Johnsonians,[8] there were six denominations that were distinctly affected by Glasite theological, ecclesiological, and practical ideas: the Scotch Baptists, the Old Scots Independents, the Inghamites, the Haldanites, the Walkerites, and the Disciples of Christ, or Campbellites. Though none of these groups accepted Glasite teachings wholesale, they nevertheless reproduced or imitated, to varying degrees, certain aspects of the Glasite system. The most influential of these is doubtless the Disciples of Christ, which emerged from the theology of Thomas Campbell (1763–1854) and his son, Alexander (1788–1866), originally of County Antrim, Ireland. Alexander had spent a year attending the University of Edinburgh, where he absorbed the similar theologies of Glas and Sandeman, as well as Robert and James Haldane, becoming convinced that "gospel Christianity" had to be restored. The Campbells formally repudiated the Presbyterian Church shortly after their emigration to Pennsylvania in the early 1800s, and began forming an ecumenical, "Restorationist" primitive Christian movement around 1820. Both Campbells had had contact with Sandemanians, and had read some of Glas's works, as well as gaining further familiarity with Sandemanianism through its influences on the Haldanes, with whom they were on friendly terms. Greater still were the connections between Sandemanian theology and that espoused by the Campbells' close associate Walter Scott (1796–1861) who, while living in Scotland, thoroughly absorbed Sandemanian and Haldanite thought. So similar did Campbellite and Sandemanian theology seem that a critic remarked in a letter to the Campbellite publication *The Christian Baptist* that "you [Campbellites] are substantially ... Sandemanian or Haldanian.... [I]n substance you occupy their ground."[9]

It has been sufficiently demonstrated that the Glasite-Sandemanian movement has had greater effects than is generally acknowledged. Whatever may be thought of the movement as a whole, it possessed features that appealed to the minds and hearts of many deeply religious and thoughtful people. Though the eighteenth century cannot be described as an age of constructive theological thought, it was not lacking in intellectual activity and speculative interests in the truths of divine revelation. It was a time of intellectual enlightenment and spiritual awakening, and while in some respects John Glas was a pioneer, he was also a man of his age—one who never fully escaped from the restricting influences of the traditional theology that he himself criticized so severely. While most of his ideas were derived directly and indirectly from previous thinkers, Glas had a genius for synthetic thought that he shared with his greatest disciple, Robert Sandeman, whose abilities were such that the movement gradually lost its founder's name and took on that of the brilliant proselyte. Whereas Glas did cull his ideas from a myriad of previous and contemporary works, he was never a slavish copyist. His starting point was the Scriptures, specifically the New Testament, and he traveled alongside or followed others only as far as he believed they followed the gospels, and he often carried the implications of their principles beyond the point at which they stopped.

Glas was more adept at criticism than at construction, quick to perceive and expose inconsistencies in popular theology that concealed fundamental Christian truths behind veils of scholastic interpretation, shallow mysticism, and evanescent emotionalism. He strove to correct the errors of ancient and contemporary theology, and to emphasize the historic foundations of the Christian faith, which for him was a transcendental and objective truth as manifested in the historical Jesus Christ. He suspected all claims to religious experience that rested on a purely subjective basis, which signified to him how Christianity had lost its way and needed to be brought back into conformity with the simple and definite faith of the Apostles. Consequently, he retreated to the New Testament, and it was his call for Christians to do so that caught the attention of his contemporaries. There was that in his presentation of the gospel that impressed the minds of religious people to whom the popular preaching seemed inadequate, and who desired the positive note in the exposition of Christian truth. Andrew Fuller, a critic of the Glasite system, admitted that "The principles taught by Messrs. Glass and Sandeman ... did certainly give a new turn and character to almost everything pertaining to the religion of Christ, as must appear to any one who reads and understands their publications."[10]

As important as John Glas was in founding and leading the movement that originally bore his name, doubly so was his son-in-law, Robert Sandeman, in broadcasting Glasite principles to England, Wales, and North America. Though not nearly as prolific a writer as Glas, Sandeman had a talent for honing his mentor's theological principles down to essential concepts. The *Letters on Theron and Aspasio* generated far greater discussion and controversy than anything Glas had published, with the possible exception of *The Testimony of the King of Martyrs*, particularly as it affected the nascent Methodist movement. The very public debate that erupted between Sandeman and John Wesley did more than anything else to advertise Glasite theology and church organization, and caused Wesley to refine Methodism in such a way as to further differentiate it from a merely evangelical Anglicanism. People who might never had otherwise had occasion to hear of the *Letters on Theron and Aspasio* were exposed to it due to Sandeman's rhetorical scuffle with the Methodists, with Independents particularly drawn to this new form of primitive Christianity. This led to the establishment of several churches in England, and a few in Wales, before Sandeman traveled to New England and met some success in Massachusetts, New Hampshire, and especially Connecticut. By that point Sandeman had come to be so identified with the Glasite movement that Englishmen began calling it "Sandemanian," which replaced the appellation "Glasite" by the latter half of the eighteenth century.[11]

Those who were attracted to the movement were most attracted to its antiauthoritarian characteristics and relative lack of hierarchy, and this constitutes the primary reason for the movement's early success. Scottish Presbyterians who chaffed against ministers, presbyteries, synods, and the General Assembly with its endless committees, found among the Glasites a refreshing simplicity. The same can be said of the English Independents Sandeman converted, who bristled at the overbearing manner of their ministers. The spread of enthusiastic, evangelical Christianity during the Great Awakening and Glas's and Sandeman's acerbic criticism of it drew like-minded clerics and laymen into the movement from both Britain and New England. Connecticut offers an ideal example of the magnetic appeal of Sandemanianism to New England Congregationalists who had grown fed up with the rigidity of that region's social structure, reinforced as it was by religious orthodoxy and political organization. Regardless of which part of the Atlantic World they lived in, Glasites and Sandemanians refused to accept the worldliness that had accrued to Protestant Christianity, particularly in its overtly politicized nature, and the Sandemanian emphasis on the separation of church and state became just as attractive as its highly streamlined structure of church authority.

Conversely, for all the appeal and interest it generated, the Glasite-Sandemanian movement attracted intense controversy and opposition from the established churches. Evangelicals in Britain and America had every reason to deride a theology that smacked of the very conservatism and intellectualism they were so busy repudiating, and establishment leaders likewise excoriated a movement that aimed at tearing them down. In the cases of John Glas and Robert Sandeman, the aggressive manner in which they went about propagating their theology clearly made them more enemies than friends, the former of whom were as disconcerted by the leaders' zealotry as by opposition to their theological and ecclesiological principles. Indeed, both seemed to revel in rhetorical combat and the occasionally harsher treatment meted out to them, though that was generally confined to the presses. However, one can imagine that Glas felt a sort of confirmation in 1733 when in Perth he suffered physical abuse from angry citizens who spattered ordure upon him and his companions as they walked to the newly established Glasite church there. Both he and Sandeman constantly compared themselves and their disciples to the apostles in the numerous letters they left behind, and evidently found in resistance and antagonism the verification that they were blazing the right trail.

Robert Sandeman, however, who had been so forward in his attacks on James Hervey and John Wesley, when he went to New England somehow lost his combative edge. This was more than compensated for by the abrasiveness of Nathaniel and Colburn Barrell in facing their theological and political enemies, with Sandeman putting himself in the unusual position of imploring them to restraint, even as he admitted to his preference for "spirited conduct." The American Sandemanians suffered the misfortune of being a pacifist, apolitical sect in a place and time where passivity and nonparticipation in politics were most unwelcome. Men like Ebenezer White and his son Ebenezer Russell White joined the Sandemanian church on account of their frustration with the constitution of the Congregational Church, and along with the Barrells found themselves put on the defensive for their heterodoxy, to which they responded with all the angry zeal of the newly converted. The outbreak of the Revolutionary War compounded their troubles, and the combativeness of the Barrells is contrasted with the humility and composure of Hopestill Capen and John Sparhawk.

The experience of the Sandemanians in revolutionary America was not unique, but part of a well-established pattern in New England of harassing the heterodox. The systematic abuse of Quakers, Baptists, and various sectarian groups was deemed socially acceptable, and found sanction in the law. Cursed as heretics and deviants, minority sectarians and schismatics existed at the margins of their societies, and the religious and civil authorities made sure they stayed there. When political agitation against British authority erupted in the 1760s and 1770s, those who dared to support British policy or remind Americans of their allegiance to George III and obedience to Parliament found themselves pushed out to the margins, as well. There they became fair game for the Sons of Liberty and the revolutionary committees formed to galvanize colonial opposition to British rule and compel unanimous support for the Revolution. The tactics utilized in persecuting Quakers and Baptists in the seventeenth and eighteenth centuries in New England differed very little from those used to intimidate Loyalists and Neutrals throughout the rebelling colonies during the Revolution.

In this sense, and in many other ways, religion played a pervasive role in the American Revolution. The debate over the extent of that relationship has been and continues to be a lively one, but some scholars' assertions to the absence of any relationship cannot be supported by the preponderance of evidence to the contrary. This is not to deny that in some respects religion was subordinated to politics in the latter half of the eighteenth century, or that political leaders cannily utilized religious language to garner support for radical Whig ideology. However, it was in religion that colonial Americans found a language to enrich political dialogue—one that could be understood by the masses who did not attend college or were familiar with the career of John Wilkes or the writings of Trenchard and Gordon. Indeed, as Patricia U. Bonomi conclusively stated, "the state of mind in which American colonials moved toward separation [from Britain] is nowhere better seen than in the realm of religion." It was in Protestant idioms that eighteenth-century Americans, as much as their forebears, understood the world, and that some artisans and merchants, farmers and mechanics, laborers and slaves, and others believed the War for Independence to be—as J. C. D. Clark called it—"the last great war of religion" should not be surprising, though many historians of revolutionary America reject such an interpretation.[12]

It has been said here that the American Revolution nearly destroyed the Sandemanians, and to a certain extent this is undeniably true. But hostility of those like of Ezra Stiles and Samuel Langdon did not play a greater role than the fact that the Sandemanian churches had no opportunity to consolidate themselves doctrinally before their religious principles were put to the test by outside events. Add to that a system of church government that mingled exclusionism, dogmatism, and intolerance, and the outcome could not have been other than it was. Langdon commented on the prevalence of internal quarrels and dissensions in the Sandemanian churches, and predicted their eventual demise unless "they are ... drove firm together by some kind of persecution." Ironically, persecution only worsened their instability, and before his death Sandeman refused to play the role of sectarian leader sufficiently to hold the churches "firm together." After 1771, the rudderless churches were left to flail around devoid of a strong connection to their theological root, and the relative absence of communication from Britain is significant on this score. John Glas's death in 1773 further robbed the American Sandemanians of a doctrinal and disciplinary arbiter as they faced the Revolution. However, Glas was as reluctant as Sandeman to put on the mantle of sectarian leader, so it is pointless to speculate on his potential influence had he lived through the 1770s. In the end, as the final section explains, Sandemanianism was far too rigid and unyielding a form of Christianity to attract or maintain adherents, and the wonder is that it managed to survive as long as it did.

Why, then, with such apparently able leaders and devoted disciples, did the movement decline and eventually vanish from New England? The answer lies not in the external attacks on it, but on internal factors. From its beginning, the Glasite movement was subjected to all the dangers that beset what has been described as particularism, by which is meant the tendency of new religious movements to make the emphasis of particular aspects of truth or details of practice the supreme consideration in their life and work. Such movements generally originate in the conviction that important matters of faith and order have been neglected, and their avowed purpose is to restore what is lacking in contemporary religious observance. They concentrate on minutiae that have been ignored, and in so doing tend to generate new minutiae that receive too great an emphasis in the effort to effect a restoration of "pure" religion. Rather than identifying themselves as orthodox, such movements become defined by these minutiae, which get the lion's share of attention from supporters and detractors alike. The Glasite-Sandemanian movement was decidedly particularist, having claimed a rediscovery of the truth and the restoration of neglected but essential practices. It stood over against other religious denominations as *the* one body that offered a pure and complete reproduction of primitive Christianity. Particularists tend to become narrow and dogmatic, hypercritical and intolerant, exclusive and self-righteous, and glory in adversity and isolation, which were traits of the Glasites and Sandemanians, and this offers a key to understanding their ultimate failure.

The Glasite-Sandemanian doctrine of faith, intended to exalt the truth of sovereign grace, led to an overemphasis of faith as "simple belief" of the testimony of the gospels. Glas and Sandeman made faith primarily the intellectual apprehension of objective revelation. In so doing they failed to see that faith has affective and volitional aspects as well as cognitive—that faith is the response of the whole person as a thinking, emotive, and willing personality. In the Glasite theology, no distinction is drawn between faith and belief, which were regarded as identical terms that may be used interchangeably. Moreover, there is little or no appreciation of the different shades of meaning attached to the word "faith" by the various New Testament writers. "Faith" on the lips of Jesus, or in the utterances and letters of the apostles, is regarded as meaning "simple belief." But the conception of faith is not as simple as Glas and Sandeman had made it appear. The terms "faith" and "belief" do not always have the same connotation. In the Synoptic Gospels, "faith" and "belief" indicate a receptive state of mind toward Christ and his message, devoid of any prerequisites or active effort. Faith is the natural response of the human spirit when brought into contact with divine truth, while belief is an act of surrender to Jesus Christ. It may be readily admitted that "faith," in the common sense of the term, is "belief" or intellectual assent to something presented to the mind, but "saving faith" in the New Testament means something else. Belief in and of itself possesses no moral power. That which is accepted as true by the mind must also receive the approbation of the will and the loving trust of the heart, and not just belief in a series of propositions or a system of theology. Glas was obliged to affirm that mere belief, such as the faith of devils, possesses no saving quality—that belief of the truth is "of a different nature from their belief," as is shown by its fruits, though he would not allow that "there must be more in faith, than the belief of the truth of the gospel." This doctrine of faith, expounded and amplified by Sandeman, won the adherence of numerous disciples, but it made no general appeal as did his teaching on the spiritual nature of Christ's kingdom.

The Glasites and Sandemanians stood for an excessive literalism in the interpretation of the New Testament which led them to exalt the letter above the spirit and to introduce a new form of legalism. The New Testament became a new code of laws and regulations, departure from which was looked upon as a setting aside of the divine commandments. No practice was held to be permissible unless it rested on some explicit injunction of Christ or the apostles, or some precedent exemplified in the primitive churches. Doctrine and conduct, organization and order were permanently fixed. No room was left for development or modification in view of changing times or conditions. Nothing might be added to or taken from what was written in the inspired word of God. Therefore, the Glasites sought to reproduce in exact detail the church order and customs of the New Testament churches, conformity to scriptural precedent meaning uniformity in practice. So tenaciously did the Glasites and Sandemanians observe this rule that, during the whole course of their history, they scarcely deviated from the standpoint and customs that characterized them at their first formation.

In his extensive criticism of the Sandemanians, Andrew Fuller showed how punctilious adherence to the letter of scripture might lead to neglect of the weightier matters that Christ enjoined.[13] The Glasites were so anxious to reproduce the apostolic practices and methods that they forgot the apostolic warning "the letter killeth, but the spirit giveth life." However praiseworthy a course of action might appear to others, if it were not definitely enjoined or exemplified in the New Testament, the Glasites and Sandemanians felt themselves under no obligation to follow it. On the other hand, they restored practices that had a temporary or local significance—such as foot-washing, the kiss of charity, and love-feasts—representing them as permanently obligatory of all Christians of every age and place, solely because Christ or his apostles had observed them. By their rigid conformity to express precept and precedent the Glasites and Sandemanians fell into the error of Judaic legalism that Jesus had condemned. Jesus and his apostles laid down no hard and fast rules intended to regulate every detail of personal conduct or church order, but rather they enunciated great spiritual principles that were to find expression according to peculiar conditions and needs. To reduce Christian life and fellowship to a system is to produce a mechanical uniformity that destroys the soul of religion.

Glasite and Sandemanian discipline was so strict and severe that many revolted against it and were either excommunicated or else voluntarily withdrew themselves from the fellowship. Small as the churches were, they suffered constant depletion in their numbers. Some members were "put away" on moral grounds—as can happen in any church—but in many instances excommunications took place on account of differences of opinion respecting some point of doctrine or practice. Remarkably, a considerable number of the leading elders themselves suffered either temporary or permanent excommunication, so intolerant were they of diversity of sentiment within the fellowship. If any members were foolish or bold enough to express views contrary to those commonly acknowledged as the beliefs and practices of the churches, they were obliged either to recant or sever their connection. In all decisions unanimity was essential, but if this could not be secured by persuasion, recourse was had to the expulsion of the dissidents. Like most particularist denominations, the Glasites and Sandemanians were characterized by controversy and division. They prided themselves on the strictness of their discipline, but their severity deterred more liberal-minded people from joining such a rigid and stern fellowship, and drove out those whose support and influence might have aided the movement as a religious force. Liberty of thought and action had no place in these churches, and as new societies arose with broader platforms they absorbed many who held some of the Glasite principles but could not conform to its rigid *orthopraxy*.

John Glas looked to the New Testament as his primary, and indeed only, guide to true Christianity and frequently compared himself, Sandeman, and other Glasite missionaries to the apostles, particularly in instances where they suffered abuse or persecution. Much as Paul had to contend with churches that threatened to wander away from orthodoxy as he defined it, so Glas found a similar dynamic afflicting the fledgling Sandemanian churches, mainly those established in England. Particularly vexing was the Calvinist doctrine of predestination, to which Glas strongly adhered. A large number of the members of James Allen's church, for instance, found themselves generally unwilling to accept it, and Glas counseled Allen not to be distracted by or drawn into "foolish questions and disputes raised by this fiery dart of Satan driven toward free will in opposition to the scripture doctrine of grace." Better that the Glasite churches remain small and composed of true believers than prone to controversy: "I know not but that it may be said of you as to Gideon,—the people are yet too many; the Lord may work by fewer." Nonetheless, despite the strenuous efforts of Sandeman's successors in Britain in the mid-1760s, discipline issues, excommunications, and doctrinal disputes kept the Sandemanian churches small and often locked in some sort of contention. Glas's relations with James Allen suffered because of the latter's inability to solve these recurrent problems. Much the same tribulations plagued the American churches, which did not communicate with either Glas or other British brethren, and upon the death of Sandeman in 1771 any connection that might have existed was effectively severed.[14]

For all of John Glas's and Robert Sandeman's efforts to extend the movement inside and outside of Great Britain, the insular and exclusionary nature of the movement as it solidified in the 1750s produced self-contained and isolated churches that did little to attract potential converts. Regarding all other bodies as corrupt, the Glasites and Sandemanians refused to hold any fellowship with them or to cooperate in the promotion of work conducted by Bible or missionary societies. Association with other Christians brought immediate excommunication. The churches were exclusive coteries of believers intent on the enjoyment of common fellowship and the exercise of the religious life, but their liberality did not extend beyond their own communion. They showed no interest in reaching out to unchurched sinners or non-Christians. Sandeman traveled to England and America, and John Barnard to Wales, but only on invitation and never of their own volition. When invited to explain their principles they were prepared to respond—usually by letter—but "We are utterly against aiming to promote the cause we contend for, either by creeping into private houses, or by causing our voice to be heard in the streets or in the fields, or by officiously obtruding our opinions upon others in conversation." If inquirers wished to know more of the order and fellowship of the churches they were welcome to attend the open meetings, but no effort was made to induce anyone to join. This left the Glasites and Sandemanians wide open to the charge that they exhibited a callous disregard for the salvation of sinners. Andrew Fuller leapt on this feature when he wrote that to "worldly men indeed, who make no pretence to religion, the system seems to bear a friendly aspect: but it discovers no concern for *their* salvation. It would seem to have no tears to shed over a perishing world: and even looks with a jealous eye on those that have, glorying in the paucity of its numbers!" But this apparent unconcern arose from the belief that God knows his own elect, and that the sinner can do nothing but wait until God reveals Christ to him. Consequently, the Glasites and Sandemanians were in no serious way perturbed by their small and diminishing numbers.[15]

Had John Glas been content to place the supreme emphasis upon the great spiritual principles with which he commenced his career, he might have become one of the truly outstanding theologians of the eighteenth century, a religious leader on the scale of John Wesley, and the founder of a powerful and growing denomination. But he was ensnared by the pitfalls that beset religious particularism, repelling many who otherwise would have followed him in a great spiritual adventure of faith and service. Glas had been too focused on severing all connections to Presbyterianism, and then again to the English Independents he likewise abhorred, to cultivate his movement properly. Had he been less dogmatic, one wonders what impact he might have had on Independency in both England and Scotland, not to mention Scottish Presbyterianism.

Glas's particularism lost him an opportunity of becoming a great leader. However, his life and work had not been in vain. He recalled attention to the fundamental principles of New Testament Christianity. The Independency for which he contended has continued in the spin-off groups and Glasite-influenced denominations of Britain and America, while his emphasis on the spiritual nature of Christ's kingdom and the primacy of the New Testament as the criterion of faith and order are widely held Christian precepts.

One is struck by the opportunities on which John Glas and Robert Sandeman failed to capitalize. Glas established a primitive Christian church founded on the strictest adherence to the New Testament and infused with his reflexive suspicion of ecclesiastical authority, which resulted in churches riven by contention and lapses in discipline that were harshly punished. Both he and Sandeman generally refused to interfere in doctrinal disputes apart from gentle exhortations, and acted more forcefully only after it was already too late to heal the rifts that inevitably appeared. Devoid of properly asserted authority, it is a wonder that the Glasites and Sandemanians managed to maintain their congregations against the attacks leveled at them by their opponents, as well as survive the stresses that always threatened to tear them apart from within. But manage they did, though only barely, which should not eclipse the artful simplicity of Glasite-Sandemanianism, nor diminish John Glas's stature as an astute eighteenth-century theologian worthy of standing alongside the Wesleys, Jonathan Edwards, or Andrew Fuller.

The devastating impact of the American Revolution cannot be discounted, however, in assessing the Sandemanians in America. Given its basic simplicity, rationalism, and egalitarianism, on its surface Sandemanianism would seem to have generated enormous appeal from revolutionary New Englanders coming into an acute political awareness based on Lockean philosophy. That it failed to do so, and instead generated hostility and opposition from the inheritors of both Old Light and New Light beliefs—particularly those who had become Whigs—underscores the essential paradox of the American Revolution: of how one governs a democratic, libertarian society so wary of governing authority. The thirteen colonies that separated themselves from the British Empire by 1783 barely endured the experience of revolution and the War for Independence, and the United States of America teetered on the brink of dissolution during the "Critical Period" in which it struggled with its independence before 1790. In this sense, the ordeal of the Sandemanians in revolutionary America offers just one of many indicators of the difficulties that came to plague American society as it made the uneasy transition from a provincial to a national identity. However,

Sandemanian exclusionism and the determination of its adherents to a confused position on involvement in worldly political affairs—especially a professed loyalty to a monarch the Whigs decided was a tyrannical puppet of shadowy, caesaropapist forces—certainly did little to broaden their appeal.

The Sandemanian impact on the late eighteenth-century American religious landscape has been easily dismissed—the sect worthy in most historians' eyes of no notice at worst, and of an article or two at best. However, despite their seeming insignificance, one must respect that their effect on their environment was out of proportion to their size. The vast majority of them had fled the Revolution for the safety of Nova Scotia before 1780, where they managed to reestablish their communities and continue through the first half of the nineteenth century. Barrells, Winslows, Fosters, Benedicts, and other Sandemanian families of distinguished New England bloodlines attempted to recapture in Canada some measure of what they had reluctantly left behind in the United States. However, like so many Loyalist exiles scattered throughout the British Empire, the Canadian Sandemanians could not exchange their identity entirely, and the anguished lament of Edward Foster undoubtedly echoed in the memories of his coreligionists as they pondered what had befallen them.[16]

They do, however, beg comparison with a Christian sect that bears a superficial resemblance to the Sandemanians—the Society of Friends. The first Quakers in New England suffered far greater hostility and opposition under the Puritan establishment yet they grew steadily, a growth accelerated by the foundation of New Jersey and Pennsylvania under the auspices of William Penn. Political control and economic success in Pennsylvania radiated power to Quakers in New England as the eighteenth century opened and progressed, enabling them to challenge the establishment and increase their numbers. A reform movement that began at mid-century resulted in a Quakerism that was much more pietistic and spiritual, one that repudiated the worldliness accruing from materialism and political power. In Pennsylvania, the assembly gradually lost its Quaker membership, no doubt hastened by competition from Presbyterians who leveled the most strident attacks on the Friends in the legislature who refused to allocate funds to prosecute the French and Indian War. Some Quakers resisted this reform movement, insistent on retaining their governmental authority, which allowed propagandists to characterize all Quakers as demagogues starving for political power and willing to stoop as low as possible to maintain it.[17] As the imperial crisis erupted in the 1760s, the Quakers were again divided over opposition to British policy, particularly Philadelphia merchants who refused to join the Nonimportation Agreement. The Sons of Liberty harassed all Quakers they encountered, pushing many of them into sympathy with the Tories. Those who espoused Whig principles were censured by the Philadelphia Yearly Meeting and forced to withdraw from the Continental Association, and this further accelerated the Quaker withdrawal from provincial politics.[18]

The outbreak of the American Revolution forced Quakers to declare their political positions, which for a majority became loyalism, while most of the remainder opted for neutrality based on apolitical opinions. A small minority of Whig Quakers called themselves "Free Quakers," but their loyalty to the United States was always suspect in the eyes of the Patriots, and the Pennsylvania Assembly largely ignored and eventually discredited them. The Yearly and Quarterly Meetings likewise disowned active Whig Friends—the greatest number of disownments since the onset of the reform movement. Other Friends were regularly assailed in the streets and in the press for their pacifism, lack of patriotism, or outright loyalism, and they were inordinately distrained by the revolutionary authorities for their refusals to enlist in the Continental Army or pay for substitutes. Nothing brought worse mistreatment than the institution of oaths to the state and the Continental Congress implemented by the revolutionary committees, that brought additional distraints, while mobs routinely vandalized Quakers' houses for their refusal to observe fast or thanksgiving days during the war. Through all of this the Friends persevered, growing stronger and more confident in the rectitude of their path after the Revolution. Sectarianism, rather than weakening the Society of Friends as it had the Sandemanians, may have proved the latter's ultimate salvation, though it must be acknowledged that the Friends had more than a century of experience to guide them.

Another point of comparison can clearly be drawn with the Shakers, properly known as The United Society of Believers in Christ's Second Appearing, who arrived in New York as a small group of English Quaker sectarians under the leadership of "Mother" Ann Lee in 1774. Establishing a community at Niskayuna, northeast of Albany by 1776, they—like the Sandemanians—generated rampant gossip for their obvious shunning of worldliness and the rumored peculiarity of their liturgical practices. This strangeness, combined with their Englishness and pacifism, as well as their refusal to comment on or participate in the socio-political concussions of the day, served to render them deeply suspicious to the Patriot-dominated local governments around Albany, which investigated them closely. Amos Taylor, an itinerant printer who had briefly joined the Shaker community at Shirley, Massachusetts, in search of spiritual enlightenment, became disaffected and published an expose, *A Narrative of the Strange Principles, Conduct and Character of the People known by the Name of Shakers* (1782) that confirmed what most of their neighbors had already decided: that the Shakers were an alien, dangerous group to be eradicated. That Ann Lee, radically violating established gender norms and most Christian precepts, vaguely identified herself as Christ reincarnate and performed healing miracles sealed at least her fate, if not that of her sect. Partly for these reasons, including inciting riots—usually caused by nothing more than their mere presence—as well as their vigorous missionary efforts in Massachusetts, she and several of her more senior disciples were arrested as probable Loyalists. Languishing in jail, Lee experienced revelatory visions even as she suffered from a head wound inflicted by a member of a mob who had thrown a large rock at her. She endured almost two years' incarceration before Gov. George Clinton decided to release her in 1783 on a promise that the Shakers would do nothing to aid the British. Her injury and privations seem to have precipitated a rapid decline in her health, and she died in 1784 at the age of forty-eight. The Shakers' devout apoliticism and refusal to leave the United States mark the key to their longer term success, and of course highlights the Sandemanians' ultimate failure. Had those who opted to emigrate to Nova Scotia remembered and obeyed Sandeman's repeated exhortations to avoid politics, and thus remained behind, it is likely the Sandemanians would have fared at least as well as the Shakers did.[19]

There remains, however, the question of just how sectarianism could have preserved the Quakers and the Shakers, but apparently doomed the Sandemanians. Were the Sandemanians a sect, as they have been defined in this work, or were they—as they defined themselves—a church? Ernst Troeltsch made a distinction between the two, having interpreted them as separate expressions of the Christian tradition. According to Troeltsch, a sect, interpreting Jesus Christ's teachings in a literal and radical manner, is a small, voluntary fellowship of converts who seek to realize the divine law in their own behavior. It is a community apart from and in opposition to the world around it. It emphasizes the eschatological features of Christian doctrine, espouses the ideals of frugality and poverty, prohibits participation in legal or political affairs, and shuns any exercise of dominion over others. Religious equality of believers is stressed and a sharp distinction between clergy and laity is not drawn. It appeals principally to the lower classes. A church, meanwhile, stresses the redemptive and forgiving aspects of the Christian tradition, compromising the more radical teachings of Christ and accepting many features of the secular world as at least relatively good. It seeks to dominate all elements within society, to teach and guide them, and to dispense saving grace to them by means of sacraments administered by ecclesiastical officeholders. Although it contains organized expressions of the radical spirit of Christianity in its monastic system, it does not require its members to realize the divine law in their own behavior. It is conservative and allied to the upper and ruling classes.[20]

Troeltsch based his definitions of sect and church on his analysis of the history of European Christianity prior to 1800, and tended to interpret the two phenomena as static and mutually exclusive, which drew a fair amount of criticism. H. Richard Niebuhr offered the most cogent critique of Troeltsch's sect–church distinction, arguing that it was far too inflexible. In regard to the definition of sect, Niebuhr argued that it tends to be unstable and thus results in virtually every sectarian movement either shrinking into dissolution or growing into a church over time, but never remaining merely a sect in accord with Troeltsch's definition.[21] State-sponsored churches such as the Catholic and Anglican churches, and minority movements such as the Amish or the Hutterites, lulled Troeltsch into perceiving pronounced differences between a sect and a church, but the Sandemanians offer an example of how a sect may neither be purely a sect, nor a church. While Sandemanianism was literalist and exclusionary, antiauthoritarian and egalitarian, it did not emphasize any eschatology, and distinguished between a membership and other congregants. It retained the sacraments of baptism and the Eucharist. It banned Christian fellowship with outsiders, but otherwise placed no restrictions on other types of social interaction—certainly not to the point of creating closed communities, as did the Amish, for example. Finally, its appeal ranged all across the socioeconomic spectrum, though most commonly attracted adherents from among the merchant and artisan classes.

One element that was of vital importance to Troeltsch's definition of a sect does hold true with the Glasites and Sandemanians, and that was the near-constant state of tension and conflict in which they grew and developed throughout the greater part of the eighteenth century. The Quakers, by contrast, experienced a high degree of hostility and opposition in seventeenth-century New England, but over the course of the eighteenth century came to be an increasingly tolerated and accepted part of their communities, particularly in New Jersey and Pennsylvania where they enjoyed political power. Such gradual acceptance eluded the Sandemanians in late colonial and revolutionary America, and did not come to them until the nineteenth century. The Shakers likewise coped with hostility and violence, but weathered those storms and—while never integrating—achieved a modicum of respect for their relative separateness. Regarding these movements, the variance of their respective beliefs and practices from accepted Protestant norms confirmed sectarian identity upon them if one accepts Troeltsch's schema. Churches, on the other hand, comprehend the society at large, and are at ease within it because they accept the dominant value system. However, while both Quakers and Sandemanians leveled sharp criticism at the prevalent Protestant denominations, neither sought to undermine societal foundations, much less displace any or all other denominations. Depending on one's Troeltschian perspective, Quakerism, Shakerism, and Sandemanianism were as much churches as they were sects.

Finally, some summary comparisons and contrasts should be drawn between the Sandemanians and the Methodists, who arose virtually parallel to one another and wrangled over theology in the late 1750s in ways that shaped both movements. Here in the Wesleyan movement one finds a sect that grew out of an established Protestant tradition—Anglicanism—and in a short space of time grew into a church during the Revolution. Committed to a more fundamentalist Calvinism and evangelicalism, they likewise attracted suspicion and persecution on account of John Wesley's vocal opposition to the Revolution and its republican politics. Apart from the emphasis on spiritual perfectionism and cultivation of charismatic practices, there was little to Methodism that would have struck the average Congregationalist, Presbyterian, or Baptist as particularly strange. In fact, on the surface their Calvinism was fairly traditional, though they did repudiate predestination and the doctrine of limited atonement, basically contending that God offered free grace to all that people—in full possession of free will—variously accepted or rejected. But a pietistic shunning of worldly entanglements meant a sanctimonious, tacit loyalism similar to that of the Sandemanians that nevertheless drew the Patriots' ire. Methodists endured rhetorical attacks in the press, verbal and physical assaults in the streets, and an opprobrium of loyalism applied by the Whigs with a broad paintbrush, much as did other pietistic and pacifist religious groups. However, unlike the Sandemanians, the Methodists did not flee the Revolution or the creation of the United States, eventually tempering the more radical aspects of their theology and watching as popular evangelicalism caught up with them during the Second Great Awakening in the early 1800s.[22]

Another factor that must be taken into account in assessing the Sandemanians is the difference between late eighteenth-century America and Europe. Popular religious interest markedly declined in Europe during this period, while in America it was sustained through the Revolution and increased by the turn of the century. The European state churches tended to identify themselves strongly with reactionary values and interests during the stressful transition to industrialism and democracy, whereas the established American churches—especially the Episcopal (Anglican) Church—had to ameliorate themselves to changes in the status quo brought on by the Revolution. In revolutionary France, for example, the Catholic Church's retrograde posture made it an early target of the radicals, and its inability to adjust to the rapidly changing situation condemned it to a temporary reconstitution in the First Republic. The sociological interpretation of religious development owes much to Max Weber's, as well as Troeltsch's, suppositions that secularization went hand-in-hand with modernization—a supposition that is confounded by the further development and popularity of religion in the early national United States, and has challenged sociologists and historians of religion in the latter half of the twentieth century.[23]

The Sandemanians, therefore, defy easy categorization because to some extent they refused to identify themselves as anything other than Christians. This holds true not only for the modern scholar, but also for the Sandemanians' contemporaries, who variously regarded them along a continuum running from curiosity, to suspicion, to hostility. In a very cogent sense, then, in their "primitive" Christianity the Sandemanian experience neatly paralleled that of the first-century Christians to whom they looked as exemplars. John Glas looked to the New Testament as his primary, and indeed only, guide to true Christianity and frequently compared himself, Sandeman, and other Glasite missionaries to the apostles, particularly in instances when they suffered abuse or persecution. Much as Paul had to contend with churches that threatened to wander away from orthodoxy as he defined it, so Glas found a similar dynamic afflicting the fledgling Sandemanian churches, mainly those established in England. Particularly vexing was the doctrine of predestination, to which Glas strongly adhered. A large number of the members of James Allen's church found themselves generally unwilling to accept it, and Glas counseled Allen.[24] The Sandemanians managed to persevere until well into the twentieth century, but as never more than a Protestant fringe group despite the eloquence of Glas's and Sandeman's florid prose and intellectual acumen, or the fame of Michael Faraday as a scientist. To a degree the Sandemanians reveled in their tiny, sectarian identity, and were energized by controversies both religious and political to which they offered incisive commentaries, and it remains something of a mystery that they failed to attract a larger following among those dissatisfied with the better-established Protestant denominations. On the other hand, the excessive zeal of the newly converted, the strangeness of their ritual worship, and their confused political stance in America were disconcerting to those who might otherwise have been interested in the movement. The great influence of the mainline denominations cannot be underestimated in this regard, for their successful campaigns to discredit the Sandemanians and their leaders effectively squelched anything more than a marginal appeal the Sandemanians might have generated.

Nearly all of the Boston Sandemanians joined Edward Foster on the British transports that evacuated others of the city's Loyalists to Halifax, Nova Scotia, in 1776. The Sandemanian churches in Portsmouth and New Haven fell apart as a result of the stress generated by the Revolution, while the Danbury and Newtown churches managed to survive into the nineteenth century before they too receded into oblivion. The culprit again was internal dissension such as afflicted the Danbury church, when in 1788 Oliver Burr relocated from Newtown and built a house, and a faction protested that this violated the tenet against "laying up treasures on earth." A majority supported Burr and excommunicated the minority who refused to accept the congregation's judgment. The controversy did not end there, however, and a conference organized in Taunton in February 1789 and composed of delegates from Danbury, Newtown, Boston, Portsmouth, and Taunton met to issue a final ruling on the matter.[25] They upheld the decision of the Danbury church, but the subject of materialism refused to go away. Ebenezer Russell White gradually drifted into a strict interpretation of seeking wealth similar to that of Oliver Burr's critics, and he found himself and his small cadre of supporters unable to convince the rest of the church. He determined that he was "compelled to separate from such a corrupt society" and withdrew to form a new church in March 1798. "White's church" fell apart twenty years later when most of its membership adopted Baptist principles, one of whom, Levi Osborn, became a leading member of the Campbellite Disciples of Christ in Danbury.

☙

One by one, the Sandemanian churches in New England languished and died, with precious few new members attracted to the churches to replace those who left or passed away. Eliezer Chater, an elder of the London church, in an exceedingly rare surviving transatlantic correspondence, wrote to Daniel Salmon of Trumbull, Connecticut, in 1809 that "There seems to be little attention in these days to the concerns of the profession. It seems to be overlooked or swallowed up either about national concerns or in that enthusiastic zeal of the religious world striving to excell each other in promoting self-righteousness." He lamented that "The bren. in this country are few & feeble, scattered up & down in many places, & we have only one Elder in America [Ezra Peck], & he is more than sixty years of age." He did note hopefully the establishment of a church in Harpersfield, New York. According to Williston Walker, the Sandemanian movement effectively ceased to exist to any significant degree by 1830, though the Danbury church did hang on until the 1890s before it finally vanished.[26]

Epilogue

"Our Father's Fortunes Would Almost Teach Us to Renounce His Principles"

> For thirty years he was my instructor, my play fellow, almost my daily companion. To him I owe my fondness for reading, my familiarity with the Bible, my knowledge of old Colonial and American incidents and characteristics. He left me nothing but his example and the memory of his many virtues, for all that he ever earned was given to the poor. He was too good for this world; but remembrance of his childlike simplicity, and truly Christian character, is never absent from my mind.
>
> —Joseph Howe, *The Speeches and Public Letters of Joseph Howe*

Edward Foster's sorrow at leaving Boston was at first hardly assuaged while he settled into his new home and situation in Halifax, Nova Scotia. Efforts to reestablish the Sandemanian churches initially met with frustration and lethargy. The disappointment Robert Sandeman faced in 1764–1765 confronted the New England Sandemanians between 1776 and 1783, as the war remained foremost in the anguished expatriates' minds. The hope for a speedy end to the war and the prospects of returning to their homes, which had been confiscated by the revolutionary governments of Massachusetts, Connecticut, and New Hampshire, faded with each passing year, and were dashed at last with the American victory and the signing of the Treaty of Paris in 1783. Once the Sandemanians had made their own peace with the new realities, conditions began to improve. Foster noted in 1784 with a pride mingled with a lingering frustration that in the Halifax church "We have on Sabbath days considerable audience, and some appear attentive: but none have confidence enough in the truth to become professors of it." In sharp contrast to the experience of Loyalist expatriates in Britain, those who removed to Nova Scotia eventually prospered, particularly the Sandemanians, who settled mainly in Halifax and Shelburne. The experience of John Howe, the Loyalist printer, is at once indicative both of the successes enjoyed by the Sandemanian exiles, as well as their inability to adhere to Glas's and Sandeman's admonishments against mixing in political affairs.[1]

Howe's knack for success did not fail him in Halifax, marred as it was with the pain of exile and personal tragedy. He began publishing the *Halifax Journal* in December 1780, which became famous for the clarity of its layout and the quality of the typesetting, and this success eventually led to his establishing the *Nova Scotia Magazine and Comprehensive Review of Literature, Politics and News* in 1789. He lost his wife, Martha, to childbirth complications in November 1790; his grief was compounded by the failure of his ambitious magazine project in 1792. Despite this setback, the success of the *Halifax Journal* and his other printing enterprises compensated for the collapse of the *Nova Scotia Magazine*, and in October 1798 he remarried, only to see his first daughter follow her mother in death while giving birth a few months later. Howe's fortunes improved again in 1801, when he was appointed King's Printer, responsible for publishing the *Nova Scotia Royal Gazette* and the *Debates of the House of Assembly*. Later that year he was appointed Postmaster of Halifax, a position that was extended in 1803 to Deputy Postmaster-General of Nova Scotia, Cape Breton, Prince Edward Island, New Brunswick, and the Bermudas. As if this were not enough, he also volunteered to travel throughout the United States in the years immediately preceding and during the War of 1812, collecting intelligence for the British-Canadian government on New England Federalist resistance to the Nonintercourse Act (1807) and opposition to the Jeffersonian Republicans, as well as president James Madison's administration. Throughout this period, Howe occupied an eldership in the Halifax church, assisting in its growth, eventually becoming a preacher to a substantial community of former runaway slaves from the United States during the late 1810s and 1820s.[2]

In addition to his already prodigious civic contributions, Howe took it upon himself to spearhead a campaign to create a police force in Halifax, which had since its founding in 1749 lacked one. Being a port city, Halifax inevitably attracted sailors of questionable morals and respect for authority, as well as a healthy share of privateers and pirates, which gave the city a reputation for general lawlessness. Henry Alline, the evangelical Baptist who founded the Seventh-Day Baptist denomination, remarked of a 1783 visit that while "there were two or three souls that received the Lord Jesus Christ ... the people in general are almost as dark and vile as Sodom." Little had changed by the time Howe was appointed a Justice of the Peace, as well as Justice of the Inferior

Court of Common Pleas in 1810. According to a leading historian of Halifax, in the 1810s: "The upper streets were full of brothels. Grogshops and dancing houses were to be seen in every part of the town.... [Brunswick] street was known as 'Knock Him Down Street' in consequence of the affrays and even murders committed there." A committee, of which Howe was a part, established a professional police force, a court, and Bridewell penitentiary by 1820. Howe became Bridewell's unofficial chaplain, preaching every Sunday to the inmates and becoming increasingly appalled by deteriorating conditions and the corruption among those chosen to operate the prison. Those who had served their terms benefited from Howe's continued philanthropy; he ceaselessly worked to find them jobs. His efforts to clean up the prison and its administration, however, failed. He retained his judicial appointments through the 1820s and early 1830s, as well as becoming Health Warden in 1832. Howe died a man of high reputation and repeatedly noted piety and charity, in 1835. While New Englanders regarded Sandemanianism as a handicap, Nova Scotians clearly considered it an asset. Howe's sons, though men of equally high standing through similar careers spanning much of the rest of the 1800s, could not refrain from critiquing their father's Sandemanian commitment to simple living and charity. Joseph Howe, in a letter to a friend, complained that "Our father's fortunes would almost teach us to renounce his principles," though ultimately they chose to honor them.[3]

Once more firmly established, the Barrells, Fosters, and Howes, among other Sandemanian families, cultivated the modest growth and health of the Nova Scotia churches. Altogether, Sandemanianism fared reasonably well there, persisting into the early twentieth century before finally dissipating with the passing of two elderly women, who constituted the last church in Halifax, in 1905 and 1906. It endured still longer in Britain, with its most famous adherent the mid-nineteenth-century scientist Michael Faraday, and meetings are noted to have continued in Edinburgh and London until the 1990s, though evidence for this remains anecdotal. Though seemingly "few & feeble," the Sandemanians cast a long and imposing shadow over the evolution of Protestant Christianity, especially in America. Though the churches declined swiftly, one cannot escape the long reach of its fundamental theology as interpreted by the Campbells and Walter Scott, all of whom were intimately familiar with the theology of the Haldanes and Sandeman.[4]

In the 1790s, Alexander Campbell had had his fill of politicized Scottish Presbyterianism, much as John Glas had in the 1720s, and decided to emigrate to the newly born United States, where he supposed Presbyterianism existed less tainted by worldliness. However, all he found in

Pennsylvania was the same distraction of politics, and finally disconnected himself and his son from the church. Meanwhile, they met Walter Scott, who blended Haldanite and Sandemanian theologies with Lockean and Scottish Enlightenment philosophy, claiming to have arrived at a theology that was eminently rational, yet available not just to the learned, but especially to the uneducated. Scott and the Campbells found natural allies in Elias Smith (1769–1846) and Barton Warren Stone (1772–1844), both of whom expressed frustration with the dominance of clerical elites closely tied to the Federalist Party, and with theological erudition in general as deliberately impeding ordinary people from believing that they could achieve salvation but for the ministrations of "political Tories." So was born the Restorationist movement and the denomination of the Disciples of Christ. Like the Sandemanians, the Disciples insisted on referring to themselves simply as "Christians," and variously maintained much of Sandemanian theology and liturgical practice, most notably the holy kiss and foot-washing. The Restorationists were avid publishers of newspapers and journals such as Smith's *Herald of Gospel Liberty* (1808–1817), Campbell's *Christian Baptist* (1823–1830) and *Millennial Harbinger* (1830–1870) and Stone's *Christian Messenger* (1826–45), as well as longer theological treatises such as Smith's *New Testament Dictionary* (1812), Campbell's *Christian System* (1835, 1839), and Scott's *The Gospel Restored* (1836).[5]

Thomas Campbell wrote the basic creed of the "Christian Association" when it was formed in 1809, employing language that could easily have been borrowed from Glas's works: "Where the holy Scriptures speak, we speak; and where they are silent, we are silent." The Restorationists quibbled about how far to take their primitivism: Campbell was extremely rigid and fundamentalist, while Stone sought compromise with like-minded groups. Some groups, most of them Baptist, practiced foot-washing and the kiss of charity while others did one or the other, or neither, and all disagreed on the specific demands of communalism. Campbell, going slightly farther than either Glas or Sandeman, relied on the New Testament alone, declaring that it completely replaced the Old Testament, and he based his argument on the Baconian rationale that the ancients had incomplete knowledge of God. He believed in the Bible's infallibility, and insisted that Christians "speak of Bible things by Bible words because we are always suspicious that if the word is not in the Bible, the idea which it represents is not there." The Bible is an immanently simple and understandable book that must be taken literally, and not simply as "a book of ... opinions, theories, abstract generalities, nor of verbal definitions." Jesus Christ stood at the absolute center of the Bible, the truth of which he boiled down to three facts: Jesus was cruci-

Epilogue

fied, buried, and rose from the dead. He pushed Lockean theory to its limits in insisting, as Glas and Sandeman had, that reason can prove the existence of God, based on his idea that human reason cannot conceive of an uncaused Creator capable of creating the cosmos *ex nihilo*, and that only God could have imparted the idea of God to the minds of men. The truths of Christianity are all provable based on the traditional evidences being utilized by other theologians, and consequently Christianity for Campbell and the western Restorationists was a reasonable one hostile to the "headless" piety of the raucous revivals and the excessive emotionalism of the evangelicals. The eastern Christian movement was friendly toward revivalism, and the rapprochement between the two sides came only in the 1830s from an agreement that the Holy Spirit operates through the Word, from which neither can be wholly separated from the other.[6]

The Restorationists were imminently practical in their theology, and they were agreed in their opposition to Calvinism, particularly the doctrines of predestination and reprobation. Here their distinction from Sandemanianism is most clear. They rejected innate depravity based on a rejection of the Calvinist insistence that all were equally sinful, and their rejection of predestination depended on their belief in free will, and their belief that faith must precede justification. Campbell took the Restorationist lead in differing with the Calvinists on the sacrament of baptism, which he understood to be a requisite for justification as a remittance of past sins. This opened him up to the charge of exclusionism by implying that the unbaptized remained unforgiven, from which he backed away in his "Lunenberg Letter" (1837) to suggest that faith and love were the only absolute prerequisites for justification, though immersion remained a necessary rite. This cost him some followers, who thought he had waffled. The Restorationists leaned heavily toward Universalism, as well as Unitarianism—in fact the Christian Connection was also known as the "Evangelical Unitarians"—but most tended to avoid any speculation on nonscriptural issues, taking their lead again from Campbell, who questioned Trinitarianism but conceded that the scriptures spoke of "a society in God himself, a plurality as well as unity in the Divine nature" that could justify both Trinitarian and Unitarian doctrines.[7]

◊

Sandemanianism ultimately did not succeed in becoming a bona-fide denomination in the United States, but there is no mistaking the disproportionate influence of John Glas's and Robert Sandeman's theology on the later development of primitive Christian Restorationism through the nineteenth century and beyond. Other movements espousing similar theologies and ecclesiologies preceded and succeeded Sandemanianism, most of them associated with varieties of Baptist churches, but it is in the formation of the Disciples of Christ that one finds an unbroken thread of direct Glasite-Sandemanian influence. Officially known as the Christian Church (being essentially the same appellation Glas selected for himself and his followers), the Disciples have retained most of Glas's theology, as well as the high degree of lay participation and leadership. The relative egalitarianism of the Sandemanian churches has since expanded among the Disciples to give women more visible roles, as well as to embrace racial and ethnic diversity. However, the rejection of "enthusiasm" by Glas and Sandeman was itself rejected by their nineteenth-century heirs, who embraced evangelical revivalism and the charismatic style that typified the Second Great Awakening and radical American Protestantism into the present day.

The Sandemanians, and the Glasites from which they evolved, were diminished by the blinding glare of a quickened pace of political, cultural, social, and economic changes that spawned two revolutions. Upheavals that gave birth to the United States, as well as multiple personal failings among the sect's adherents, effectively prevented the Sandemanians from becoming a more permanent feature on the American religious landscape, even if many of their ideas survived in—sometimes radically—altered forms. They were rendered minor and obscure not by any judgment against the force of their ideas by the generations that have followed, but simply because brighter galaxies and stars command our gaze. Yet, as I have endeavored to show, there is ample reason to study the Sandemanians and recover their place in history. As a case study in the difficult relationship between church and state, as an enlightening vignette in the history of religion and ideas in the eighteenth century, as an object lesson in the nature of sectarian leadership, and as a morality tale warning against religious and political zealotry and persecution, the story of the Sandemanians is rich with meaning. History has been likened to archaeology, where tangible artifacts of the past are unearthed, each time enhancing our understanding of the past and occasionally altering it permanently. To borrow from L. P. Hartley and the New Testament, each new discovery and challenging interpretation allows us to see that distant "foreign country" through the glass a little less darkly.

Notes

INTRODUCTION

1. E. Alfred Jones, *The Loyalists of Massachusetts: Their Memorials, Petitions and Claims* (London, 1930), 137.
2. Joseph Fish, *Christ Jesus the Physician, and his Blood the Balm recommended for the Healing of a diseased People* (New London, 1760), 45; Patricia U. Bonomi, *Under the Cope of Heaven: Religion, Society, and Politics in Colonial America*, rev. ed. (New York, 2003), 162–168.
3. Arminianism is a variety of Christian theology first propagated by Jacobus Arminius (1560–1609), and is a rejection of Calvinist predestination. Arminian theologians contended that Christ's death was an atonement for the sins of all humanity, rather than for the Elect only, as Calvin asserted, and that individuals retained a free will to choose or reject God's grace, as well as lose that grace if once favored with it. Consequently, salvation depends in the Arminian scheme upon the presence and lifelong cultivation of faith, which strict Calvinists equate with an effort of the will, a species of "works." To them, it denied God his omnipotence and omniscience. See Alan P. F. Sell, *The Great Debate: Calvinism, Arminianism, and Salvation* (Grand Rapids, Mich., 1982).
4. On the history of the development of toleration in New England during the eighteenth century, see Chris Beneke, *Beyond Toleration: The Religious Origins of American Pluralism* (New York, 2006), esp. chaps. 1–2.
5. Exceptions include Battista Mondin, *Storia della teologica*, 4 vols. (Bologna, 1996–1997); Wilhelm Gräb, *Religion als Therma der Theologie: Geshcichte, Standpunkte und Perspektiven theologischer Religionskritik* (Gütersloh, 1999); Jonathan Hill, *The History of Christian Thought* (Oxford, 2003); and Anthony N. S. Lane, ed., *A Concise History of Christian Thought*, rev. ed. (London, 2006).
6. The two leading exceptions are Robin Gill, ed., *Readings in Modern Theology: Britain and America* (Nashville, 1995), Mark A. Noll, *America's God: From Jonathan Edwards to Abraham Lincoln* (New York, 2002), and E. Brooks Holifield, *Theology in America: Christian Thought from the Age of the Puritans to the Civil War* (New Haven,

2003), though Holifield's work is primarily focused on the United States as part of a larger transatlantic intellectual community, a theme underscored in this work.

7. Sydney E. Ahlstrom, "The Problem of Religious History in America," *Church History* 39 (1970), 224; Holifield, *Theology in America*, viii, 13; Susan O'Brien, "A Transatlantic Community of Saints: The Great Awakening and the First Evangelical Network, 1735–1755," *American Historical Review* 91 (1986), 811–832.

8. Representative examples include Sydney E. Ahlstrom, *Theology in America: The Major Protestant Voices from Puritanism to Neo-Orthodoxy* (Cincinnati, 1967); Perry Miller, *The New England Mind: The Seventeenth Century* (New York, 1939; reprint 1961); idem, *The New England Mind: From Colony to Province* (Cambridge, Mass., 1953; reprint 1961); William G. McLoughlin, *Soul Liberty: The Baptists' Struggle in New England, 1630–1833*, 2 vols. (Hanover, 1991); William H. Brackney, *Baptists in North America: A Historical Perspective* (Oxford and Malden, Mass., 2006); William Warren Sweet, *Methodism in American History* (1938, rev. New York, 1954); Dee Andrews, *The Methodists and Revolutionary America, 1760–1800: The Shaping of an Evangelical Culture* (Princeton, 2000).

9. Holifield, *Theology in America*, 25. The abundance of works on New England's religious history is far too great to distill to a few representative examples, though arguably it began with Perry Miller's *The New England Mind* and concretized by Sacvan Bercovitch's *The Puritan Origins of the American Self* (New Haven, 1975). A comment on the South's denigration is found in Jack P. Greene, *Pursuits of Happiness: The Social Development of Early Modern British Colonies and the Formation of American Culture* (Chapel Hill, 1988), "Prologue."

10. A good example is the 1970 discovery of Sirius B, a "dark" companion star in orbit around Sirius A, the "Dog Star" in the constellation Canis Major. Irregularities in the motion of Sirius A hinted at its companion's existence. Robert K. G. Temple, *The Sirius Mystery* (New York, 1976).

11. A small sampling includes Rufus M. Jones, *The Quakers in the American Colonies* (New York, 1911, 1966); Edward Deming Andrews, *The People Called Shakers: A Search for the Perfect Society*, rev. ed. (New York, 1963); Gillian L. Gollin, *Moravians in Two Worlds: A Study of Changing Communities* (New York, 1967); Jacob R. Marcus, *The Colonial American Jew, 1492–1776*, 3 vols. (Detroit, 1970); Richard K. MacMaster, Samuel L. Horst, and Robert F. Ulle, eds., *Conscience in Crisis: Mennonites and Other Peace Churches in America, 1739–1789* (Scottsdale, Penn., 1979); Jon Butler, *The Huguenots in America: A Refugee People in New World Society* (Cambridge, Mass., 1983);

12. R. R. Palmer, *The Age of the Democratic Revolution: A Political History of Europe and America, 1760–1800*, 2 vols. (Princeton, 1959, 1964).

13. Williston Walker, "The Sandemanians of New England," *American Historical Association Annual Report for 1901* (Washington, D.C., 1902); Charles St. C. Stayner, "The Sandemanian Loyalists," *Collections of the Royal Nova Scotia Historical Society* 29 (1951), 62–123; Jean F.

Hankins, "A Different Kind of Loyalist: The Sandemanians of New England during the Revolutionary War," *New England Quarterly* 60 (1987), 224–248; idem, "Connecticut's Sandemanians and the Revolution," in Robert M. Calhoon, ed., *Loyalists and Community in North America* (Westport, Conn., 1994), 56–79; Geoffrey N. Cantor, *Michael Faraday, Sandemanian and Scientist: A Study of Science and Religion in the Nineteenth Century* (New York, 1991); John Howard Smith, "'Sober Dissent' and 'Spirited Conduct': The Sandemanians and the American Revolution, 1765–1781," *Historical Journal of Massachusetts* 28 (2000), 142–166.

14. Ned C. Landsman, *Scotland and Its First American Colony* (Princeton, 1985); idem, *Nation and Province in the First British Empire: Scotland and the Americas, 1600–1800* (Lewisburg, Penn., and London, 2001). The bulk of scholarship on Scottish philosophical influences in America is devoted to the political facets of the American Revolution and early national period, rather than the colonial period alone. Examinations of the intellectual connections between Scotland and America in the prerevolutionary period is best represented by Richard B. Sher and Jeffrey R. Smitten, eds., *Scotland and America in the Age of Enlightenment* (Princeton, 1990).

15. I prefer to call the Revolutionary War the "War *for* Independence" rather than the "War *of* Independence," which has become the most common usage among early Americanist historians in the past twenty years. This is not to imply, however, that I believe the American Revolution to have been essentially a conservative one designed to preserve and refine the constitution of the colonial political systems. Colonial America, despite some obvious deviations from European sociopolitical organization, retained a highly traditional British orientation and identity—one that grew over the course of the eighteenth century rather than diminished. In this sense, the American Revolution is simply the culmination of a process begun by the English Glorious Revolution of 1688, which introduced Lockean natural rights philosophy and Whig political theory to prominence in the Atlantic World. However, the fundamental nature of the Revolution was radical. See Gordon S. Wood, *The Radicalism of the American Revolution* (New York, 1991); J. C. D. Clark, *The Language of Liberty, 1660–1832: Political Discourse and Social Dynamics in the Anglo-American World* (Cambridge, 1994); and Brendan McConville, *The King's Three Faces: The Rise and Fall of Royal America, 1688–1776* (Chapel Hill, 2006).

16. Clark, *The Language of Liberty*, 225.

CHAPTER 1

1. Various terms have been used in scholarly literature to refer to the Church of Scotland, such as the Scottish Church, the National Church, the Kirk, and the Establishment. Appearances of the terms National Church and the Establishment in this chapter are specific references to the Church of Scotland.

2. The sect Glas founded was referred to by outsiders as "Glasites," a term I use in reference to the movement until its refinement by Robert Sandeman in the 1760s, at which point they became most commonly known as the "Sandemanians." Glas and Sandeman simply referred to themselves and their adherents as "Christians."
3. Gordon Donaldson, *The Scottish Reformation* (Cambridge, 1960), 29, 43–60; James Edward McGoldrick, "Patrick Hamilton, Luther's Scottish Disciple," *Sixteenth Century Journal* 18 (1987), 81–88; Thomas S. Freeman, "'The reik of Maister Patrik Hammyltoun': John Foxe, John Winram, and the Martyrs of the Scottish Reformation," *Sixteenth Century Journal* 27 (1996), 43–60.
4. Donaldson, *The Scottish Reformation*, 53–65, 144; Stewart Lamont, *The Swordbearer: John Knox and the European Reformation* (London, 1991), 99–110, 116–117, 123–126, 13–142; W. Stanford Reid, "John Knox's Theology of Political Government," *Sixteenth Century Journal* 19 (1988), 529–540; Callum G. Brown, *Religion and Society in Scotland since 1707*, rev. ed. (Edinburgh, 1997), 68; Robert M. Healey, "Waiting for Deborah: John Knox and Four Ruling Queens," *Sixteenth Century Journal* 25 (1994), 371–379.
5. King James VI of Scotland, *Basilikon Doron* (1598) quoted in C. H. McIlwain, ed., *The Political Works of James I* (Cambridge, Mass., 1918), 24–25, 62–70; Maurice Lee, Jr., *Government by Pen: Scotland under James VI and I* (Urbana, Ill., 1980), 20–23. John Coffey argues forcefully that the radical Presbyterians were to James's mind identical to the English Puritans in terms of "ethos and spirituality," in *Politics, Religion and the British Revolutions: The Mind of Samuel Rutherford* (Cambridge, 1997), 17–18; Donaldson, *The Scottish Reformation*, 144–148; Maurice Lee, Jr., *The Road to Revolution: Scotland under Charles I, 1625–1637* (Urbana, Ill., 1985), 130–131, 200–216.
6. F. D. Dow, *Cromwellian Scotland, 1651–1660* (Edinburgh, 1979), 9–12, 39–42; Julia Buckroyd, *Church and State in Scotland, 1660–1681* (Edinburgh, 1980), 7–11. Charles Stuart's supporters were also called the "Resolutionists," while his opponents were the "Protesters" who ignored the Solemn League and Covenant and worked to whittle it away. See also David Stevenson, *The Scottish Revolution, 1637–1644: The Triumph of the Covenanters* (Newton Abbot, 1973); idem, *Revolution and Counter-Revolution in Scotland, 1644–1651* (London, 1977); and Walter Makey, *The Church of the Covenant, 1637–1651* (Edinburgh, 1979).
7. Dow, *Cromwellian Scotland*, 268–270; Buckroyd, *Church and State in Scotland*, 22–30, passim; Elizabeth Hannan Hyman, "A Church Militant: Scotland, 1661–1690," *Sixteenth Century Journal* 26 (1995), 49–74; William Ferguson, *Scotland's Relations with England: A Survey to 1707* (Edinburgh, 1977), 142–165; Brown, *Religion and Society in Scotland since 1707*, 31. The best introduction to the interplay of religion and politics in Scotland in the seventeenth century remains G. D. Henderson, *Religious Life in Seventeenth-Century Scotland* (Cambridge, 1937).
8. Hogg quoted in Arthur Fawcett, *The Cambuslang Revival: The Scottish Evangelical Revival of the Eighteenth Century* (London, 1971), 14–15;

"Sir John Clerk's Observation on the Present Circumstances of Scotland, 1730," ed. T. C. Smout, in *Miscellany of the Scottish History Society* 10 (1965), 175–212; Brown, *Religion and Society in Scotland since 1707*, 18.

9. J. H. S. Burleigh, *A Church History of Scotland* (London, 1960), 200, 287–308; Brown, *Religion and Society in Scotland since 1707*, 18; John McKerrow, *History of the Secession Church* (Edinburgh, 1854), 73ff. Anonymously published, *The Marrow of Modern Divinity* was most likely written by one Edward Fisher of Gloucester.

10. Fawcett, *The Cambuslang Revival*, 19–21; McKerrow, *History of the Secession Church*, 11–17; Thomas Boston, *Memoirs of the Life, Times and Writings of Thomas Boston*, ed. John McKerrow (Aberdeen, 1852), 331–350; Brown, *Religion and Society in Scotland since 1707*, 28.

11. John Glas, *A Continuation of Mr. Glas's Narrative* (Dundee, 1828), 138; Robert Wodrow, *Analecta; or Materials for a History of Remarkable Providences; Mostly Relating to Scotch Ministers and Christians*, 4 vols. (Edinburgh, 1842–1843), 3:323; Hew Scot, ed., *Fasti Ecclesiae Scoticanae: The Succession of Ministers in the Church of Scotland from the Restoration to the Revolution*, 8 vols. (Edinburgh, 1915–1950), 5:370.

12. Writing in 1729, Glas reflected that "I had looked a little into the episcopal controversy, and was fully satisfied, that in the word of God there was no foundation for prelacy and that the presbyterians had the better of them by the Scriptures.... I had not then considered the controversy betwixt the presbyterians and them of the congregational way, but took up the common report against the congregational business, that it is mere confusion, and was the mother of all the sectaries.... Thus I thought myself a sound presbyterian, and accordingly declared myself so, by subscribing to the Formula." *A Continuation of Mr. Glas's Narrative*, 138–139.

13. Glas, *A Narrative of the Rise and Progress of the Controversy about the National Covenants, and of the Ways that have been taken about It on both Sides* (Edinburgh, 1728), 2. The Westminster Shorter Catechism was devised by an assembly of divines held at Westminster as part of the covenanted uniformity that united the churches of England, Scotland, and Ireland, and was approved by the General Assembly of the Church of Scotland in 1648. Its roots extend as far back as the National Covenant of 1581, which was renewed in 1638–1639 in what is known as the "Second Scottish Reformation." See Michael Lynch, *Edinburgh and the Reformation* (Edinburgh, 1981) and James Church, *Patterns of Reform: Continuity and Change in the Reformation Church* (Edinburgh, 1989).

14. Ernest Stoeffler, *The Rise of Evangelical Pietism* (Leiden, 1965); Johannes Wallmann, "Was ist Pietismus?" in *Pietismus und Neuzeit: Ein Jahrbuch zur Geschichte des neueren Protestantismus* (1974–), vol. 21 (Göttingen, 1994); George Becker, "Pietism's Confrontation with Enlightenment Rationalism: An Examination of the Relation between Ascetic Protestantism and Science," *Journal for the Scientific Study of Religion* 30 (1991), 139–158; Robert D. Preus, *The Theology of Post-Reformation Lutheranism*, 2 vols. (St. Louis, 1970), 1:129–135.

15. Glas, *Narrative*, 3. The Cameronians developed a fierce reputation in southern Scotland for their reactionary ecclesiology, particularly for "rabbling," the oftentimes violent removal of allegedly unregenerate clergy from their churches. Inured to violence in the harsh landscape of the Borderlands of England and Scotland, they were famous for fighting with a sword in one hand and a Bible in the other, and for routing forces sent against them despite being usually outnumbered. After the Glorious Revolution, they were harnessed to fight the Jacobites in the Highlands, resulting in the creation of Cameronian regiments in the British army that existed into the twentieth century. See R. M. Barnes, *The Uniforms and History of the Scottish Regiments* (London, 1960), 37, 42–45; and Hyman, "A Church Militant." Either John Glas was able to placate them or he exaggerated their presence in his church.
16. Glas, *Narrative*, 4, 8.
17. Glas, *Narrative*, 9–11; John Macleod, "The Reformed Faith in Modern Scotland," *Princeton Theological Review* 24 (1926), 180.
18. [Anonymous], *An Account of the Life and Character of Mr. John Glas* (Edinburgh, 1813), x. Matthew 18:15–17 in the King James Bible reads: "Moreover if thy brother shall trespass against thee, go and tell him his fault between thee and him alone: if / he shall hear thee, thou hast gained thy brother. / But if he will not hear thee, then take with thee / one or two more, that in the mouth of two or three witnesses / every word may be established. / And if he shall neglect to hear them, tell it unto the church: but if he neglect to hear the church, let him be unto / thee as an heathen man and a publican."
19. Glas, *Narrative*, 9.
20. Glas, *Narrative*, 21, 32.
21. Glas, *Narrative*, 35–36; Wodrow, *Analecta*, 3:323; John Willison, *The Balm of Gilead* in John Willison, *Practical Works*, ed. W. M. Hetherington (Glasgow, 1844), 404.
22. Glas, *Narrative*, 37–40.
23. Wodrow, *Analecta*, 3:357. Glas also apportioned a large share of the blame on Willison's wife who, ironically, many years later was comforted at her deathbed by a Glasite maid. Robert Sandeman noted this information in John Glas, Robert Sandeman et al., *Letters in Correspondence* (Dundee, 1851), 58.
24. The counter-queries are reproduced in Glas, *Narrative*, 48–62.
25. Willison, *The Afflicted Man's Companion* (Dundee, 1728) in *Practical Works*, 729.
26. "Minutes of the Synod of Angus and Mearns," 19 Oct. 1727; Wodrow, *Analecta*, 3:449.
27. Glas, Appendix to the *Narrative*, 127–128.
28. Glas, Appendix to the *Narrative*, 128–134.
29. Glas, Appendix to the *Narrative*, 134.
30. Glas, Appendix to the *Narrative*, 134–135.

31. Glas, *A Continuation of the Narrative* (Edinburgh, 1729), 150–164; *An Account of the Life and Character of Mr. John Glas*, xxix.
32. Glas, *A Continuation of the Narrative*, 172.
33. Glas, *A Continuation of the Narrative*, 172; Wodrow, *Analecta*, 4:3.
34. Glas, *A Continuation of the Narrative*, 182–195. In the process of defending Glas, Miller became a Glasite convert and eventually an elder in the Perth church.
35. Glas, Appendix to the *Narrative*, 195–206.
36. Glas, Appendix to the *Narrative*, 210. The list of charges is provided on pp. 230–231.
37. Glas, Appendix to the *Narrative*, 234–237; Glas, *Remarks upon the Memorial of the Synod of Angus against Mr. Glas and the Sentence of the Commission Deposing him from the Ministry* (Edinburgh, 1730), 339.
38. Glas, *A Continuation of the Narrative*, 240–241.
39. Wodrow, *Analecta*, 4:3; *The Scots Magazine. Containing a General View of the Religion, Politicks, Entertainment, &c. in Great Britain*, I (Edinburgh, 1739), 233.
40. Jean Smellon, a young Glasite disciple who lived in Edinburgh, walked to Dundee once every month in order to take Communion. She later married Glas's son Thomas, and became a "ministering widow" after her husband's death. See John Glas, Robert Sandeman, et al., *Letters in Correspondence*, 5–6.
41. John Owen, *The True Nature of a Gospel Church and Its Government* in *Works of John Owen*, 16 vols. (Edinburgh, 1843), 16:79–81; John Glas, Robert Sandeman, et al., *Supplementary Volume of Letters of John Glas, Robert Sandeman, etc.* (Perth, 1865), iv.
42. Glas, "A Letter to Mr. John Willison concerning Illiterate Ministers," in *The Works of Mr. John Glas*, 2nd ed., 5 vols. (Perth, 1782), 2:256–278 (hereafter cited as *Works*); *Letters in Correspondence*, 22–23.
43. *An Account of the Life and Character of Mr. John Glas*, xlvi–xlvii.

CHAPTER 2

1. Primitive Christianity in this context refers to the broad spectrum of fundamentalist sectarianism that places emphasis on the dilution of authority and enhanced lay participation in the churches, indicative of first-century Christianity as described in the New Testament. See Carter Lindberg, *The European Reformations* (Malden, Mass., 1996), esp. chap. 8.
2. See chapters 3 and 4 for discussions of the Great Awakening.
3. Soteriology is the blanket term for doctrines of Christian salvation.
4. Glas, *A Treatise on the Lord's Supper* in *Works*, 5:210, 206, 207–208. Unless otherwise noted, all primary source references in this chapter are from Glas's *Works*. Regarding universalism, it appears that the majority of early Christian churches espoused this theology, influenced by the

Gnostics centered at Alexandria, Egypt, and spread by Origen of Alexandria in the third century, and Gregory of Nyssa and Ambrose of Milan in the fourth century. It was forcefully refuted in the exegetical and polemical works of Augustine of Hippo and Basil the Great, and officially made anathema by the Fifth Ecumenical Synod of Constantinople in 553. See *The Cambridge History of Christianity*, Vol. II: *Constantine to 600*, Augustine Casiday and Frederick W. Norris, eds. (Cambridge, 2007), 19–22, and chap. 20.

5. *A Treatise on the Lord's Supper*, 210; Jean Calvin, *Institutes of the Christian Religion*, ed. John T. McNeill, trans. Lewis Battles, 2 vols. (Philadelphia, 1960), 2:934; Glas, *An Answer to Some Objections . . . against the "Plea for Pure and Undefiled Religion"* in *Works*, 2:57.
6. *Notes on Scripture Texts, No. II* in *Works*, 3:80, 84; *The Scheme of Justification by Faith agreeable to Commonsense* in *Works*, 5:355–356, 358, 362–363.
7. *The Testimony of the King of Martyrs* (Edinburgh, 1729), 141, 142–143.
8. *The Testimony of the King of Martyrs*, 145; *The Usefulness of Catechisms* in *Works*, 2:95. Question 86: "What is faith in Jesus Christ?" Answer: "Faith in Jesus Christ is a saving grace whereby we receive and rest upon him alone for salvation, as he is offered to us in the gospel."
9. *The Usefulness of Catechisms Further Considered* in *Works*, 2:119, 121–122.
10. Antinomianism was an epithet hurled by religious legalists at those holding liberal theological beliefs, especially those who appeared to believe that salvation relieved the believer of any responsibility or obligation to adhere to any scriptural or secular laws or codes of ethics. It has been used with virtual indiscriminateness since the solidification of Christian theology by various factions with differing shades of opinions concerning soteriology. For a fair example of how English Calvinists defined Arminianism, see *The Declaration of the Congregational Ministers, in and about London, against Antinomian Errours, and Ignorant and Scandalous Persons Intruding Themselves into the Ministry* (London, 1699).
11. *The Usefulness of Catechisms*, 138; *Notes on Scripture Texts No. I* in *Works*, 3:100–101; *The Usefulness of Catechisms*, 96–109.
12. *Testimony of the King of Martyrs*, 143–145; *A Treatise on the Lord's Supper*, 213.
13. *A Treatise on the Lord's Supper*, 217–221, 226.
14. *Notes on Scripture Texts No. I*, 89.
15. *An Explication of the Proposition . . . that a Church of Jesus Christ . . . is, in its Discipline subject to no Jurisdiction under Heaven* (1728) in *Works*, 1:194; *The Testimony of the King of Martyrs*, 65.
16. *A Second Letter to Mr. Aytone, Containing Remarks upon his "Review of the Observations on the original Constitution of the Church"* in *Works*, 1:432, 433; *Some Observations upon the Original Constitution of the Christian Church* in *Works*, 1:345; *An Explication of the Proposition*, 187, 188.

17. *An Explication of the Proposition*, 210; *Notes on Scripture Texts No. VI* in *Works*, 3:297; *An Explication of the Proposition*, 195, 214, 281; *A Treatise on the Lord's Supper*, 185.
18. *An Explication of the Proposition*, 184–185; *The Speech of Mr. John Glas*, 285.
19. *Narrative*, 11–14, 17; *A Supplement to Mr. Ebenener Erskine's Synodical Sermon* in *Works*, 2:290; *A Grave Dialogue Betwixt Three Freethinkers* in *Works*, 4:262.
20. *An Explication of the Proposition*, 185–186; *Testimony of the King of Martyrs*, 110–119.
21. *A Supplement to Mr. Ebenener Erskine's Synodical Sermon*, 292–293.
22. *The Speech of Mr. John Glas before the Commission*, 284; *Tradition by the Succession of Bishops* in *Works*, 5:336 ff.; *A View of the Heresy of Aerius* in *Works*, 4:470 ff.; *Notes on Scripture Texts No. VI*, 300. It must be noted that with regard to Glasite-Sandemanianism, specific occurrences of women being included among the membership and leadership go largely unmentioned in the extant primary source materials. However, based on feminine participation (and in rare cases leadership) in eighteenth-century British-American Protestantism, I am inclined to assume that women did play an important role in the Glasite and Sandemanian churches, though presumably not as eldresses. See Marilyn J. Westerkamp, *Women and Religion in Early America, 1600–1850: The Puritan and Evangelical Traditions* (London: Routledge, 1999), chaps. 5–6.
23. *A Commentary on Acts xv. 1–11* in *The Christian Advocate and Scotch Baptist Repository*, 2 vols. (reprint Dundee, 1847), 2:4; "The Right of the Christian People, and the Power of their Pastors, in the Ordination of Ministers of the Gospel Asserted" in *Works*, 2:229–255.
24. *The Right of the Christian People, and the Power of their Pastors, in the Ordination of Ministers*, 234–245.
25. *A Dissertation on Infant Baptism* in *Works*, 2:356.
26. *A Dissertation on Infant Baptism*, 329, 358–359, 371, 376–378; *Short Notes on Baptism* in James Morison, ed., *A Supplementary Volume of Letters of John Glas* (Perth, 1865), xxxix.
27. *A Treatise on the Lord's Supper*, 27, 156, 157, 166; *Some Observations upon the Original Constitution of the Christian Church*, 330–331.
28. "A Letter to Mr. Randie ... concerning Frequent Communicating" (1749) in *Works*, 2:301; *A Treatise on the Lord's Supper*, 9, 75, 90.
29. *An Explication of the Proposition*, 215–216; *The Three Divine Rests* in *Works*, 3:438–440.
30. *The Three Divine Rests*, 440, 442, 447–449.
31. The "elements" are the bread and wine used in the service.
32. Romans 16:16, I Corinthians 16:20, II Corinthians 13:12, I Thessalonians 5:26, I Peter 5:14.
33. *A Treatise on the Lord's Supper*, 49, 50.
34. John 13:1–17.
35. I Timothy 5:10.

36. *A Treatise on the Lord's Supper*, 182; *An Explication of the Proposition*, 217–218; "A Letter to a Minister of the Established Church, in Answer to one from him on Forbearance" in *Works*, 2:174–175; *An Explication of the Proposition*, 234; *A Treatise on the Lord's Supper*, 183–184, 185.
37. *A Treatise on the Lord's Supper*, 185, 192–193, 197; *An Explication of the Proposition*, 238.
38. John Glas to James Cant, [n.d.], in *The Christian Advocate and Scotch Baptist Repository*, 3 vols. (reprint Dundee, 1851) 3:187–188; *Notes on Scripture Texts No. VI*, 298–299; *A Treatise on the Lord's Supper*, 184.
39. *Some Observations upon the Original Constitution of the Christian Church*, 369; *The Testimony of the King of Martyrs*, 152–153; *An Explication of the Proposition*, 213.
40. "A Letter to a Minister of the Established Church," 175; "Catholic Charity" in *Works*, 2:180–195.
41. "The Rule of Forbearance Defended" in *Works*, 2:196–212; *A Grave Dialogue*, 246; *The Scheme of Justification by Faith*, 418.
42. *The Unlawfulness of Blood-eating* in *Works*, 2:164, 167–168, 171–172.
43. *The Unlawfulness of Blood-eating*, 165.
44. *A Plea for Pure and Undefiled Religion* in *Works*, 2:4–5, 12, 13.
45. *A Plea for Pure and Undefiled Religion*, 13–14, 17.
46. *An Explication of the Proposition*, 201–202; *An Answer to Some Objections*, 47–48; *The Three Divine Rests*, 440.
47. *Letters in Correspondence*, 88.
48. *A National Fast Sermon at Dundee, Jan. 9th 1740* in *Works*, 2:324.
49. *A National Fast Sermon*, 324; *A Second Fast Sermon at Dundee, Feb. 4th 1741* in *Works*, 2:337.
50. *A National Fast Sermon*, 326–327.
51. Holifield, *Theology in America*, chap. 4.

CHAPTER 3

1. However, some Sandemanians did use this term in explaining the church to outsiders.
2. Michael J. Crawford, ed., "The Spiritual Travels of Nathan Cole," *William and Mary Quarterly*, 3rd Ser., 33 (1976), 89–126.
3. These are the terms employed with reference to the Awakening in New England among Congregationalists and Baptists, primarily, whereas among Presbyterians in New York, New Jersey, and Pennsylvania the revivalists were known as "New Side" and their opponents as "Old Side" Presbyterians. In this context, "New Light" is to be equated with "New Side," since the ideological and theological emphasis was essentially the same. A much less distinct terminology identified the supporters and detractors of the revivals in Britain, and is thus not used in this work. For a fuller explication of the difficulties in distinguishing New Lights from Old Lights, and New Side from Old Side, see Christopher Grasso, *A Speaking Aristocracy: The Transformation of Public Discourse in Eigh-*

teenth-Century Connecticut (Chapel Hill, 1999), 87–88, 101, 105–107, 147.

4. John Sage, *The Fundamental Charter of Presbytery, as It Hath Been Lately Established, in the Kingdom of Scotland, Examin'd and Disprov'd* (London, 1695), 370–371, 373; Clydesdale Synod Records, 6 Apr. 1697, 4 Oct. 1705, Scottish Record Office, Edinburgh, 1:170, 2:48; Wodrow, *Analecta*, 1:20–21, 178, 4:4; George Wemyss, "The Preface to the Reader," in John Spalding, *Synaxis Sacra; Or, A Collection of Sermons Preached at Several Communions; Together with Speeches at the Tables, both before, at, and after that Work* (Edinburgh, 1703), preface unpaginated; Leigh Eric Schmidt, *Holy Fairs: Scotland and the Making of American Revivalism*, 2nd ed. (Grand Rapids, Mich., 2001), 44–45.

5. The Camisards, also known as the "French Prophets," were a millenarian Huguenot sect from the southern French province of Languedoc. Famous for their enthusiasm, the Camisards during worship often fell into trances, spoke in tongues, and were also notable for their inclusion of women as "prophets," who most often were the ones who experienced the charisms. See Hillel Schwartz, *The French Prophets: The History of a Millenarian Group in Eighteenth-Century England* (Berkeley, 1980). Wesley later retreated from Camisard beliefs in preference for particular aspects of Moravian theology and practice. Certain Camisard ideas, specifically their apocalypticism, deeply influenced the advent of Shakerism.

6. See Richard P. Heitzenrater, *Mirror and Memory: Reflections on Early Methodism* (Nashville, 1989). Methodism developed an early rift between Wesley and George Whitefield over issues of denominational discipline, Moravian influence, and Anglican Church control. The Wesleyans, being more beholden to Moravian influence than Whitefield had been comfortable with, grew rapidly in England throughout the 1740s and 1750s, as well as in the American colonies. See Andrews, *The Methodists and Revolutionary America*, 16–38.

7. Robert Sandeman, "Biography of Robert Sandeman," in *Discourses on Passages of Scripture: With Essays and Letters* (Dundee, 1857), vi.

8. Sandeman, "Thoughts on Christianity in a Letter to a Friend" (Edinburgh, 1891), 11, 13–20.

9. James Hervey, *Theron and Aspasio: or, A series of dialogues and letters upon the most important and interesting subjects* (London, 1755), 33; John Brown, *Memoirs of the Life and Character of the Late Rev. James Hervey, A.M.* (London, 1822), 58–59. Scant attention has been devoted to this formative aspect of Wesley's career, though it is clear that Wesley's reaction to Hervey's work served to solidify the Methodist doctrine of justification.

10. James Hervey, *The Works of James Hervey*, 7 vols. (London, 1787), 5:353; John Wesley to Samuel Furly, 14 Oct. 1757, in John Telford, ed., *The Letters of John Wesley*, 8 vols. (London, 1931), 3:230; John Wesley to James Hervey, 29 Nov. 1758.

11. Hervey quoted in Sandeman, *Letters on Theron and Aspasio* (Edinburgh, 1757; reprint New York, 1838), 312–313. Emphasis in original.

12. Sandeman, *Letters*, 411, 282, 232; idem, *Discourses*, 93.

13. Sandeman, *Letters*, 366–367, 336, 80, 20, 316, 334, 338, 91–92.
14. Sandeman, *Letters*, 339, 309, 359; idem, *Discourses*, 96.
15. Sandeman, *Letters*, 257, 72, 257.
16. Sandeman, *Discourses*, 130–131; idem, *Letters*, 285, 336–337, 355.
17. Sandeman, *Letters*, 349; *Discourses*, 168–169; *Letters*, 259, 349, 358.
18. *Letters in Correspondence*, 66; Sandeman, *Discourses*, 209; idem, *Letters*, 349, 375.
19. Wesley, *Letters*, 3:231; *Remarks* quoted in Luke Tyerman, *The Oxford Methodists* (London, 1873), 293–294.
20. Robert Sandeman to John Cranstoun, Jul. 1758 in *Letters in Correspondence*, 38–39.
21. Samuel Pike, *An Epistolary Correspondence between S. P[ike] and R. S[andeman]* (London, 1759), 3–41, 66–79, 84–101.
22. Glas, Sandeman, et al., *Supplementary Letters*, 93–94. Sandemanian doctrine explicitly stipulated that there could only be one true Christian church in any one city, and so while Pike and his supporters retained their sanctuary on Thames Street, they could not create a Sandemanian church there since the one at the Bull-and-Mouth had already been established.
23. *Supplementary Letters*, 16, 18, 19–24.
24. *Letters in Correspondence*, 34, 35.
25. Robert Sandeman to William Cudworth quoted in William Jones, ed., *The New Evangelical Magazine*, 21 vols. (London, 1793–1823), 9:140; *Supplementary Letters*, 89–90.
26. *Supplementary Letters*, 82; *Letters in Correspondence*, 36.
27. *Letters in Correspondence*, 75, 4, 5.
28. *Letters in Correspondence*, 5; Robert Sandeman to Samuel Churchill quoted in *The Christian Advocate and Scotch Baptist Repository*, 5 vols. (Beverly and London, 1849–1853), 2:155.
29. *Supplementary Letters*, 59, 60.
30. Samuel Pike, "An Address by Mr. Samuel Pike to a Christian Church in London" (Edinburgh, 1766), 6; *Supplementary Letters*, 63, 65. The church moved its quarters to St. Paul's Alley, in the Barbican district, in 1778, and again to Barnsbury Grove. A schism in the nineteenth century resulted in two Sandemanian churches that existed until well into the twentieth century. The noted chemist Michael Faraday was an elder in one of them. See Geoffrey Cantor, *Michael Faraday, Sandemanian and Scientist*.
31. Pike, *A Plain and Full Account*, 20, 24.
32. Pike, *A Plain and Full Account*, 29, 28, 29–30.
33. Jones, *The Evangelical Magazine*, 15:106, 187–188; *The Christian Advocate*, 1:173.
34. *Letters in Correspondence*, 48, 45.
35. *Letters in Correspondence*, 44–45, 47–48; *Supplementary Letters*, 7.
36. See their letters to each other in *Letters in Correspondence*, 82–88.
37. *Letters in Correspondence*, 82–88; *The Christian Advocate*, 1:173–174.

38. *Letters in Correspondence*, 29. Rowlands had just lost a number of followers to the Sandemanians.
39. Strangely, the *Letters on Theron and Aspasio* was not one of them.
40. *Supplementary Letters*, 64.
41. *Letters in Correspondence*, 29.
42. *Letters in Correspondence*, 29–33; *Supplementary Letters*, 71; Thomas Rees, *The History of Protestant Nonconformity in Wales*, 2nd ed. (London, 1833), 385.
43. William Jones, ed., *Memoir of Archibald M'Lean* (London, 1817), xx-xxii.
44. Jones, *The New Evangelical Magazine*, 1:295; idem, *Memoir of Archibald M'Lean*, xxxiv, xlii, xliv; idem, ed., *Memoir of John Richard Jones*, in *The New Evangelical Magazine*, 15:321–328.
45. James Smith and Robert Ferrier, *The Case of James Smith, late Minister at Newburn, and of Robert Ferrier, late Minister at Largo, truly represented and defended* (Edinburgh, 1768); Robert Ferrier, Preface to *Testimony of the King of Martyrs* (Edinburgh, 1777), 19.
46. Ferrier, Preface to *Testimony of the King of Martyrs*, 19, 20; Donald Beaton, "The Old Scots Independents," in *Records of the Scottish Church History Society*, 7 vols. (Edinburgh, 1929), 3:140–141. Scottish Glasites and English Sandemanians influenced, both directly and indirectly, such sects as the Haldanites, the Walkerites, and in the United States the Campbellites. All aspired to some adherence to primitive Christian principles, church organization, and practice. Irish and Scottish Baptists, the latter still exhibiting Sandemanian influence, introduced to the United States the now familiar practice among some current Baptist denominations of foot-washing. Alex Haldane, *Lives of Robert and James Alexander Haldane*, 4th ed. (Edinburgh, 1855); E. I. Carlyle, "John Walker," in Sydney Lee, ed., *Dictionary of National Biography*, 66 vols. (London, 1885–1901), 65:59; James A. Haldane, *Strictures upon "Primitive Christianity" by Mr. John Walker* (Edinburgh, 1820); Jesse R. Kellems, *Alexander Campbell and the Disciples* (New York, 1930); Edwin S. Gaustad and Philip Barlow, *New Historical Atlas of Religion in America* (New York, 2000), 178–187. See the epilogue in this book.

CHAPTER 4

1. I am indebted to Seth Cotlar, who granted me access to some of his research, and whose conference paper, "Reconceiving Community in the Commercial Empire: The Sandemanian Controversy of the 1760s in New England," I had the pleasure of commenting on at the Omohundro Institute of Early American History and Culture Seventh Annual Conference, Glasgow, Scotland, July 2001. Much of this chapter builds on themes Cotlar and I have independently explored.

2. Perry Miller, *The New England Mind: From Colony to Province*, chaps. 20–22; Cotton Mather, *Ratio Disciplinae Fratrum Nov-Anglorum* (Boston, 1726).
3. John J. McCusker and Russell Menard, *The Economy of British America, 1607–1789* (Chapel Hill, 1985), 248–255, 262–276, 278–330; Stephanie Grauman Wolf, *As Various as Their Land: The Everyday Lives of Eighteenth-Century Americans* (New York, 1993), 88–94; Richard D. Brown, *Knowledge Is Power: The Diffusion of Information in Early America, 1700–1865* (New York, 1989), 36–39, 127–128; Charles E. Clark, *The Public Prints: The Newspaper in Anglo-American Culture, 1665–1740* (New York, 1994), 6–9, 134–137, 141–143, 179–181, 185; Michael Warner, *Letters of the Republic: Publication and the Public Sphere in Eighteenth-Century America* (Cambridge, Mass., 1990), 34–72; Edward M. Cook, Jr., *The Fathers of the Towns: Leadership and Community Structure in Eighteenth-Century New England* (Baltimore, 1976); Jon Butler, *Becoming America: The Revolution before 1776* (Cambridge, Mass., 2000), 134–184.
4. *The Public Records of the Colony of Connecticut, 1636–1776*, 15 vols., 1–3 ed. J. H. Trumbull, vols. 4–15 ed. C. J. Hoadly (Hartford, 1850–1890), 3:299; Richard L. Bushman, *From Puritan to Yankee: Character and the Social Order in Connecticut, 1690–1765* (Cambridge, Mass., 1967), chap. 11. Rogers's group, known as the Rogerenes, was an outgrowth of the handful of Seventh-Day Baptists who lived in Connecticut at the time. See John R. Bolles and Anna B. Williams, *The Rogerenes, Some Hitherto Unpublished Annals Belonging to the Colonial Society of Connecticut* (Boston, 1904).
5. J. William T. Youngs, Jr., "Congregational Clericalism: New England Ordinations before the Great Awakening," *William and Mary Quarterly*, 3rd Ser., 31 (1974), 481–482; Eliphalet Adams, *The Gracious Presence of Christ with the Ministers of the Gospel, a ground of great Consolation to Them. As it was Represented in a Sermon Preach'd at Groton, On Occasion of the Ordination of the Reverend Mr. John Owen, Pastor of the First Society there* (New London, Conn., 1730), 37; Bushman, *From Puritan to Yankee*, 155–163; Holifield, *Theology in America*, 25–26, 80–84; John Corrigan, *The Prism of Piety: Catholic Congregational Clergy at the Beginning of the Enlightenment* (New York, 1991), 9–31; Harry S. Stout, *The New England Soul: Preaching and Religious Culture in Colonial New England* (New York, 1986), 148–165; Cotton Mather, *Ratio Disciplinae Fratrum Nov-Anglorum. A Faithful Account of the Discipline Professed and Practised; In The Churches of New England* (Boston, 1726), 5.
6. Arianism refers to the belief in Christ as a purely human individual only touched by divinity, rather than being an embodiment of it. Eighteenth-century Deists inclined to this belief. Deism was the rationalist religious philosophy that posited a mechanical universe crafted by God to run without his interference. Arminianism is the theological doctrine that the soul can be prepared for the reception of divine grace through the doing of "good works." Pelagianism is a belief in free will that discountenances

the doctrine of original sin, insisting that the individual can affect his or her own salvation. Socinianism was another rationalist theology that denied the divinity of Christ, trinitarianism, the power of the sacraments, vicarious atonement, and the resurrection of the body.

7. Ned C. Landsman, "Revivalism and Nativism in the Middle Colonies," *American Quarterly* 34 (1982), 155–156; Archibald Alexander, *Biographical Sketches of the Founder and Principal Alumni of the Log College* (Philadelphia, 1851), 127–134, 150–152; Elias Boudinot, *The Life of William Tennent, Late Pastor of the Presbyterian Church at Freehold, N.J.*, improved ed. (Trenton, N.J., 1833), 20–24. William Tennent Sr. stressed that the spiritual transformation of regeneration precipitated a similar physical transformation, sometimes attended by extended trance states, visions, waking dreams, and sudden changes in bodily constitution. John Tennent's conversion apparently shattered his health, rendering him dependant upon his brothers for physical support. He interpreted the catastrophic diminution of physical strength as a consequence of a complimentary increase in his spiritual fortitude. See John Tennent, *The Nature of Regeneration Opened* (Boston, 1735). In a "Prefatory Discourse" to this treatise (pp. i–ix), Gilbert Tennent related how John would pace a room clutching a Bible to his chest and weeping uncontrollably, and that William Jr. had at one point died and then was brought back to life.

8. Connecticut Archives, Ecclesiastical Affairs, XI, 35a, Connecticut State Library, Hartford, Conn.; Ebenezer Frothingham, *The Articles of Faith and Practice, with the Covenant, That is confessed by the Separate churches of Christ in general in this Land ...* (Newport, 1750); C. C. Goen, *Revivalism and Separatism in New England, 1740–1800* (New Haven, 1962); Gaustad and Barlow, *New Historical Atlas of Religion in America*, 22; Andrews, *The Methodists and Revolutionary America*, 31–38.

9. William Tennent Sr. believed that conversion was a long, drawn-out process that required constant prayer and meditation. William Jr., Gilbert, and John all endured experiences that included trance states and physical shocks that left William Jr. permanently weakened and dependent upon Gilbert for the rest of his life. For them, conversion was a physical as well as a spiritual trial, and they made this an integral part of the revivals. See Alexander, *Biographical Sketches*, 71–72, 112–115.

10. Fawcett, *The Cambuslang Revival*, 64–74, 97–112.

11. Jonathan Edwards, *The Distinguishing Marks Of a Work of the Spirit of God ...* (Boston, 1741); *The Nature of True Virtue* (c. 1755), in Richard L. Bushman, ed., *The Great Awakening: Documents on the Revival of Religion, 1740–1745* (Chapel Hill, 1970), 153–157; Edwards, *Some Thoughts concerning the Present Revival of Religion in New England* (Boston, 1742); Thomas Prince, Jr., ed., *The Christian History*, 2 vols. (Boston, 1743–1745), 2:95; Jonathan Edwards, "Notes on Revelation" and *An Humble Attempt to promote Explicit Agreement and Visible Union of God's People in Extraordinary Prayer for the Revival of Religion and the Advancement of Christ's Kingdom on Earth, pursuant to Scripture-Promises and Prophecies*

concerning the last Time (Boston, 1747), in Stephen J. Stein, ed., *The Works of Jonathan Edwards*, Vol. 5 (New Haven, 1977), 427, 253–284; John Howard Smith, "The Promised Day of the Lord: American Millennialism and Apocalypticism, 1735–1783," in Richard Connors and Andrew Colin Gow, eds., *Anglo-American Millennialism, from Milton to the Millerites* (Leiden, 2004), 118–119.

12. Jonathan Edwards, *An Humble Inquiry into the Rules of the Word of God* (1749); Harry S. Stout and Peter Onuf, "James Davenport and the Great Awakening in New London," *Journal of American History* 70 (1983), 556–578; Bonomi, *Under the Cope of Heaven*, 159–160.

13. Jonathan Edwards to James Robe, 12 May 1743, in Edwards, *The Works of Jonathan Edwards*, Vol. 16, ed. George S. Claghorn (New Haven, 1998), 134–135; Thomas Prince, *Extraordinary Events the Doings of God...* (Boston, 1745), 20; Thomas Sewall, *The Lamb Slain...* (Boston, 1745), 29; Charles Chauncy, *Marvellous Things done by the right Hand and holy Arm of God...* (Boston, 1745), 21; Edwin Scott Gaustad, *The Great Awakening in New England* (New York, 1957), 79; S. E. Dwight, *The Life of President Edwards...* (New York, 1830), 243–244, 212, 262, 278, 287, 412; Cotton Mather, *A Discourse Concerning the Covenant which God will remember, in the Times of Danger passing over his Church* (London, 1714); Aaron Burr, *A Discourse Delivered at New-Ark...* (New York, 1755); *The Watchman's Answer to the Question, What of the Night, etc...* (New York, 1757). Edwards's reference to the "enemy" comes from Isaiah 59:19: "When the enemy shall come in like a flood, the Spirit of the Lord shall lift up a standard against him."

14. Goen, *Revivalism and Separatism in New England*, chaps. 2–4; Heimert, *Religion and the American Mind from the Great Awakening to the Revolution*, pt. I; Jack D. Marietta, *The Reformation of American Quakerism, 1748–1783* (Philadelphia, 1984); James R. Tanis, *Dutch Calvinistic Pietism in the Middle Colonies: A Study in the Life and Theology of Theodorus Jacobus Frelinghuysen* (The Hague, 1967).

15. Charles. P. Hanson, *Necessary Virtue: The Pragmatic Origins of Religious Liberty in New England* (Charlottesville, 1998), chap. 5; William Haller, *The Elect Nation: The Meaning and Relevance of Foxe's Book of Martyrs* (New York, 1963); John Miller, *Popery and Politics in England, 1660–1688* (Cambridge, 1973); Jeremy Black, "The Catholic Threat and the British Press in the 1720s and 1730s," *Journal of Religious History* 12 (1983), 364–381; Francis D. Colignano, *No King, No Popery: Anti-Catholicism in Revolutionary New England* (Westport, Conn., 1995), chap. 1; Smith, "The Promised Day of the Lord," 121–122.

16. Marietta, *The Reformation of American Quakerism*, chaps. 6–8; Samuel Davies, *Virginia's Danger and Remedy* (Williamsburg, 1756); *The Curse of Cowardice* (Hanover, Va., 1758); John Ballantine, *The Importance of God's Presence with an Army...* (Boston, 1756); James Cogswell, *God, the pious Soldier's Strength and Instructor...* (Boston, 1757); Samuel Cooper, *A Sermon Preached before His Excellency Thomas Pownall, Esq ... October 16, 1759. Upon Occasion of the Success of His Majesty's Arms in the Reduction of Quebec...* (Boston, 1759), 38–39; Samuel

Langdon, *Joy and Gratitude to God for ... the Conquest of Quebec* (Portsmouth, 1760), 37–38.

17. Thomas Secker to Samuel Johnson, 27 Sept. 1758, in Herbert and Carol Schneider, eds., *Samuel Johnson: President of King's College. His Career and Writings*, 3 vols. (New York, 1929), 3:258; Ezra Stiles, *A Discourse on the Christian Union* (Boston, 1761), 28, 30, 96; Smith, "The Promised Day of the Lord," 125–127. See also Carl Bridenbaugh, *Mitre and Sceptre: Transatlantic Faiths, Ideas, Personalities, and Politics* (New York, 1962), chaps. 4–6, for a thorough discussion of the bishop controversy.
18. See Bruce Daniels, *The Connecticut Town: Growth and Development, 1635–1790* (Middletown, Conn., 1979), chap. 4.
19. Bushman, *From Puritan to Yankee*, chap. 4.
20. Records of the Ecclesiastical Society of Danbury, 3 Jan. 1755.
21. *Letters in Correspondence*, 72–74; Records of the Ecclesiastical Society of Danbury, 20 Dec. 1762.
22. The Cambridge Platform, adopted by a synod convened at Cambridge, Massachusetts, in August 1649, codified Congregational church organization and discipline, particularly regarding the admission of new members and the punishment of offenders. Connecticut sought to revise the Cambridge Platform in 1708 by granting more power to ministers and church elders at the expense of the membership, in what became the Saybrook Platform. However, unlike the Cambridge Platform, the Saybrook Platform was not generally approved, and as many societies adopted it as rejected it. Clergymen faced a greater potential for problems in congregations that stuck to the Cambridge Platform. See Williston Walker, *The Creeds and Platforms of Congregationalism* (New York, 1893), 224–225; Benjamin Trumbull, *A Complete History of Connecticut, Civil and Ecclesiastical, from the Emigration of its First Planters, from England, in the Year 1630, to the year 1764; and to the Close of the Indian Wars*, 2 vols. (New London, 1898), 1:410–414; Bushman, *From Puritan to Yankee*, 150–155.
23. Eliphalet Adams, *The Gracious Presence of Christ with the Ministers of the Gospel, a ground of great Consolation to Them. As it was Represented in a Sermon Preach'd at Groton, On Occasion of the Ordination of the Reverend Mr. John Owen, Pastor of the First Society there* (New London, 1730), 37; Thomas Clap, *The Greatness and Difficulty of the Work of the Ministry. A Sermon Preached at the Ordination of the Reverend Mr. Ephraim Little, At Colchester, September 20, 1732* (Boston, 1732), 16; Bushman, *From Puritan to Yankee*, 155–163.
24. The Committee of the First Society in Danbury, "A Vindication of the Proceedings of the Eastern Association, in Fairfield County: and of the Council that censured Mr. White, and dismissed him from his Pastoral Relation to the First Church in Danbury: in a Letter to the Reverend Joseph Bellamy" (New Haven, 1764), 11, 35, 60. White is quoted on p. 51.
25. "A Vindication of the Proceedings ... ," 10, 35, 14.
26. "A Vindication of the Proceedings ... ," 21, 20. Emphasis added.

27. "A Vindication of the Proceedings . . . ," 39. Actually, even among strict Calvinists there existed the minutest possibility that one of the unregenerate could be self-deluded about their election, or deluded by Satan, and subsequently that the community could likewise be fooled into counting one of the "goats" as one of the "sheep." While true grace did alter the soul of the recipient forever, human perception is an imperfect instrument, and thus one could be mistakenly counted among the elect, though one's future bad behavior would inevitably expose the error, and lead to such a member's excommunication. See Perry Miller, *The New England Mind: The Seventeenth Century*, chap. 13; Edmund S. Morgan, *Visible Saints: The History of a Puritan Idea* (Ithaca, 1963), 47–52.
28. "A Vindication of the Proceedings . . . ," 6, 27 (emphasis added); Ebenezer Russell White to Abel Robbins, 19 Dec. 1764; "A Vindication of the Proceedings . . . ," 73.
29. White quoted in "A Vindication of the Proceedings . . . ," 26, 64–65; Records of the Ecclesiastical Society of Danbury, 16 Apr. 1764; "A Vindication of the Proceedings . . . ," 73.
30. Records of the Ecclesiastical Society of Danbury, 16 Apr. 1764; "A Brief Narrative of the Proceedings . . . ," 24; Records of the Ecclesiastical Society of New Fairfield, Dec. 1764. The Saybrook Platform was formally abandoned in 1784.
31. Franklin B. Dexter, ed., *Extracts from the Itineraries and other Miscellanies of Ezra Stiles . . . With a Selection from his Correspondence* (New Haven, 1916), 269.
32. A typical example of this is an item published by "Jack New Li[ght]" in the *Connecticut Courant*, 5 Dec. 1768.
33. *Letters in Correspondence*, 75, 77, 80.
34. *Letters in Correspondence*, 99; James Dana to Ezra Stiles, 18 Jan. 1765, in Ezra Stiles, *Memoir of Robert Sandeman on his First Coming to America 1764*, Beinecke Library, Yale University. There is no corroborating evidence to indicate the accuracy of Dana's statement. Sandeman did not believe he had really converted anyone during his first missionary sojourn in Danbury, despite his initial high hopes upon arriving.
35. *Letters in Correspondence*, 99; James M. Bailey, *The History of Danbury* (New York, 1896), 34–35; *Letters in Correspondence*, 101.
36. Chauncy Whittlesey to Ezra Stiles, 24 Jan. 1765. This letter and others are included in the manuscript copy of the *Memoir*, which is available in microform at the Beinecke Library at Yale University. Ezra Stiles to Chauncy Whittlesey, 5 Dec. 1764, Stiles Papers, Yale University; Stiles to Benjamin Stevens, 17 Mar. 1769 quoted in Edmund S. Morgan, *The Gentle Puritan: A Life of Ezra Stiles, 1727–1795* (Chapel Hill, 1962), 209.
37. James Dana to Ezra Stiles, 7 Jan. 1765, Stiles Papers, Yale University Library; Charles Chauncy to Ezra Stiles, 3 Dec. 1764, Stiles Papers; Ezra Stiles to Chauncy Whittlesey, 5 Dec. 1764, Stiles Papers.
38. Samuel Langdon, *An Impartial Examination . . .*, 1, 2; Charles Chauncy, *Twelve Sermons on the Following Seasonable and Important Subjects . . .*

(Boston, 1765), 4; Benjamin Stevens to Ezra Stiles, 30 Oct. 1764, Stiles Papers; Stiles, *Memoir of Robert Sandeman*, 4 Dec. 1764.
39. Ebenezer Russell White to Abel Robbins, 20 Nov. 1764, Robbins Collection, Connecticut Historical Society.
40. Stiles, *Memoir of Robert Sandeman*, 44; Seth Pomeroy, Jr. to Ezra Stiles, 27 Jan. 1766, Stiles Papers; Ezra Stiles to Samuel Langdon, 24 May 1766, Stiles Papers; Benjamin Stevens to Ezra Stiles, 30 Oct. 1764, Stiles Papers; Stiles, *Memoir of Robert Sandeman*, 43; Charles Chauncy, *Twelve Sermons*, 4.
41. Alexander Garden was the Anglican commissary of South Carolina at the time of Whitefield's tours of 1739 and 1740. William Howland Kenney III, "Alexander Garden and George Whitefield: The Significance of Revivalism in South Carolina, 1738–1741," *South Carolina Historical Magazine*, 71 (1970), 12–13; [Andrew Croswell], *An Answer to the Rev. Mr. Garden's Three First Letters to the Rev. Mr. Whitefield* ... (Boston, 1741), 32; Leigh Eric Schmidt, "'A Second and Glorious Reformation': The New Light Extremism of Andrew Croswell," *William and Mary Quarterly*, 3rd Ser., 53 (1986), 217; Croswell, *What Is Christ to Me, if He Is Not Mine? or, A Seasonable Defence of the Old Protestant Doctrine of Justifying Faith* ... (Boston, 1745), 4; [Andrew Croswell], *A Letter to Mr. Robert Sandeman: By a Minister in Boston* (Boston, 1766).
42. Isaac Backus, *True Faith will produce good Works* ... (Boston, 1767), 17–20, 21. Emphases in original.
43. Backus, *True Faith will produce good Works*, 26, 24 (emphases in original); Backus, *Truth is Great and Will Prevail* (Boston, 1781), 16 (emphasis in original); William G. McLoughlin, *New England Dissent, 1630–1833: The Baptists and the Separation of Church and State*, 2 vols. (Cambridge, Mass., 1971), 2:741.
44. Samuel Langdon to Ezra Stiles, 17 Sept. 1766, quoted in Ezra Stiles, *The Literary Diary of Ezra Stiles*, 3 vols., Franklin B. Dexter, ed. (New York, 1901), 2:171n. See also Samuel Pike, *A plain and full account of the Christian practices of the Church in St. Martin's-le-Grand* (Boston, 1766).

CHAPTER 5

1. "S. W.," *The Wonderful Appearance of an Angel, Devil & Ghost* (Boston, 1774).
2. David D. Hall, *Worlds of Wonder, Days of Judgment: Popular Religious Belief in Early New England* (Cambridge, Mass., 1989), chaps. 1–2.
3. *Newport Mercury* (R.I.), 28 Oct. 1765; *Pennsylvania Journal*, 5 Sept. 1765. For similar demonstrations elsewhere in the colonies, see *Boston Gazette, Supplement*, 19 Aug. 1765; "G." in *New-York Gazette*, 29 Aug. 1765; "Colonus" in *Providence Gazette*, 24 Aug. 1765; *Portsmouth Mercury* (N.H.), 9 Sept. 1765; *South Carolina Gazette*, 31 Oct. 1765; William L. Saunders, ed., *The Colonial Records of North Carolina*, 10 vols. (Raleigh, 1886–1890), 7:123–25. For an official report from Virginia, see Gov. Fauquier's (Va.) letters to the Lords of Trade, Public

Record Office, London, CO 5/1331. See also Edmund S. and Helen S. Morgan, *The Stamp Act Crisis: Prologue to Revolution* (Chapel Hill, 1953), 121–25. Pope's Day (5 Nov.) was a popular anti-Catholic celebration in the British colonies. See Peter Shaw, *American Patriots and the Rituals of Revolution* (Cambridge, Mass., 1981), 16–18, 180–97; Dirk Hoerder, *People and Mobs: Crowd Action in Revolutionary Massachusetts, 1765–1780* (New York, 1977), 91–97; George P. Anderson, "Ebenezer Mackintosh: Stamp Act Rioter and Patriot," Colonial Society of Massachusetts, *Publications* 26 (1927), 15–64; Anne Rowe Cunningham, ed., *The Letters and Diary of John Rowe, Boston Merchant, 1759–1762, 1764–1779* (Boston, 1903; reprint, 1969), 67; Paul Gilje, *The Road to Mobacracy: Popular Disorder in New York City, 1763–1834* (Chapel Hill, 1987), 29. See also Cogliano, *No King, No Popery*, chap. 2.

4. Nathaniel Barrell to [ ], 19 Jun. 1766, Sandeman-Barrell Papers, Massachusetts Historical Society, Boston; Petition of 9 Jun. 1766, Sandeman-Barrell Papers. The other subscribers were Benjamin Hart, Moses Noble, Colburn Barrell, Nathaniel Rogers, and William Fullerton.

5. Convention at Perth Amboy to Secretary, Society for the Propagation of the Gospel in Foreign Parts Correspondence, Ser. B, XXIV, 314; Bridenbaugh, *Mitre and Sceptre*, 230–248; [Anonymous], *Liberty and Property Vindicated and the St—pm—n burnt* (New London, 1765); *Connecticut Gazette*, 30 Aug. 1765; John Adams, *Works of John Adams*, 2:197; Clarence S. Brigham, *Paul Revere's Engravings* (New York, 1969), 22–23.

6. William Patten, *A Discourse Delivered at Hallifax* ... (Boston, 1766), 21; Stephen Johnson, *Some Important Observations* ... (Newport, R.I., 1766), 15.

7. Jones, *The Loyalists of Massachusetts*, 113, 137; Samuel Peters, *General History of Connecticut*, Samuel Jarvis McCormick, ed. (London, 1781; reprint, Upper Saddle River, NJ, 1970), 267–268; John Howard Smith, "'Sober Dissent' and 'Spirited Conduct,'" 146–147.

8. Robert Sandeman to Nathaniel Barrell, 1 Oct. 1766 and 17 Nov. 1766, Sandeman-Barrell Papers.

9. Robert Sandeman to Nathaniel Barrell, 8 Jan. 1767, Sandeman-Barrell Papers.

10. *Boston Chronicle*, 4–9 Dec. 1769; Nathaniel Barrell to Gov. Benning Wentworth, Petition, 9 Jun. 1766, Sandeman-Barrell Papers; Smith, "'Sober Dissent,'" 147–148. The other four subscribers were Benjamin Hart, Moses Noble, Nathaniel Rogers, and William Fullerton. Coercion in the enforcement of the boycotts was not limited to Boston, but was generally widespread. See Michael A. McDonnell, "Mobilization and Political Culture in Revolutionary Virginia: The Failure of the Minutemen and the Revolution from Below," *Journal of American History* 85 (1998), 946–981, esp. 959–961, regarding the laboring classes' use of threats to force gentry merchants into signing Non-Importation Agreements in Williamsburg.

11. *Boston Chronicle*, 7–11 Dec. 1769 (emphasis in original); Smith, "'Sober Dissent,'" 148–149.

12. *Boston Chronicle*, 7-11 Dec. 1769; Smith, "'Sober Dissent'," 149-150.
13. *Boston Chronicle*, 7-11 Dec. 1769; Smith, "'Sober Dissent'," 150-151. Adherence to the letter of the Non-Importation Agreement was never unanimous, not even in Boston. Nonetheless, many Americans lost their businesses and trades to the boycotts. See Charles M. Andrews, "The Boston Merchants and the Non-Importation Movement," Colonial Society of Massachusetts, *Publications* 19 (Boston, 1918), 204-206; Arthur M. Schlesinger Sr., *The Colonial Merchants and the American Revolution* (New York, 1957), chaps. 11-12; Ronald Hoffman, *A Spirit of Dissension: Economics, Politics, and the Revolution in Maryland* (Baltimore, 1973), 85-87; Charles S. Olton, *Artisans for Independence: Philadelphia Mechanics and the American Revolution* (Syracuse, N.Y., 1975), 29-47; and Billy G. Smith, "Material Lives of Laboring Philadelphians, 1750-1800," *William and Mary Quarterly*, 3rd Ser., 38 (1981), 163-202.
14. *Letters in Correspondence*, 107, 108 (emphasis in original); Smith, "'Sober Dissent'," 151-152.
15. *Letters in Correspondence*, 110, 112-113 (emphasis added); Massachusetts Supreme Court of Judicature, "Indictment of Colburn Barrell for preaching about rebellion," Boston, 21 Nov. 1770, Boston Public Library, Chamberlain Collection; Hankins, "A Different Kind of Loyalist, 232; Smith, "'Sober Dissent'," 152-153. The Sandeman-Barrell Papers do not contain any letters written by Colburn Barrell to Robert Sandeman, the one-sided aspect of the correspondence and Barrell's actions leading one to the conclusion that Barrell simply ignored Sandeman's advice. It is hard to believe, though, that such was the case, and allowances must be made for the possibility that letters from Colburn Barrell to Sandeman may not have survived.
16. William Hutchinson to [Isaac Winslow, Jr.], 3 Jul. 1770, Winslow Family Papers, Massachusetts Historical Society, Boston; Simon Pease to Isaac Winslow, Jr., 29 May 1774, Winslow Collection, Massachusetts Historical Society; Smith, "'Sober Dissent'," 156-157.
17. *Boston Gazette*, 5 Sept. 1774; *Massachusetts Spy*, 8 Sept. 1774; John Andrews to William Barrell, 30 Aug. 1774 in Winthrop Sargent, ed., *Letters of John Andrews* (Cambridge, 1866), 349; Smith, "'Sober Dissent'," 157-158.
18. *Letters in Correspondence*, 102-104.
19. Samuel Andrew Peters, Declaration on Joseph Pynchon, 8 Jan. 1784, Betts Autograph Collection, Yale University Library, New Haven, Connecticut.
20. Schlesinger, *The Colonial Merchants and the American Revolution*, 156-209; Middlekauff, *The Glorious Cause: The American Revolution, 1763-1789* (New York, 1982), 186-188.
21. First Continental Congress, "To the People of Great Britain," in W. C. Ford, ed., *Journals of the Continental Congress*, 34 vols. (Washington, D.C., 1904-1937), 1:83, 88; [John Adams and Daniel Leonard], *Novanglus and Massachusettensis* (Boston, 1819), 72-74; Hanson, *Necessary Virtue*, 11-14, 61-64; Brigham, *Paul Revere's Engravings*, 124-125; *New*

Hampshire Gazette, 15 Jul. 1774; Samuel Sherwood, *The Church's Flight into the Wilderness: An Address on the Times* (New York, 1776), 33, 15.

22. Robert M. Calhoon, *The Loyalists in Revolutionary America, 1760–1781* (New York, 1965), 290–294; [John Adams and Daniel Leonard], *Novanglus and Massachusettensis*, 74 (emphasis added). On the subject of gentry leadership of the radical Whigs, see Pauline Maier, *From Resistance to Revolution: Colonial Radicals and the Development of American Opposition to Britain, 1765–1776* (New York, 1972) and Holton, *Forced Founders: Indians, Debtors, Slaves, and the Making of the American Revolution in Virginia* (Chapel Hill, 1999).

23. Sung Bok Kim, "The Limits of Politicization in the American Revolution: The Experience of Westchester, County, New York," *Journal of American History* 80 (1993), 878.

24. Hopestill Capen, Petition to Court of Inquiry, 29 Aug. 1776, Broadside, Massachusetts Historical Society; Smith, "'Sober Dissent,'" 142–143.

25. Bernard Bailyn denied that religious convictions had any serious influence on the course of the American Revolution in *The Ideological Origins of the American Revolution*, enlarged ed. (Cambridge, Mass., 1992), dismissing millenarian Puritanism as a "most limited and parochial tradition" (32). Jon Butler went further in *Awash in a Sea of Faith*, declaring that the Revolution was "a profoundly secular event" (194). For an alternative, and far more convincing opinion asserting millenarian evangelicalism's key role in the Revolution, see J. C. D. Clark, *The Language of Liberty*, chap. 4.

26. Jon Butler, *Awash in a Sea of Faith*, 188. The best examples of this interpretation of religion's relationship to the Revolution are Hatch's *The Sacred Cause of Liberty* and Melvin B. Endy Jr.'s "Just War, Holy War, and Millennialism in Revolutionary America," *William and Mary Quarterly*, 3rd Ser., 42 (1985), 3–25. The shortcoming in Hatch's study is its regional focus, which ignores contravening evidence coming from middle-colony and southern clergy, while Endy is not convincing when he dismisses similar evidence even as he admits to its existence. The majority of historians who have tackled the subject largely tend to concentrate on New England Congregationalism, from which the most strident religious rhetoric in support of the Revolution emanated. However, New England divines were not the only clergymen who were caught up in the revolutionary tempest.

27. *Minutes and Letters of the Coetus of the German Reformed Congregations in Pennsylvania, 1747–1792* (Philadelphia, 1903), 350, 352; F. Ernest Stoeffler, ed., *Continental Pietism and Early American Christianity* (Grand Rapids, 1976), 156–159, 256–264; Calhoon, *The Loyalists in Revolutionary America*, 334–369; John Murray, *Nehemiah, or the Struggle for Liberty Never in Vain, When Managed with Virtue and Perseverence* (Newburyport, Mass., 1779), 53.

28. [Herman Husband], *Proposals to Amend and Perfect the Policy of the Government of the United States of America* (Philadelphia, 1782); Ruth H. Bloch, *Visionary Republic: Millennial Themes in American Thought* (Cambridge, 1985), 99. Husband had been a philosophical leader of the North Carolina Regulators in the 1760s, fleeing to his native Maryland

when the Regulation was crushed, and from there moving to western Pennsylvania.

29. George Duffield, *A Sermon Preached in the Third Presbyterian Church, in the City of Philadelphia, On Thursday, December 11, 1783* (Philadelphia, 1784), 24; Elisha Rich, *The Number of the Beast Found out by Spiritual Arithmetic* (Chelmsford, Mass., 1775), 9; Bloch, *Visionary Republic*, 98–99.

30. Nancy L. Rhoden, *Revolutionary Anglicanism: The Colonial Church of England Clergy during the American Revolution* (New York, 1999), 89; Samuel Andrews, *A Sermon Preached at Litchfield, in Connecticut, Before a Voluntary Convention of the Clergy of the Church of England of Several Provinces in America, June 13, 1770* (New Haven, 1770), 13; William Clark to S.P.G., 1 Oct. 1770, William Stevens Perry, ed., *Historical Collections Relating to the American Colonial Church*, 5 vols. (1870–1878; reprint New York, 1969), 3:552–553.

31. Thomas Bradbury Chandler, *A Friendly Address to All Reasonable Americans, on the Subject of Our Political Confusions* (Boston, 1774), 20–22, 31, 49–52. The Münsterites were a band of millenarian Anabaptist Melchiorite peasants and workers led by Jan van Lyden and Jan Matthys during the sixteenth-century Peasant Wars sparked by the Protestant Reformation. They sacked and occupied the city of Münster in 1534 before Counter-Reformation forces defeated them the following year.

32. Thomas Jefferson, *The Papers of Thomas Jefferson*, 19 vols., ed. Julian P. Boyd et al. (Princeton, 1950), 1:165; Lyman H. Butterfield, ed., *Adams Family Correspondence*, 2 vols., (Cambridge, Mass., 1963), 1:195; Middlekauff, *The Glorious Cause*, 308–311.

33. L. Kinvin Wroth et al., eds., *Province in Rebellion: A Documentary History of the Founding of the Commonwealth of Massachusetts, 1774–1775* (Cambridge, Mass., 1975), 2077–81, microfiche. The others were John Winslow Sr., John Winslow Jr., Isaac Winslow Sr., Joshua Winslow, Samuel H. Sparhawk, and Colburn Barrell. A copy of the list of "protesters" is found in the Massachusetts Historical Society, *Proceedings* 11, 1869–1870 (Boston, 1871), 394–395. See Douglas Edward Leach, *Roots of Conflict: British Armed Forces and Colonial Americans, 1677–1763* (Chapel Hill, 1986), for details on the difficult relations between the British military and provincial militias, particularly during the French and Indian War.

34. Fairfield Superior Court Papers, Fairfield, Connecticut, bundle dated 1770–1779; Titus Hosmer to Silas Deane, 22 May 1775, in *Correspondence of Silas Deane, 1774–1776*, Connecticut Historical Society, *Collections* 31 vols. (Hartford, 1860–1967), 2:238; Trumbull Papers, Connecticut State Library, V, pt. I, 169a–c, 170a–c. See also Connecticut Archives, Revolutionary War Records, 1:420, 427, 5:397a–b, 404a, 405a–c; and James H. Trumbull, ed., *Public Records of the Colony of Connecticut, 1636–1776*, 25 vols. (Hartford, 1850–1890), 25:51–52, 54, 203–204, 439, 442; and Zeichner, *Connecticut's Years of Controversy*, 231.

35. Hopestill Capen, Petition to the Court of Inquiry, 29 Aug. 1776; Smith, "'Sober Dissent,'" 158–159.

36. Peter Force, ed., *American Archives*, 4th Ser., 6 vols. (Washington, D.C., 1833), 3:851; William H. Nelson, *American Tory* (Oxford, 1961), 97–98; Bruce E. Steiner, *Connecticut Anglicans in the Revolutionary Era: A Study in Communal Tensions* (n.p., 1978), 50; John Sparhawk to Isaac Winslow Jr., 12 Dec. 1775, Winslow Papers, Massachusetts Historical Society, Boston; Smith, " 'Sober Dissent'," 160.
37. John Sparhawk to Isaac Winslow, Jr., 12 Dec. 1775, Winslow Papers, Massachusetts Historical Society, Boston; Daniel Humphreys to Joseph Hastings, 6 Jun. 1777, Sandeman-Barrell Papers; Smith, " 'Sober Dissent'," 160–161.
38. Daniel Humphreys to Joseph Hastings, 6 Jun. 1777, Sandeman-Barrell Papers, Massachusetts Historical Society; Connecticut Archives, Revolutionary War Records, 37:136–144; Robert McDevitt, *Connecticut Attacked: A British Viewpoint, Tryon's Raid on Danbury* (Chester, Conn., 1974), 37–38. It is unclear whether the British or the Patriots burned the church along with the nineteen other buildings that were burned. White submitted a claim for the damage to the meetinghouse totaling £1,637.60.
39. Connecticut Archives, Revolutionary War Records, 8:239a–239c., 8:238b.
40. Connecticut Archives, Revolutionary War Records, 8:240a–240b, 241–242 (emphasis in original). The other subscribers were Oliver Burr, Thomas Gold, Daniel Humphreys, and Theophilus Chamberlain. Stiles, *Literary Diary*, 2:228; Smith, " 'Sober Dissent'," 159–160.
41. Joseph Howe, "Memo on My Father," Joseph Howe Papers, microfilm, reel 22, Public Archives of Nova Scotia; F. E. Crowell, "New Englanders in Nova Scotia," Public Archives of Nova Scotia Scrapbook Collection, MG 9, No. 109, 132–133; Terrence M. Punch and Allan E. Marble, "The Family of John Howe, Halifax, Loyalist and King's Printer," *The Nova Scotia Historical Quarterly* 6 (1976), 317–318; Joseph A. Chisholm, *Howe Letters*, typescript, Public Archives of Nova Scotia, 18.
42. Connecticut Archives, Revolutionary War Records, 13:285, 20:96; Smith, " 'Sober Dissent'," 161.
43. Barrell's petition quoted in E. Alfred Jones, *The Loyalists of Massachusetts*, 22. See also Lorenzo Sabine, *Biographical Sketches of Loyalists of the American Revolution*, 2 vols. (reprint Port Washington, New York, 1966), 2:430–431; Smith, " 'Sober Dissent'," 153–154.

CHAPTER 6

1. The word "sect" comes from the Latin root verb *secare*, which means to follow or obey a teacher or master as a disciple. It does not mean a group that "cuts" itself away from a larger group, specifically, though it is true that most sects derive from schismatic movements. The Glasites cannot be described as Presbyterian schismatics, as they retained almost nothing of Presbyterian theology or ecclesiology. Vergilius Ferm, ed., *An Encyclopedia of Religion* (New York, 1945), 699. See also H. Richard Niebuhr, *The Social Sources of Denominationalism* (New York, 1929).

2. The Dundee church at one point in the late 1700s had nearly 200 members, while the London church had close to 150.
3. The best known Sandemanian besides the movement's leaders is indisputably Michael Faraday, the English chemist who was also an elder in the London church. See Geoffrey Cantor, *Michael Faraday: Sandemanian and Scientist* (New York, 1991).
4. The term "Erastian" refers to the theology of Thomas Erastus (1524–1583), who opposed Calvinism, but advocated state-sponsored Christianity.
5. *Supplementary Letters*, Appendix, vi.
6. A. R. MacEwen, *The Erskines* (Edinburgh, 1900), 67.
7. Gavin Struthers, *The History of the Relief Church* (Glasgow, 1843), 179; A. J. Campbell, *Two Centuries of the Church of Scotland, 1707–1929* (Paisley, 1930), 90–91.
8. The Bereans were followers of John Barclay, who withdrew from the Church of Scotland in 1773 to form an independent church bearing some similarity to the Glasites. The Johnsonians were followers of John Johnson, a General Baptist from Liverpool, who likewise bear a likeness to the Glasites in their church organization.
9. Richard M. Tristano, *The Origins of the Restoration Movement* (Atlanta, Ga., 1988), 59; Holifield, *Theology in America*, 292–300; R[obert] B. S[emple], "Letter to the Editor," *The Christian Baptist* 3 (April 1826), 227.
10. Andrew Fuller, *Strictures on Sandemanianism* in *The Works of Andrew Fuller*, 5 vols. (London, 1831), 2:334.
11. The American churches never referred to themselves as Glasite, but as Sandemanian or Christian. It is interesting that Sandeman never made any effort to reject the use of his name in application to the movement.
12. Patricia U. Bonomi, "Religious Dissent and the Case for American Exceptionalism," in Hoffman and Albert, eds., *Religion in a Revolutionary Age* (Charlottesville, Va., 1994), 51; Clark, *The Language of Liberty*, 305.
13. Fuller, *Strictures on Sandemanianism*, 420–425.
14. *Letters in Correspondence*, 44, 46.
15. Samuel Pike, *An Account of the Christian Practices . . .* (London, 1766), 16–17; Fuller, *Strictures on Sandemanianism*, 444–445.
16. See Mary Beth Norton, *The British Americans: The Loyalist Exiles in England, 1774–1789* (Boston, 1972).
17. See the anonymously published pamphlet by David Jones, *The Quaker Unmask'd* (Philadelphia, 1764), for a prime example of this sort of literature.
18. Jack D. Marietta, *The Reformation of American Quakerism* (Philadelphia, 1984), chaps. 6–10.
19. David Jaffee, "The Village Enlightenment in New England, 1760–1820," *William and Mary Quarterly*, 3rd Ser., 47 (1990), 336.
20. Ernst Troeltsch, *The Social Teaching of the Christian Churches*, 2 vols., Olive Wyon trans. (New York, 1931), 1:328–349.

21. Niebuhr, *The Social Sources of Denominationalism*, 16–21.
22. Mark A. Noll, *America's God*, chaps. 16–17; Dee E. Andrews, *The Methodists and Revolutionary America*.
23. Max Weber, *The Sociology of Religion*, Ephraim Fischoff, trans. (Boston, 1963), chap. 14; Cyril E. Black, "Dynamics of Modernization," in Robert Nisbet, ed., *Social Change* (New York, 1972), 237–270. See also Richard D. Brown, *Modernization* (New York, 1979). On the Catholic Church in revolutionary France, see Timothy Tackett, *Religion, Revolution, and Regional Culture in Eighteenth-Century France: The Ecclesiastical Oath of 1791* (Princeton, 1986); Simon Schama, *Citizens: A Chronicle of the French Revolution* (New York, 1989), 776–779; Malcolm Crook, "Citizen Bishops: Episcopal Elections in the French Revolution," *The Historical Journal* 43 (2000), 955–976. For an astute survey of Christianity in postrevolutionary America, see Nathan O. Hatch, *The Democratization of American Christianity* (New Haven, 1989); and Noll, *America's God*. For a recent assessment of the secularization-modernization paradigm, see Steve Bruce, ed., *Religion and Modernization: Sociologists and Historians Debate the Secularization Thesis* (Oxford, 1992).
24. *Letters in Correspondence*, 44, 46.
25. Williston Walker, "The Sandemanians of New England," 158–160.
26. Eliezer Chater to Daniel Salmon, 12 May 1809, MacIntosh Collection, University of Dundee, Dundee, Scotland; Walker, "The Sandemanians of New England," 158, 161. See also James M. Bailey, *The History of Danbury* (New York, 1896), 299. I have been unable to confirm the existence of the Sandemanian church in Harpersfield. If it did exist, it must not have done so for long.

Epilogue

1. See Mary Beth Norton, *The British-Americans. Letters in Correspondence*, 130.
2. Public Archives of Nova Scotia, Commission Books, R.G. 1, vol. 172, 106, 109; Terrance M. Punch, and Allan E. Marble, "The Family of John Howe, Loyalist and King's Printer," *Nova Scotia Historical Quarterly* 6 (1976), 317–327.
3. Howe resigned from his deputies as Postmaster and King's Printer, citing health problems, in 1817. Alline quoted in Thomas H. Randall, *Halifax: Warden of the North*, rev. ed. (Toronto, 1971), 79, 150–151; H. R. Percy, *Joseph Howe* (Don Mills, 1976), 3–4, 18.
4. Stayner, "The Sandemanian Loyalists," 112; Cantor, *Michael Faraday, Sandemanian and Scientist*. I received an email from a Scotland Yard detective and student of Sandemanianism who reported having spoken in 2000 with a Gerald Sandeman of Edinburgh, who was by his own report the last surviving elder of any Sandemanian church in Britain, and that

the sect was "finished." Jeffrey Tribe to John Howard Smith, 9 Oct. 2006, email.
5. Elias Smith, *A New Testament Dictionary* (Philadelphia, 1812), 5; Alexander Campbell, *The Christian System* (1835; reprint St. Louis, 1890), 115, 168–169; idem, "Experimental Religion," *Millennial Harbinger*, 5th Ser., 4 (1861), 327; idem, "Christian Experience," *Millennial Harbinger*, 1 (1830), 498–499; Michael G. Kenny, *The Perfect Law of Liberty: Elias Smith and the Providential History of America* (Washington, D.C., 1994), 118; Nathan O. Hatch, "The Christian Movement and the Demand for a Theology of the People," *Journal of American History* 67 (1980), 545–567; Tristano, *The Origins of the Restoration Movement*, 59; Holifield, *Theology in America*, 292–295.
6. Alexander Campbell, *Memoirs of Elder Thomas Campbell* (Cincinnati, 1861), 18, n.4; Campbell, *The Christian System*, 134, 18; "The Confirmation of the Testimony," *Millennial Harbinger* 1 (1830), 9; "Experimental Religion," *Millennial Harbinger* 5th Ser., 4 (1861), 327; Holifield, *Theology in America*, 295–297.
7. Alexander Campbell, "Unitarianism as Connected with Christian Union," *Millennial Harbinger* 3rd Ser., 3 (1846), 451–452; "A Restoration of Ancient Things," *The Christian Baptist*, 2nd ed., ed. D. S. Burnet (Cincinnati, 1861), 362; Campbell and N. L. Rice, *A Debate Between Rev. A. Campbell and Rev. N. L. Rice, On the Action, Subject, Design, and Administration of Christian Baptism* (Lexington, Ky., 1844), 611; Holifield, *Theology in America*, 302–305; Noll, *America's God*, 242–244.

Bibliography

DOCUMENTS COLLECTIONS

Beinecke Rare Book and Manuscript Library. Yale University Library. New Haven, Conn.
Betts Autograph Collection. Yale University Library. New Haven, Conn.
Chamberlain Collection. Boston Public Library. Boston, Mass.
Fairfield Superior Court Papers. Connecticut State Library. Hartford, Conn.
Joseph Howe Papers. Public Archives of Nova Scotia. Halifax, N.S.
MacIntosh Collection. University of Dundee. Dundee, Scotland.
Revolutionary War Records, Ser. 1, 1763–1789. Connecticut Archives. Connecticut State Library. Hartford, Conn.
Sandeman-Barrell Papers. Massachusetts Historical Society. Boston, Mass.
Trumbull Papers. Connecticut State Library. Hartford, Conn.
Winslow Family Papers. Massachusetts Historical Society. Boston, Mass.

PRIMARY SOURCES

[   ]. *An Account of the Life and Character of Mr. John Glas.* Edinburgh: W. Coke, 1813.
[   ]. *The Wonderful Appearance of an Angel, Devil & Ghost, to a Gentleman in the Town of Boston, in the Nights of the 14th, 15th, and 16th of October, 1774.* Boston: John Boyle, 1774.
Adams, Eliphalet. *The Gracious Presence of Christ with the Ministers of the Gospel, a ground of great Consolation to Them.* . . . New London, Conn.: T. Green, 1730.
Adams, John. *Legal Papers of John Adams*, 3 vols. L. Kinvin Wroth and Hiller B. Zobel, eds. Cambridge, Mass.: Harvard University Press, 1968.
[Adams, John and Daniel Leonard]. *Novanglus and Massachusettensis.* Boston: Hews & Goss, 1819.

Andrews, Samuel. *A Sermon Preached at Litchfield, in Connecticut. Before a Voluntary Convention of the Clergy of the Church of England of Several Provinces in America, June 13, 1770*. New Haven: Thomas and Samuel Green, 1770.

Avery, David. *The Lord is to be praised for the Triumph of his Power*. Norwich, Conn.: Green & Spooner, 1778.

Backus, Isaac. *True Faith will produce good Works: A Discourse ... with some Remarks on the Writings of Mr. Sandeman*. Boston: D. Kneeland, 1767.

———. *Isaac Backus on Church, State, and Calvinism*. William G. McLoughlin, ed. Cambridge, Mass.: Harvard University Press, 1968.

———. *A History of New England with Particular Reference to the Baptists*, 2nd ed. Newton, Mass.: The Backus Historical Society, 1871, reprint New York: Arno Press, 1969.

Ballantine, John. *The Importance of God's Presence with an Army....* Boston: Edes and Gill, 1756.

Barber, Daniel. *The History of My Own Times*, 2 vols. Washington, D.C.: S. C. Ustick, 1827.

Boston Chronicle. 7–11 Dec. 1769.

Boston Gazette. 5 Sept. 1774.

Boston Gazette, Supplement. 19 Aug. 1765.

Boston, Thomas. *Memoirs of the Life, Times and Writings of Thomas Boston*. Edinburgh: J. Ogle, 1813.

Breck, Robert. *Past Dispensations of Providence Called to Mind....* Hartford, Conn.: Barlow & Babcock, 1784.

Burr, Sr., Aaron. *A Discourse Delivered at New-Ark....* New York: Hugh Gaine, 1755.

———. *The Watchman's Answer to the Question, What of the Night, etc....* New York: S. Kneeland, 1757.

Bushman, Richard L., ed. *The Great Awakening: Documents on the Revival of Religion, 1740–1745*. Chapel Hill: University of North Carolina Press, 1970.

Butterfield, Lyman H., ed. *Adams Family Correspondence*, 2 vols. Cambridge, Mass.: Harvard University Press, 1963.

Calvin, John. *Institutes of the Christian Religion*, Henry Beveridge, trans. Grand Rapids, Mich.: William B. Eerdmans, 1962.

Campbell, Alexander. "Christian Experience." *Millennial Harbinger* 1 (1830), 259–260.

———. "The Confirmation of the Testimony." *Millennial Harbinger* 1 (1830), 8–14.

———. *The Christian System*. 1839; reprint St. Louis: Christian Publishing Co., 1890.

——— and N. L. Rice. *A Debate Between Rev. A. Campbell and Rev. N. L. Rice, On the Action, Subject, Design, and Administration of Christian Baptism*. Lexington, Ken.: A. T. Skillman & Son, 1844.

———. "Unitarianism as Connected with Christian Union." *Millennial Harbinger*, 3rd Ser., (1846), 450–454.

———. "Experimental Religion." *Millennial Harbinger*, 5th Ser., (1861), 325–329.

———. *Memoirs of Elder Thomas Campbell*. Cincinnati: H. S. Bosworth, 1861.

———. "A Restoration of Ancient Things." *The Christian Baptist*, 2nd ed. D. S. Burnet, ed. Cincinnati: D. S. Burnet, 1861.

Capen, Hopestill. Petition to Court of Inquiry. 29 August 1776. Broadside.

Carmichael, John. *A Self-Defensive War Lawful, Proved in a Sermon, Preached at Lancaster, before Captain Ross's Company of Militia.* . . . Philadelphia: John Henry Miller, 1775.

Chandler, Thomas Bradbury. *A Friendly Address to All Reasonable Americans, on the Subject of Our Political Confusions*. Boston: [Mills and Hicks], 1774.

———. *What Think Ye of the Congress Now?* New York: James Rivington, 1755.

Chauncy, Charles. *Marvellous Things done by the right Hand and holy Arm of God.* . . . Boston: T. Fleet, 1745.

———. *Twelve Sermons on the Following Seasonable and Important Subjects.* . . . Boston: D. & J. Kneeland, 1765.

[Church, Benjamin]. *Liberty and Property Vindicated and the St—pm—n burnt*. New London, Conn.: [Kneeland and Adams], 1765.

Claghorne, George S., ed. *The Works of Jonathan Edwards*, Vol. 16. New Haven: Yale University Press, 1998.

Clap, Thomas. *The Greatness and Difficulty of the Work of the Ministry.* . . . Boston: Printed for John Eliot, 1732.

Cobbet, Thomas. *The Civil Magistrates Power in matters of Religion*. London: W. Wilson, 1653.

Cogswell, James. *God, the pious Soldier's Strength and Instructor.* . . . Boston: John Draper, 1757.

Committee of the First Society in Danbury, Connecticut. "A Vindication of the Proceedings of the Eastern Association, in Fairfield County: and of the Council that censured Mr. White, and dismissed him from his Pastoral Relation to the First Church in Danbury: in a letter to the Reverend Joseph Bellamy." New Haven: B. Mecom, 1764.

Connecticut Courant. 5 Dec. 1768.

Cooke, Samuel. *The Violent Destroyed: And Oppressed Delivered.* . . . Boston: Draper and Phillips, 1777.

Cooper, Samuel. *A Sermon Preached before His Excellency Thomas Pownall, Esq.* . . . *October 16, 1759. Upon Occasion of the Success of His Majesty's Arms in the Reduction of Quebec.* . . . Boston: Green & Russell and Edes & Gill, 1759.

Crawford, Michael J. ed. "The Spiritual Travels of Nathan Cole." *William and Mary Quarterly*, 3rd Ser., 33 (1976), 89–126.

Croswell, Andrew. *An Answer to the Rev. Mr. Garden's Three First Letters to the Rev. Mr. Whitefield*.... Boston: S. Kneeland and T. Green, 1741.

———. *What Is Christ to Me, if He Is Not Mine? or, A Seasonable Defence of the Old Protestant Doctrine of Justifying Faith*.... Boston: Rogers and Fowle, 1745.

———. "A Letter to Mr. Robert Sandeman ... by a Minister in Boston." Boston: Kneeland and Adams, 1766.

Davies, Samuel. *Virginia's Danger and Remedy*. Williamsburg: William Hunter, 1756.

———. *The Curse of Cowardice*. Boston: Z. Fowle and S. Draper, 1759.

Deane, Silas, et al. *Correspondence of Silas Deane, 1774–1776. Connecticut Historical Society Collections*, 3 vols. Hartford: Connecticut Historical Society, 1870.

Devotion, John. *The Duty and Interest of a People to Sanctify the Lord of Hosts*.... Hartford, Conn.: Ebenezer Watson, 1777.

[Dove, David James]. *The Quaker Unmask'd*. Philadelphia: [Andrew Steuart], 1764.

Drayton, William Henry. *A Letter from Freeman of South Carolina, to the Deputies of North-America, assembled in the high court of Congress at Philadelphia*. Charles Town, S.C.: Peter Timothy, 1774.

Duffield, George. *A Sermon Preached in the Third Presbyterian Church, in the City of Philadelphia*.... Philadelphia: F. Bailey, 1784.

Dwight, Timothy. *A Valedictory Address to the Young Gentlemen Who Commenced Bachelors of Arts, July 25th, 1776*. New Haven: Thomas & Samuel Green, 1776.

Earle, Alice, ed. *Diary of Anna Green Winslow: A Boston School Girl of 1771*. Boston: Houghton Mifflin Co., 1894.

Edwards, Jonathan. *Some Thoughts concerning the Present Revival of Religion in New England*. Boston: S. Kneeland and T. Green, 1742.

———. *An Humble Inquiry into the Rules of the Word of God*. Boston: S. Kneeland and T. Green, 1749.

"Farmer, in the State of Massachusetts-Bay." *Some Remarks on the Great and Unusual Darkness*.... Danvers, Mass.: E. Russell, 1780.

Fish, Elisha. *The Art of War Lawful, and Necessary for a Christian People, Considered and Enforced*.... Boston: Thomas and John Fleet, 1774.

Fish, Joseph. *Christ Jesus the Physician, and his Blood the Balm recommended for the Healing of a diseased People*. New London, Conn.: Timothy Green, 1760.

[Fisher, Edward?]. *The Marrow of Modern Divinity*. London: "R. W.," 1645.

Force, Peter, ed. *American Archives*, 4th Ser., 6 vols. Washington, D.C.: Government Printing Office, 1833.

Ford, W. C., ed. *Journals of the Continental Congress, 1774–1789*, 34 vols. Washington, D.C.: Government Printing Office, 1904–37.

———, ed. *Warren-Adams Letters, being chiefly a correspondence among John Adams, Samuel Adams, and James Warren ..., 1743–1814*. Massachusetts Historical Society, *Collections*, 2 vols. Boston: Massachusetts Historical Society, 1917–1925.

———, ed. *Letters of William Lee* . . . , *1766–1783*, 3 vols. Reprint New York: New York Times, 1971.

Frothingham, Ebenezer. *The Articles of Faith and Practice, with the Covenant.* . . . Newport, Conn.: J. Frankiln [sic], 1750.

Fuller, Andrew. *The Works of Andrew Fuller*, 5 vols. London: Holdsworth and Ball, 1831.

Gatchel, Samuel. *The Signs of the Times.* . . . Danvers, Mass.: E. Russell, 1781.

General Court of Massachusetts. *A Proclamation for a Public Thanksgiving.* Watertown, Mass.: Benjamin Edes, 1775.

Glas, John. *The Works of Mr. John Glas*, 5 vols., 2nd ed. Perth: R. Morison & Son, 1782.

———. *Remarks upon the Memorial of the Synod of Angus against Mr. Glas and the Sentence of the Commission Deposing Him from the Ministry.* Edinburgh: James Davidson & Co., 1730.

Gordon, William. *History of the Rise, Progress, and Establishment of the Independence of the United States of America* . . . , 3 vols. London: Charles Dilly & James Buckland, 1788.

Haldane, John A. *Strictures upon "Primitive Christianity" by Mr. John Walker.* Edinburgh: W. Oliphant, 1820.

Hervey, James. *The Works of James Hervey*, 7 vols. London: F. & C. Rivington, 1787.

Howe, Joseph. *The Speeches and Public Letters of Joseph Howe*, 3 vols. Joseph A. Chisholm, ed. Halifax, N.S.: Chronicle Publishing Co., 1909.

[Husband, Herman]. *Proposals to Amend and Perfect the Policy of the Government of the United States of America.* Baltimore: Mary Katherine Goddard, 1782.

Jefferson, Thomas. *The Papers of Thomas Jefferson*, 19 vols. Julian P. Boyd et al., eds. Princeton: Princeton University Press, 1950.

Jensen, Merrill, ed. *English Historical Documents, Vol. IX: American Colonial Documents to 1776.* New York: Oxford University Press, 1955.

Johnson, Stephen. *Some Important Observations.* . . . Newport, R.I.: Samuel Hall, 1766.

Jones, David. *Defensive War in a just Cause Sinless.* Philadelphia: Henry Miller, 1775.

Jones, William ed. *The New Evangelical Magazine, and Theological Review*, Vol. 9. London: T. Tegg, 1815.

[Kennedy, John]. *A Scriptural Account of the uncommon Darkness that happened on FRIDAY May 19th, 1780.* Boston: Thomas and John Fleet, 1780.

Keteltas, Abraham. *God Arising and Pleading His People's Cause.* Newburyport, Mass.: John Mycall, 1777.

Langdon, Samuel. *Joy and Gratitude to God for* . . . *the Conquest of Quebec.* Portsmouth, N.H.: Daniel Fowle, 1760.

———. *Government Corrupted by Vice, and recovered by righteousness.* . . . Watertown, Mass.: Benjamin Edes, 1775.

Massachusetts Historical Society. *Proceedings*, Vol. XI. Boston: Massachusetts Historical Society, 1871.

Massachusetts Spy. 8 Sept. 1774.

Mather, Cotton. *A Discourse Concerning the Covenant which God will remember, in the Times of Danger passing over his Church.* Boston: B. Green, 1712.

———. *Ratio Disciplinae Fratrum Nov-Anglorum.* Boston: S. Gerrish, 1726.

Mays, John David, ed. *Letters and Papers of Edmund Pendleton,* 2 vols. Charlottesville: University of Virginia Press, 1967.

Mellwain, C. H., ed. *The Political Works of James I.* Cambridge, Mass.: Harvard University Press, 1918.

Meigs, Josiah. *An Oration Pronounced before a Public Assembly in New Haven.* . . . New Haven: Thomas and Samuel Green, 1782.

Murray, John. *Nehemiah, or the Struggle for Liberty Never in Vain, When Managed with Virtue and Perseverance.* Newburyport, Mass.: John Mycall, 1779.

The New England Magazine and Theological Review, 10 vols. London: T. Tegg, 1815–1824.

Newport Mercury (R.I.). 28 Oct. 1765.

New-York Gazette. 29 Aug. 1765.

Owen, John. *Works of John Owen,* 24 vols. Edinburgh: Johnstone and Hunter, 1843.

Parkman, Ebenezer. *The Diary of Ebenezer Parkman, 1703–1782.* Harriette M. Forbes, ed. Westborough, Mass.: Westborough Historical Society, 1899.

Patten, William. *A Discourse Delivered at Halifax.* . . . Boston: D. Kneeland, 1766.

Pennsylvania Journal. 5 Sept. 1765.

Perry, William Stevens, ed. *Historical Collections Relating to the American Colonial Church,* 5 vols. 1870–1878; reprint New York: AMS Press, 1969.

Peters, Samuel. *General History of Connecticut.* Samuel Jarvis McCormick, ed. London, 1781; reprint Upper Saddle River, N.J.: Prentice-Hall, 1970.

Philbrick, Norman, ed. *Trumpets Sounding: Propaganda Plays of the American Revolution.* New York: B. Blom, 1972.

Pike, Samuel. *An Epistolary Correspondence between S. P(ike) and R. S(andeman).* London: Printed for J. Johnson, 1764.

———. *A plain and full account of the Christian practices of the Church in St. Martin's-le-Grand.* Boston: Z. Fowle, 1766.

Portsmouth Mercury (N.H.). 9 Sept. 1765.

Prince, Thomas. *Extraordinary Events the Doings of God.* . . . Boston: D. Henchman, 1745.

"Printshop Boys." *North End, South End Forever . . . a Commemoration of the fifth of November.* . . . Boston: [n.p.], 1768.

Providence Gazette. 24 Aug. 1765.

Rich, Elisha. *The Number of the Beast Found out by Scriptural Arithmetic.* Chelmsford, Mass.: Nathaniel Coverly, 1775.

Robbins, Ammi R. *Journal of the Rev. Ammi R. Robbins, A Chaplain in the American Army, in the Northern Campaign of 1776.* New Haven: B. L. Hamlen, 1850.

Rowe, John. *The Letters and Diary of John Rowe, Boston Merchant, 1759–1762, 1764–1779.* Anne Rowe Cunningham, ed. Boston, 1903; reprint New York: New York Times, 1969.

Sage, John. *The Fundamental Charter of Presbytery, as It Hath Been Lately Established, in the Kingdom of Scotland, Examin'd and Disprov'd.* London: Printed for C. Brome, 1695.

Sandeman, Robert. *Letters on Theron and Aspasio. Addressed to the Author.* Edinburgh, 1757; reprint New York: John S. Taylor, 1838.

———, John Glas et al. *Letters in Correspondence.* Dundee: Hill & Alexander, 1851.

———. *Discourses on Passages of Scripture: with Essays and Letters.* Dundee: George Sandeman, 1857.

——————— and John Glas. *Supplementary Volume of Letters of John Glas, Robert Sandeman, etc.* Perth: Morison and Duncan, 1865.

———. *Thoughts on Christianity in a Letter to a Friend from Robert Sandeman.* Edinburgh: George Waterson & Sons, 1891.

Sargent, Winthrop, ed. *Letters of John Andrews.* Cambridge: Cambridge University Press, 1866.

Saunders, William L., ed. *The Colonial Records of North Carolina*, 10 vols. Raleigh: P. M. Hale, 1886–1890.

Schneider, Herbert and Carol, eds. *Samuel Johnson: President of King's College. His Career and Writings*, 3 vols. New York: Columbia University Press, 1929.

Seabury, Samuel. *Letters of a Westchester Farmer, 1774–1775.* Clarence H. Vance, ed. White Plains, N.Y.: Westchester County Historical Society, 1930.

Sedgwick, Romney, ed. *Letters from George III to Lord Bute, 1756–1766.* London: Macmillan and Co., 1939.

Sherwood, Samuel. *The Church's Flight into the Wilderness: An Address on the Times.* New York: S. Loudon, 1776.

Shurtleff, N. B., ed. *Records of the Governor and Company of the Massachusetts Bay in New England*, 5 vols. Boston: W. White, 1853–1854.

Smith, James, and Robert Ferrier. *The Case of James Smith, late Minister at Newburn, and of Robert Ferrier, late Minister at Large, truly presented and defended.* Edinburgh: A. Donaldson, 1768.

South Carolina Gazette. 31 Oct. 1765.

Spalding, John. *Synaxis Sacra; Or, A Collection of Sermons Preached at Several Communions; Together with Speeches at the Tables, both before, at, and after that Work*. Edinburgh: Printed by the Heirs and Successors of Andrew Anderson, 1703.

Stein, Stephen J. ed. *The Works of Jonathan Edwards*, Vol. 5. New Haven: Yale University Press, 1977.

Stevens, Elisha. *Fragments of Memoranda Written by him in the War of the Revolution*. Meriden, Conn.: H. Wales Lines, 1922.

Stiles, Ezra. *A Discourse on the Christian Union*. Boston: Edes and Gill, 1761.

———. *The Literary Diary of Ezra Stiles*, 3 vols. Franklin B. Dexter, ed. New York: Charles Scribner's Sons, 1901.

———. *Extracts from the Itineraries and other Miscellanies of Ezra Stiles ... with a Selection from his Correspondence*. Franklin B. Dexter, ed. New Haven: Yale University Press, 1916.

Tennent, John. *The Nature of Regeneration Opened*. Boston, 1735.

Trumbull, James H., ed. *The Public Records of the Colony of Connecticut, 1636–1776*, 15 vols. Hartford: Lockwood & Brainerd Co., 1851.

[Various]. *The Declaration of the Congregational Ministers, in and about London, against Antinomian Errours, and Ignorant and Scandalous Persons Intruding Themselves into the Ministry*. London: Printed for John Harley, 1699.

Ward, Nathaniel. *The Simple Cobbler of Agawam*, 5th ed. Boston: Printed for Daniel Henchman, 1713.

Washington, George. *The Papers of George Washington: Colonial Series*, 10 vols. W. W. Abbot, ed. Charlottesville: University Press of Virginia, 1983–1995.

Wesley, John. *The Letters of John Wesley*. John Telford, ed., 8 vols. London: Epworth Press, 1931.

West, Samuel. *An Anniversary Sermon. Preached at Plymouth, December 22nd, 1777*. Boston: Draper and Folsom, 1778.

Williams, Roger. *The Bloody Tenent of Persecution*. London: Matthew Symmons, 1647.

———. *The Bloody Tenent Yet More Bloody*. London: Printed for Giles Calvert, 1652.

Willison, John. *The Whole Practical Works.* ... W. M. Hetherington, ed. Aberdeen: Mackay, Bachelor and Co., 1817.

Winchester, Elhanan. *Thirteen Hymns Suited to the Present Times*. Baltimore: M. K. Goddard, 1776.

Wodrow, Robert. *Analecta: or Materials for a History of Remarkable Providences: Mostly Relating to Scotch Ministers and Christians*, 4 vols. Edinburgh: Matiland Club, 1842.

Wroth, Kinvin L. et al., eds. *Province in Rebellion: A Documentary History of the Founding of the Commonwealth of Massachusetts, 1774–1775*. Cambridge, Mass.: Harvard University Press, 1975 (microform).

Zubly, John Joachim. *The Law of Liberty: A Sermon on American Affairs preached at the opening of the Provincial Congress of Georgia.* Philadelphia: Henry Miller, 1775.

SECONDARY SOURCES

Ahlstrom, Sydney E. *Theology in America: The Major Protestant Voices from Puritanism to Neo-Orthodoxy.* Indianapolis: Bobbs-Merrill Co., 1967.
———. "The Problem of Religious History in America." *Church History* 39 (1970), 224–235.
———. *A Religious History of the American People.* New Haven: Yale University Press, 1972.
Albanese, Catherine L. *Sons of the Fathers: The Civil Religion of the American Revolution.* Philadelphia: Temple University Press, 1976.
Albion, Robert G. *Forests and Sea Power.* Cambridge, Mass.: Harvard University Press, 1926.
Alexander, Archibald. *Biographical Sketches of the Founder and Principal Alumni of the Log College.* Philadelphia: Presbyterian Board of Publication, 1851.
Alexander, Jon T. "Christian Attitudes toward War in Colonial America." *Church and Society* 64 (1974), 16–24.
Anderson, George P. "Ebenezer Mackintosh: Stamp Act Rioter and Patriot." *Publications of the Colonial Society of Massachusetts* 26. Boston: Colonial Society of Massachusetts, 1927.
Andrews, Charles M. "The Boston Merchants and the Non-Importation Movement." *Publications of the Colonial Society of Massachusetts* 19. Boston: Colonial Society of Massachusetts, 1916–1918.
Andrews, Dee E. *The Methodists and Revolutionary America, 1760–1800.* Princeton: Princeton University Press, 2000.
Andrews, Edward Deming. *The People Called Shakers: A Search for the Perfect Society,* rev. ed. New York: Dover Publications, 1963.
Bailey, James M. *The History of Danbury.* New York: Burr Printing House, 1896.
Bailyn, Bernard. *The Ideological Origins of the American Revolution.* Cambridge, Mass.: Harvard University Press, 1967.
———. "Religion and Revolution: Three Biographical Studies." *Perspectives in American History* 4 (1970), 83–169.
Barnes, R. M. *The Uniforms and History of the Scottish Regiments.* London: Sphere, 1960.
Beaton, Donald. "The Old Scots Independents." *Records of the Scottish Church History Society,* Vol. 3. Edinburgh: Scottish Church History Society, 1929.
Becker, George. "Pietism's Confrontation with Enlightenment Rationalism: An Examination of the Relation between Ascetic Protestantism and Science." *Journal for the Scientific Study of Religion* 30 (1991), 139–158.

Beneke, Chris. *Beyond Toleration: The Religious Origins of American Pluralism.* New York: Oxford University Press, 2006.

Bercovitch, Sacvan. *The Puritan Origins of the American Self.* New Haven: Yale University Press, 1975.

———. *The American Jeremiad.* Madison: University of Wisconsin Press, 1978.

Berens, John F. *Providence and Patriotism in Early America, 1640–1815.* Charlottesville: University Press of Virginia, 1978.

Bernstein, Barton J., ed. *Towards a New Past: Dissenting Essays in American History.* New York: Pantheon Books, 1968.

Black, Jeremy. "The Catholic Threat and the British Press in the 1720s and 1730s." *Journal of Religious History* 12 (1983), 364–381.

Bloch, Ruth H. *Visionary Republic: Millennial Theme in American Thought.* Cambridge: Cambridge University Press, 1985.

Bolles, John R., and Anna B. Williams. *The Rogerenes. Some Hitherto Unpublished Annals Belonging to the Colonial Society of Connecticut.* Boston: Stanhope Press, 1904.

Bonomi, Patricia U. *Under the Cope of Heaven: Religion, Society, and Politics in Colonial America.* New York: Oxford University Press, 1986.

Boudinot, Elias. *The Life of William Tennent, Late Pastor of the Presbyterian Church at Freehold, N.J.,* rev. ed. Trenton, N.J.: E. B. Adams, 1833.

Brackney, William H. *Baptists in North America: A Historical Perspective.* Oxford and Malden, Mass.: Blackwell, 2006.

Bridenbaugh, Carl. *Mitre and Sceptre: Transatlantic Faiths, Ideas, Personalities, and Politics.* New York: Oxford University Press, 1962.

———. *Cities in Revolt: Urban Life in America, 1743–1776.* New York: Oxford University Press, 1964.

Brigham, Clarence. *Paul Revere's Engravings.* New York: Atheneum Books, 1969.

Brock, Peter C. *Pacifism in the United States from the Colonial Era to the First World War.* Princeton: Princeton University Press, 1968.

Brock, W. R. *Scotus Americanus: A survey of the sources for links between Scotland and America in the eighteenth century.* Edinburgh: Edinburgh University Press, 1982.

Brooke, John. *King George III.* New York: McGraw-Hill, 1972.

Brown, Callum G. *Religion and Society in Scotland since 1707,* rev. ed. Edinburgh: Edinburgh University Press, 1997.

Brown, John. *Memoirs of the Life and Character of the Late Rev. James Hervey, A.M.* London: Ogle, Duncan and Co., 1822.

Brown, Richard D. *Revolutionary Politics in Massachusetts: The Boston Committee of Correspondence and the Towns, 1772–1774.* Cambridge, Mass.: Harvard University Press, 1970.

———. *Modernization: The Transformation of American Life, 1600–1865.* New York: Hill and Wang, 1979.

———. *Knowledge Is Power: The Diffusion of Information in Early America, 1700–1865*. New York: Oxford University Press, 1989.
Brown, Wallace. *The Good Americans: The Loyalists in the American Revolution*. New York: William Morrow and Co., 1969.
Bruce, Steve, ed. *Religion and Modernization: Sociologists and Historians Debate the Secularization Thesis*. Oxford: Oxford University Press, 1992.
Buckroyd, Julia. *Church and State in Scotland, 1660–1681*. Edinburgh: J. Donald, 1980.
Burleigh, J. H. S. *A Church History of Scotland*. Oxford: Oxford University Press, 1960.
Bushman, Richard L. *From Puritan to Yankee: Character and the Social Order in Connecticut, 1690–1765*. Cambridge, Mass.: Harvard University Press, 1967.
Butler, Jon. "Enthusiasm Described and Decried: The Great Awakening as Interpretative Fiction." *Journal of American History* 69 (1982), 305–325.
———. *The Huguenots in America: A Refugee People in New World Society*. Cambridge, Mass.: Harvard University Press, 1983.
———. *Awash in a Sea of Faith: Christianizing the American People*. Cambridge, Mass.: Harvard University Press, 1990.
———. *Becoming America: The Revolution before 1776*. Cambridge, Mass.: Harvard University Press, 2000.
Calhoon, Robert M. *The Loyalists in Revolutionary America, 1760–1781*. New York: Harcourt Brace Jovanovich, 1973.
———, Timothy M. Barnes, and George Rawlyk, eds. *Loyalists and Community in North America*. Wesport, Conn.: Greenwood Press, 1994.
Campbell, A. J. *Two Centuries of the Church of Scotland, 1707–1929*. Paisley: A. Gardner, Ltd., 1930.
Cantor, Geoffrey. *Michael Faraday: Sandemanian and Scientist*. New York: St. Martin's Press, 1991.
Casiday, Augustine, and Frederick W. Norris, eds. *The Cambridge History of Christianity, Vol. II: Constantine to 600*. Cambridge: Cambridge University Press, 2007.
Church, James. *Patterns of Reform: Continuity and Change in the Reformation Church*. Edinburgh: University of Edinburgh Press, 1989.
Clark, Charles E. *The Public Prints: The Newspaper in Anglo-American Culture, 1665–1740*. New York: Oxford University Press, 1994.
Clark, J. C. D. *The Language of Liberty, 1660–1832: Political Discourse and Social Dynamics in the Anglo-American World*. Cambridge: Cambridge University Press, 1993.
Coffey, John. *Politics, Religion and the British Revolutions: The Mind of Samuel Rutherford*. Cambridge: Cambridge University Press, 1997.
Cogliano, Francis D. *No King, No Popery: Anti-Catholicism in Revolutionary New England*. Westport, Conn.: Greenwood Press, 1995.

Cook, Jr., Edward M. *The Fathers of the Towns: Leadership and Community Structure in Eighteenth-Century New England.* Baltimore: Johns Hopkins University Press, 1976.

Corrigan, John. *The Prism of Piety: Catholic Congregational Clergy at the Beginning of the Enlightenment.* New York: Oxford University Press, 1991.

Crook, Malcolm. "Citizen Bishops: Episcopal Elections in the French Revolution." *The Historical Journal* 43 (2000), 955–976.

Daniels, Bruce. *The Connecticut Town: Growth and Development, 1635–1790.* Middletown, Conn.: Wesleyan University Press, 1979.

Davidson, James West. *The Logic of Millennial Thought: Eighteenth-Century New England.* New Haven: Yale University Press, 1977.

Davis, Natalie Zemon. *Society and Culture in Early Modern France: Eight Essays by Natalie Zemon Davis.* Stanford: Stanford University Press, 1975.

Donaldson, Gordon. *The Scottish Reformation.* Cambridge: Cambridge University Press, 1960.

———. "Scotland's Conservative North in the Sixteenth and Seventeenth Centuries." *Transactions of the Royal Historical Society*, 5th Ser., 16 (1966), 65–80.

Douglas, Ann. *The Feminization of American Culture.* New York: Alfred A. Knopf, 1977.

Dow, F. D. *Cromwellian Scotland, 1651–1660.* Edinburgh: Edinburgh University Press, 1979.

Dwight, S. E. *The Life of President Edwards....* New York, 1830.

Eaton, W. H. *The Famous Mather Byles: The Noted Boston Tory Preacher, Poet, and Wit, 1707–1788.* Boston: Butterfield, 1914.

Endy, Jr., Melvin B. "Just War, Holy War, and Millennialism in Revolutionary America," *William and Mary Quarterly*, 3rd Ser., 42 (1985), 3–25.

Ellis, John Tracy. *Catholics in Colonial America.* Baltimore: Johns Hopkins University Press, 1965.

Fawcett, Arthur. *The Cambuslang Revival: The Scottish Evangelical Revival of the Eighteenth Century.* London: Banner of Truth Trust, 1971.

Ferguson, William. *Scotland's Relations with England: A Survey to 1707.* Edinburgh: Edinburgh University Press, 1977.

Ferm, Vergilius, ed. *An Encyclopedia of Religion.* New York: The Philosophical Library, 1945.

Freeman, Thomas S. "'The reik of Maister Patrik Hammyltoun': John Foxe, John Winram, and the Martyrs of the Scottish Reformation." *Sixteenth Century Journal* 27 (1996), 43–60.

Gaustad, Edwin Scott. *The Great Awakening in New England.* New York: HarperCollins, 1957.

———, and Philip Barlow. *New Historical Atlas of Religion in America.* New York: Oxford University Press, 2000.

Gildrie, Richard P. *The Profane, the Civil & the Godly: The Reformation of Manners in Orthodox New England, 1679–1749.* University Park: Pennsylvania State University Press, 1994.

Gilje, Paul. *The Road to Mobacracy: Popular Disorder in New York City, 1763–1834.* Chapel Hill: University of North Carolina Press, 1987.

Gill, Robin, ed. *Readings in Modern Theology: Britain and America.* Nashville: Abingdon Press, 1995.

Gipson, Lawrence H. *The British Empire before the American Revolution,* Vol. 10: *The Triumphant Empire: Thunder-Clouds Gather in the West, 1763–1766.* New York: Alfred A. Knopf, 1961.

Goen, C. C. *Revivalism and Separatism in New England, 1740–1800.* New Haven: Yale University Press, 1962.

Gollin, Gillian L. *Moravians in Two Worlds: A Study of Changing Communities.* New York: Columbia University Press, 1967.

Gow, Andrew Colin, and Richard Connors, eds. *Anglo-American Millennialism from Milton to the Millerites.* Leiden: Brill Academic Publishers, 2004.

Grasso, Christopher. *A Speaking Aristocracy: The Transformation of Public Discourse in Eighteenth-Century Connecticut.* Chapel Hill: University of North Carolina Press, 1999.

Greene, Jack P., and J. R. Pole, eds. *Colonial British America: Essays in the New History of the Early Modern Era.* Baltimore: Johns Hopkins University Press, 1984.

———. *Pursuits of Happiness: The Social Development of Early Modern British Colonies and the Formation of American Culture.* Chapel Hill: University of North Carolina Press, 1988.

Gura, Philip F. *A Glimpse of Sion's Glory: Puritan Radicalism in New England, 1620–1660.* Middletown, Conn.: Wesleyan University Press, 1984.

Haldane, Alex. *Lives of Robert and James Haldane,* 4th ed. Edinburgh, 1855; reprint Edinburgh: Banner of Truth Trust, 1990.

Hall, David D. *Worlds of Wonder, Days of Judgment: Popular Religious Belief in Early New England.* Cambridge, Mass.: Harvard University Press, 1989.

Haller, William. *The Elect Nation: The Meaning and Relevance of Foxe's Book of Martyrs.* New York: Harper and Row, 1963.

Hankins, Jean F. "A Different Kind of Loyalist: The Sandemanians of New England during the Revolutionary War." *New England Quarterly* 60 (1987), 223–249.

Hanson, Charles P. *Necessary Virtue: The Pragmatic Origins of Religious Liberty in New England.* Charlottesville: University Press of Virginia, 1998.

Hatch, Nathan O. *The Sacred Cause of Liberty: Republican Thought and the Millennium in Revolutionary New England.* New Haven: Yale University Press, 1977.

———. "The Christian Movement and the Demand for a Theology of the People." *Journal of American History* 67 (1980), 545–567.

———. *The Democratization of American Christianity*. New Haven: Yale University Press, 1989.

Healey, Robert M. "Waiting for Deborah: John Knox and Four Ruling Queens." *Sixteenth Century Journal* 25 (1994), 371–386.

Heimert, Alan. *Religion and the American Mind from the Great Awakening to the Revolution*. Cambridge, Mass.: Harvard University Press, 1966.

Heitzenrater, Richard P. *Mirror and Memory: Reflections on Early Methodism*. Nashville: University of Tennessee Press, 1989.

Henderson, G. D. *Religious Life in Seventeenth-Century Scotland*. Cambridge: Cambridge University Press, 1937.

Hill, Jonathan. *The History of Christian Thought*. Oxford: Oxford University Press, 2003.

Hoerder, Dirk. *People and Mobs: Crowd Action in Revolutionary Massachusetts, 1765–1780*. New York: Academic Press, 1977.

Hoffman, Ronald. *A Spirit of Dissension: Economics, Politics, and the Revolution in Maryland*. Baltimore: Johns Hopkins University Press, 1973.

———, and Peter J. Albert, eds. *Religion in a Revolutionary Age*. Charlottesville: University of Virginia Press, 1994.

Holifield, E. Brooks. *Theology in America: Christian Thought from the Age of the Puritans to the Civil War*. New Haven: Yale University Press, 2003.

Holton, Woody. *Forced Founders: Indians, Debtors, Slaves & the Making of the American Revolution in Virginia*. Chapel Hill: University of North Carolina Press, 1999.

Hyman, Elizabeth Hannan. "A Church Militant: Scotland, 1661–1690." *Sixteenth Century Journal* 26 (1995), 49–74.

Ingram, Martin. "Ridings, Rough Music, and the 'Reform of Popular Culture' in Early Modern England." *Past and Present* 105 (1984), 79–113.

Isaac, Rhys. "Evangelical Revolt: The Nature of the Baptists' Challenge to the Traditional Order in Virginia, 1765–1775." *William and Mary Quarterly*, 3rd Ser., 31 (1974), 345–368.

———. *The Transformation of Virginia, 1740–1790*. Chapel Hill: University of North Carolina Press, 1982.

Jaffee, David. "The Village Enlightenment in New England, 1760–1820." *William and Mary Quarterly*, 3rd Ser., 47 (1990), 327–346.

Jones, E. Alfred. *The Loyalists of Massachusetts: Their Memorials, Petitions and Claims*. London: St. Catherine's Press, 1930.

Jones, Rufus M. *The Quakers in the American Colonies*. Reprint, New York: W. W. Norton, 1966.

Jones, William, ed. *Memoir of Archibald M'Lean*. London: Printed for William Jones, 1823.

Kellems, Jesse R. *Alexander Campbell and the Disciples*. New York: R. R. Smith, Inc., 1930.

Kenney III, William Howland. "Alexander Garden and George Whitefield: The Significance of Revivalism in South Carolina, 1738–1741. *South Carolina Historical Magazine* 71 (1970), 3–28.

Kenny, Michael G. *The Perfect Law of Liberty: Elias Smith and the Providential History of America*. Washington, D.C.: Smithsonian Institution Press, 1994.

Kim, Sung Bok. "The Limits of Politicization in the American Revolution: The Experience of Westchester County, New York." *Journal of American History* 80 (1993), 868–889.

Kirk, James. *Patterns of Reform: Continuity and Change in the Reformation Kirk*. Edinburgh: T. & T. Clark, 1989.

Knollenberg, Bernard. "The Revolutionary Correspondence of Nathanael Greene and John Adams." *Rhode Island History* 1 (1942), 44–83.

Kurtz, Stephen G., and James H. Hutson, eds. *Essays on the American Revolution*. Chapel Hill: University of North Carolina Press, 1973.

Lambert, Frank. *"Pedlar in Divinity": George Whitefield and the Transatlantic Revivals, 1737–1770*. Princeton: Princeton University Press, 1994.

———. *Inventing the "Great Awakening."* Princeton: Princeton University Press, 1999.

Lamont, Stewart. *The Swordbearer: John Knox and the European Reformation*. London: Hodder & Stoughton, 1991.

Landsman, Ned C. "Revivalism and Nativism in the Middle Colonies." *American Quarterly* 34 (1982), 149–164.

———. *Scotland and Its First American Colony, 1683–1765*. Princeton: Princeton University Press, 1985.

———. *Nation and Province in the First British Empire: Scotland and the Americas, 1600–1800*. Lewisburg, Penn. and London: Associated University Presses, 2001.

Lane, Anthony N. S., ed. *A Concise History of Christian Thought*, rev. ed. London and York: T. and T. Clark, 2006.

Leach, Douglas Edward. *Roots of Conflict: British Armed Forces and Colonial Americans, 1677–1763*. Chapel Hill: University of North Carolina Press, 1986.

Lee, Jr., Maurice. *Government by Pen: Scotland under James VI and I*. Urbana: Illinois University Press, 1980.

———. *The Road to Revolution: Scotland under Charles I, 1625–1637*. Urbana: Illinois University Press, 1985.

Lee, Sydney, ed. *Dictionary of National Biography*, 66 vols. London: Smith, Elder & Co., 1885–1901.

Lossing, Benson J. *The Life and Times of Philip Schuyler*, 2 vols. New York: Sheldon & Co., 1873.

Lynch, Michael. *Edinburgh and the Reformation*. Edinburgh: Edinburgh University Press, 1981.

MacEwen, A. R. *The Erskines*. Edinburgh: Oliphant, Anderson & Ferrier, 1900.

Macleod, John. "The Reformed Faith in Modern Scotland." *Princeton Theological Review* 24 (1926), 177–205.

MacMaster, Richard K., Samuel L. Horst, and Robert F. Ulle, eds. *Conscience in Crisis: Mennonites and Other Peace Churches in America: Interpretations and Documents, 1739–1789*. Scottsdale, Penn.: Herald Press, 1979.

Maier, Pauline. "Popular Uprisings and Civil Authority in Eighteenth-Century America." *William and Mary Quarterly*, 3rd Ser., 27 (1970), 3–35.

———. *From Resistance to Revolution: Colonial Radicals and the Development of American Opposition to Britain, 1765–1776*. New York: Vintage Books, 1972.

Makey, Walter. *The Church of the Covenant, 1637–1651*. Edinburgh: John Donald Publishers, 1979.

Marcus, Jacob R. *The Colonial American Jew, 1492–1776*, 3 vols. Detroit: Wayne State University Press, 1970.

Marietta, Jack D. *The Reformation of American Quakerism, 1748–1783*. Philadelphia: University of Pennsylvania Press, 1984.

Marini, Stephen A. *Radical Sects of Revolutionary New England*. Cambridge, Mass.: Harvard University Press, 1982.

Martin, James Kirby. *Benedict Arnold, Revolutionary Hero: An American Warrior Reconsidered*. New York: New York University Press, 1997.

McConville, Brendan. *The King's Three Faces: The Rise and Fall of Royal America, 1688–1776*. Chapel Hill: University of North Carolina Press, 2006.

McCusker, John J., and Russell Menard. *The Economy of British America, 1607–1789*. Chapel Hill: University of North Carolina Press, 1985.

McDevitt, Robert. *Connecticut Attacked: A British Viewpoint. Tryon's Raid on Danbury*. Chester, Conn.: Pequot Press, 1974.

McDonnell, Michael A. "Mobilization and Political Culture in Revolutionary Virginia: The Failure of the Minutemen and the Revolution from Below." *Journal of American History* 85 (1998), 946–981.

McGoldrick, James Edward. "Patrick Hamilton, Luther's Scottish Disciple." *Sixteenth Century Journal* 18 (1987), 81–88.

McKerrow, John. *History of the Secession Church*. Edinburgh: A. Fullarton, 1854.

McLoughlin, William G. "The American Revolution as a Religious Revival: 'The Millennium in One Country.'" *New England Quarterly* 40 (1967), 99–110.

———. *New England Dissent, 1630–1833: The Baptists and the Separation of Church and State*, 2 vols. Cambridge, Mass.: Harvard University Press, 1971.

———. "'Enthusiasm for Liberty': The Great Awakening as the Key to the Revolution." *Proceedings of the American Antiquarian Society* 87 (1977), 69–96.

———. *Soul Liberty: The Baptists' Struggle in New England, 1630–1833*, 2 vols. Hanover, N.H.: University Press of New England, 1991.

McRee, Griffith J. *Life and Correspondence of James Iredell*, 2 vols. New York: D. Appleton, 1857.
Middlekauff, Robert. *The Glorious Cause: The American Revolution, 1763–1789*. New York: Oxford University Press, 1982.
Miller, John. *Popery and Politics in England, 1660–1688*. Cambridge: Cambridge University Press, 1973.
Miller, Perry. *The New England Mind: The Seventeenth Century*, 2nd ed. Cambridge, Mass.: Harvard University Press, 1953.
———. *The New England Mind: From Colony to Province*, 2nd ed. Cambridge, Mass.: Harvard University Press, 1961.
Morgan, Edmund S., and Helen S. Morgan. *The Stamp Act Crisis: Prologue to Revolution*. Chapel Hill: University of North Carolina Press, 1953.
———. *Visible Saints: The History of a Puritan Idea*. Ithaca, N.Y.: Cornell University Press, 1963.
Nelson, William H. *The American Tory*. Oxford: Oxford University Press, 1961.
Niebuhr, H. Richard. *The Social Sources of Denominationalism*. New York: Henry Holt and Co., 1929.
Nisbet, Robert, ed. *Social Change*. New York: Harper and Row, 1972.
Noll, Mark A. *Christians in the American Revolution*. Grand Rapids, Mich.: William B. Eerdmans, 1977.
———. *America's God: From Jonathan Edwards to Abraham Lincoln*. New York: Oxford University Press, 2002.
Norton, Mary Beth. *The British Americans: The Loyalist Exiles in England, 1774–1789*. Boston: Little, Brown Co., 1972.
O'Brien, Susan. "A Transatlantic Community of Saints: The Great Awakening and the First Evangelical Network, 1735–1755." *American Historical Review* 91 (1986), 811–832.
Olton, Charles S. *Artisans for Independence: Philadelphia Mechanics and the American Revolution*. Syracuse, N.Y.: Syracuse University Press, 1978.
Palmer, R. R. *The Age of the Democratic Revolution: A Political History of Europe and America, 1760–1800*, 2 vols. Princeton: Princeton University Press, 1959, 1964.
Percy, H. R. *Joseph Howe*. Don Mills, Ont.: Fitzhenry & Whiteside, 1976.
Preus, Robert D. *The Theology of Post-Reformation Lutheranism*, 2 vols. St. Louis: Concordia Publishing House, 1970.
Punch, Terrance M., and Allan E. Marble. "The Family of John Howe, Loyalist and King's Printer." *Nova Scotia Historical Quarterly* 6 (1976), 317–327.
Raboteau, Albert J. *Slave Religion: The "Invisible Institution" in the Antebellum South*. New York: Oxford University Press, 1978.
Randall, Thomas H. *Halifax: Warden of the North*, rev. ed. Toronto: McClelland and Stewart, 1971.
Rees, Thomas. *The History of Protestant Nonconformity in Wales*, 2nd ed. London: John Snow, 1833.

Reid, W. Stanford. "John Knox's Theology of Political Government." *Sixteenth Century Journal* 19 (1988), 529–540.

Rhoden, Nancy L. *Revolutionary Anglicanism: The Colonial Church of England Clergy during the American Revolution.* New York: New York University Press, 1999.

Royster, Charles M. *A Revolutionary People at War: The Continental Army and the American Character, 1775–1783.* Chapel Hill: University of North Carolina Press, 1979.

Sabine, Lorenzo. *Biographical Sketches of Loyalists of the American Revolution, with an Historical Essay,* 2 vols. 1864; reprint Port Washington, N.Y.: Kennikat Press, Inc., 1966.

Schama, Simon. *Citizens: A Chronicle of the French Revolution.* New York: Vintage Books, 1989.

Schlesinger, Sr., Arthur M. *The Colonial Merchants and the American Revolution.* New York: F. Ungar, 1957.

Schlesinger, Jr., Arthur M., and Morton White, eds. *Paths of American Thought.* Boston: Houghton Mifflin, 1963.

Schmidt, Leigh Eric. "'A Second and Glorious Reformation': The New Light Extremism of Andrew Croswell." *William and Mary Quarterly,* 3rd Ser., 43 (1986), 214–244.

———. *Holy Fairs: Scotland and the Making of American Revivalism,* 2nd ed. Grand Rapids, Mich.: William B. Eerdmans, 2001.

Schwartz, Hillel. *The French Prophets: The History of a Millenarian Group in Eighteenth-Century England.* Berkeley: University of California Press, 1980.

Scot, Hew, ed. *Fasti Ecclesiae Scoticanae,* 7 vols. Edinburgh: W. Paterson, 1915.

Sell, Alan P. F. *The Great Debate: Calvinism, Arminianism, and Salvation.* Grand Rapids, Mich.: William B. Eerdmans, 1982.

Shaw, Peter. *American Patriots and the Rituals of Revolution.* Cambridge, Mass.: Harvard University Press, 1981.

Sher, Richard B., and Jeffrey R. Smitten, eds. *Scotland and America in the Age of Enlightenment.* Princeton: Princeton University Press, 1990.

Shipton, Clifford K. *Sibley's Harvard Graduates,* 18 vols. Boston: Massachusetts Historical Society, 1933.

Smith, Billy G. "Material Lives of Laboring Philadelphians, 1750–1800." *William and Mary Quarterly,* 3rd Ser., 38 (1981), 163–202.

Smith, John Howard. "'Sober Dissent' and 'Spirited Conduct': The Sandemanians and the American Revolution, 1765–1783." *Historical Journal of Massachusetts* 28 (Summer 2000), 3–25.

Smout, T. C., ed. *Miscellany of the Scottish History Society,* 10 vols. Edinburgh: T. & A. Constable, 1893–1965.

Sobel, Mechal. *Trabelin' On: The Slave Journey to an Afro-Baptist Faith.* Westport, Conn.: Greenwood Press, 1979.

Stayner, Charles St. C. "The Sandemanian Loyalists." *Collections of the Royal Nova Scotia Historical Society* 29 (1951), 62–123.

Steiner, Bruce E. *Connecticut Anglicans in the Revolutionary Era: A Study in Communal Tensions.* Hartford: American Revolution Bicentennial Commission of Connecticut, 1978.

Stevenson, David. *The Scottish Revolution, 1637–1644: The Triumph of the Covenanters.* Newton Abbot: David and Charles, 1973.

———. *Revolution and Counter-Revolution in Scotland, 1644–1651.* London: Royal Historical Society, 1977.

Stoeffler, F. Ernest, ed. *Continental Pietism and Early American Christianity.* Grand Rapids, Mich.: William B. Eerdmans, 1976.

Stout, Harry S. *The New England Soul: Preaching and Religious Culture in Colonial New England.* New York: Oxford University Press, 1986.

———, and D. G. Hart, eds. *New Directions in American Religious History.* New York: Oxford University Press, 1997.

Struthers, Gavin. *The History of the Relief Church.* Glasgow: L. A. Fullarton, 1843.

Sweet, William Warren. *Methodism in American History*, rev. ed. New York and Nashville: Abingdon Press, 1954.

Tackett, Timothy. *Religion, Revolution, and Regional Culture in Eighteenth-Century France: The Ecclesiastical Oath of 1791.* Princeton: Princeton University Press, 1986.

Tanis, James R. *Dutch Calvinistic Pietism in the Middle Colonies: A Study in the Life and Theology of Theodorus Jacobus Frelinghuysen.* The Hague: Martinus Nijhoff, 1967.

Tristano, Richard M. *The Origins of the Restoration Movement: An Intellectual History.* Atlanta: Glenmary Research Center, 1988.

Troeltsch, Ernst. *The Social Teaching of the Christian Churches*, 2 vols. Olive Wyon, trans. New York: Macmillan, 1931.

Trumbull, Benjamin. *A Complete History of Connecticut, Civil and Ecclesiastical, from the Emigration of Its First Planters. . . .*, 2 vols. New London, Conn.: Utley, 1898.

Tyerman, Luke. *The Oxford Methodists.* London: Harper and Row, 1873.

Walker, Williston. *The Creeds and Platforms of Congregationalism.* New York: Charles A. Scribner, 1893.

———. "The Sandemanians of New England." *American Historical Association Annual Report for 1901.* Washington, D.C.: American Historical Association, 1902.

Wallmann, Johannes. *Pietismus und Neuzeit: Ein Jahrbuch zur Geschichte des neueren Protestantismus.* Bielfeld: Luther-Verlag, 1974.

Warner, Michael. *Letters of the Republic: Publication and the Public Sphere in Eighteenth-Century America.* Cambridge, Mass.: Harvard University Press, 1990.

Weber, Max. *The Sociology of Religion.* Ephraim Fischoff, trans. Boston: Beacon Press, 1963.

Wells, Ronald A., ed. *The Wars of America: Christian Views.* Grand Rapids, Mich.: William B. Eerdmans, 1981.

Westerkamp, Marilyn J. *Women and Religion in Early America, 1600–1850: The Puritan and Evangelical Traditions* (London: Routledge, 1999).

Wolf, Stephanie Grauman. *As Various as Their Land: The Everyday Lives of Eighteenth-Century Americans*. New York: HarperCollins Publishers, 1993.

Wood, Gordon S. *The Radicalism of the American Revolution*. New York: Vintage Books, 1991.

Youngs, Jr., J. William T. "Congregational Clericalism: New England Ordinations before the Great Awakening." *William and Mary Quarterly*, 3rd Ser., 31 (1974), 481–490.

Zeichner, Oscar. *Connecticut's Years of Controversy, 1750–1776*. Chapel Hill: University of North Carolina Press, 1949.

Index

Act of Settlement (1690), 14
Act of Toleration (1689), 14, 94
Act of Union (1707), 14, 15
Adams, Eliphalet, 96
Adams, James, 25
Adams, John, 125, 135–136, 142
Ahlstrom, Sydney E., 3
Allen, James, 84–87 *passim*, 112, 165, 173–174
Alline, Henry, 178
American Revolution, 121–151 *passim*, 161–162; Loyalists and, 136, 161; Neutrals and, 136–137, 161; War for Independence, 139, 185n15
Amish, 171
Anabaptists, 19, 49, 62
Andrews, John, 132
Andrews, Samuel, 141
Anti-Catholicism, 102
Antinomianism, 41, 190n10
Archibald, Francis, 21, 22, 25, 34
Arianism, 97, 196–197n6
Arminianism, 38, 39, 62, 71–72, 97, 102, 183n3, 197n6
Arminius, Jacobus, 38
Arnold, Benedict, vii, 138–139

Backus, Isaac, 118–119, 140
Bailyn, Bernard, 204n25
Ballantine, John, 103
Baptists, 101, 161; Seventh-Day Baptists, 178

Barnard, John, 78, 79–80, 81, 82, 83, 86, 87–88, 166
Barrell, Colburn, 113–114, 123, 126, 127–131, 133, 143, 149, 150, 151, 160
Barrell, Nathaniel, 113–114, 124, 126–127, 150, 160
Barrell, William, 132
Batty, William, 84–85
Bayly, Lewis, 19
Beebe, James, 104
Benedict, Comfort, 148–149, 150
Benedict, Hezekiah, 146
Benedict, Thomas, 133
Bereans, 157, 207n8
Betoun, David, 10, 11
Black, Thomas, 21
Böhme, Jacob, 19
Bonomi, Patricia U., 161
Boston Association of Loyalists, 138
Boston, Thomas, 16
Boycotts, 125–126, 202–203n10, 203n13. *See* Solemn League and Covenant
Bradshaw, William, 43
Brooks, Thomas, 104
Burr, Aaron Sr., 101
Burr, Oliver, 147, 174
Butler, Jon, 204n25

Calhoon, Robert M., 5
Calvin, John, 11, 38; *Institutes of the Christian Religion, The*, 38

Index

Calvinism, 38, 42, 69, 94, 107–110 passim, 165, 181, 183n3
Calvinists, 39, 62, 114, 183n3, 200n27
Cambridge Platform, 107, 199n22
Cameron, Richard, 14, 16
Cameronians, 14, 20–21, 154, 188n15
Camisards, 193n5
Campbell, Alexander, 6, 180
Campbell, John, 6
Campbell, Thomas, 157, 180–181; "Lunenberg Letter," 181
Campbellites, 157–158, 195n46
Cant, James, 55
Cantor, Geoffrey, 5
Capen, Hopestill, 137–138, 142, 143, 150, 161
Cargill, James, 112, 113, 114
Carmichael, Robert, 89
Carleton, Sir Guy, 149
"Catholick" Calvinists, 62
Chamberlin, Theophilus, 133, 146, 147
Chandler, Thomas Bradbury, 141
Charles I (King of England), 12
Charles II (King of England), 13–14
Chater, Eliezer, 175
Chauncy, Charles, 115
Church, Asa, 133
Church of England, 11–12, 68, 101; Book of Common Prayer, 12; Westminster Shorter Catechism, 19, 20, 98, 187n13
Church of Scotland, 11–14, 36, 185n1; Confession of Faith, 11–12, 25, 26, 30, 155, 157; First Booke of Discipline, 11; Formula of 1711, 21, 25, 26; Moderatism, 15–16; National Covenant, 23, 45; Oath of Abjuration, 15; Oath of Allegiance, 13; Second Booke of Discipline, 12; Solemn League and Covenant, 13–14, 24, 45, 187n13
Churchill, Samuel, 81, 82
Civil War, English, 13
Clap, Thomas, 107
Clark, Charles E., 95
Clark, J. C. D., 5, 161
Clark, William, 141

Clinton, Gov. George, 170
Coercive Acts (1774), 121
Cogswell, James, 103
Cole, Anne, 66
Cole, Nathan, 66
Continental Congress, First, 135, 142
Continental Congress, Second, 135
Cooper, Samuel, 103
Covenanters, 14, 16, 20, 67–68
Cromwell, Oliver, 13
Croswell, Andrew, 117–118
Cudworth, William, 70, 71, 77, 78, 80, 86
Cumming, Alexander, 104, 115
Cutler, Timothy, 95

Dale, David, 90
Dana, James, 113, 115
Danbury, Connecticut, 105–106; Ecclesiastical Society of, 105, 106
Davenport, James Jr., 100
Davies, Samuel, 103
Davis, Benjamin Sr., 126, 142
Deism, 197n6
Dickinson, Jonathan, 3
Disciples of Christ, 157, 180–182. See Campbellites; Restorationism
Dove, John, 79
Duffield, George, 140
Dunkers, 141
Dutch Reformed Church, 101

East Fairfield Association, 111
Edwards, Jonathan, 3, 66, 98, 100 103, 167; "Notes on the Apocalypse," 100
Elizabeth I (Queen of England), 12
English Civil War, 13
Erskine, Ebenezer, 16, 77, 155–156
Erskine, John, 99
Erskine, Ralph, 16
Evangelicalism, 67–68

Faraday, Michael, 5, 174, 194–195n30, 207n3
Ferrier, Robert, 90–91
Fitch, Eleazer, 143
Foster, Edward, 1–2, 126, 142, 174, 177

Index

Foxe, John, 102; *Actes and Monuments of ... Great Persecutions against the True Martyrs of Christ ...*, 102
Francis II (King of France), 12
Francke, August Hermann, 20
French and Indian War. *See* Seven Years' War
"French Prophets." *See* Camisards
Fuller, Andrew, 90, 159, 164, 167
Fuller, William, 79, 83
Fullerton, William, 202n10

Gage, Gen. Thomas, 138, 142
Garden, Alexander, 117, 201n41
George III (King of England), 120, 134
Gillespie, Thomas, 155
Glas, Alexander, 17, 21
Glas, Catherine, 21
Glas, Christian, 17
Glas, George, 79, 80, 81, 112
Glas, John, 2, 9–10, 17, 36, 37, 44, 62, 66, 68, 69, 73, 77, 81, 82, 85–87 *passim*, 91, 112, 137, 153, 155–157 *passim*, 162, 163, 165–167 *passim*, 173, 174, 179, 181, 182, 187n12; ministry of, 18–19, 20–22, 34–35; on assurance, 42–43; on baptism, 49–50; on charity, 58–60; on Christian fellowship, 51–53, 55–56; on church discipline, 53–55; on church-state relations, 20, 22, 25, 27–28, 30, 32, 45–47; 60–62; on dietary restrictions, 56, 57–58; on the Eucharist, 50–51, 56–57; on faith, 41–42; on justification, 38–41; on ministerial office, 35, 47–49; on sociability, 60; on wealth, 58–59; trial and deposition of, 26–33. *See* Glasites, ecclesiology of; Glasites, practices of
Glas, John, works of: *A Continuation of Mr. Glas's Narrative*, 30; *A Narrative of the Rise and Progress of the Controversy about the National Covenants*, 29–30; *Notes on Scripture Texts No. II*, 39; *Scheme of Justification by Faith, The*, 39; *Testimony of the King of Martyrs, The*, 39–40, 89,

90, 157, 159; *Tradition by the Succession of Bishops*, 47; *Usefulness of Catechisms Considered, The*, 40
Glasites, 2, 34, 61, 182; discipline among, 86; ecclesiology of, 43–57; practices of, 57–62
Gold, Thomas, 147
Goodsir, James, 20, 22
Gordon, Thomas, 161
Gorell, Edward, 86
Gorham, Stephen, 143
Great Awakening, First, 37, 63, 66–68, 94–103, 192–193n3
Great Awakening, Second, 172
Gregory, Elhanan, 104
Gregory, Munson, 145
Guy Fawkes Day, 102

Haldane, Robert, 155, 157–158
Haldane, James Alexander, 155, 157–158
Haldanites, 157, 195n46
Halifax, Nova Scotia, 177, 178–179
Hamilton, Patrick, 10
Hankins, Jean F., 5
Harris, Howell, 87
Hart, Benjamin, 202n10
Hatch, Nathan O., 204n26
Hebronites, 15
Heimert, Alan, 102
Henry VIII (King of England), 10
Hepburn, John, 15, 16, 21
Hervey, James, 65, 68, 69–71, 77, 78, 80, 160; *Preservative against Unsettled Notions in Religion, A*, 70; *Theron and Aspasio: or, A series of Dialogues and Letters upon the most important and interesting Subjects*, 68, 69, 70–72, 80, 87
Hitchens, George, 81
Hogg, James, 14, 16
Holified, E. Brooks, 3, 4, 183–184n6
"Holy Club" (Oxford Methodists), 68, 69
Home, Henry (Lord Kames), 65
Hooker, Richard, 16
Hosmer, Titus, 143

Howe, Gen. William, 1, 142, 148
Howe, John, 148, 178–179
Howe, Joseph, 179
Howe, Martha, 178
Hoyt, Samuel, 146
Huguenots, 4
Hume, David, 65
Humphreys, Daniel, 145, 147
Husband, Herman, 139–140, 204–205n28
Hutcheson, Francis, 62, 65
Hutcheson, Patrick, 157
Hutchinson, Thomas, 138
Hutterites, 171

Ingersoll, Jared, 125
Ingham, Benjamin, 84
Inghamites, 85, 86, 157

James V (King of Scotland), 10
James VI (King of Scotland), 12, 17
Jefferson, Thomas, 142
Johnson, Stephen, 125
Johnsonians, 157, 207n8
Jones, David, 88
Jones, John Richard, 90
Jones, William, 90
Judson, David, 104, 111, 115

Ker, Walter, 98
Kerr, James, 21
King George's War, 101
Knox, John, 10–12

Landsman, Ned C., 5
Langdon, Samuel, 103, 115, 120, 162
Laud, William, 12
Lee, "Mother" Ann, 136, 169–170
Leland, John, 140
Leonard, Daniel, 135
Locke, John, 14
Lords of the Congregation, 11
Lowman, Moses, 100
Loyal American Associators, 142
Luther, Martin, 10
Lyon, Bailie, 32

MacLean, Archibald, 89, 90
Marrow of Modern Divinity, The, 16
Marstes, John, 113
Mary II (Queen of England), 14
Mary of Guise, 11
Mary, Queen of Scots, 11–12
Mather, Cotton, 95, 103
McCulloch, William, 99
Mennonites, 4, 139
Methodism, 66, 68, 85, 193n6
Methodists, 66, 68, 101
Millenarianism, 19, 99–100, 139–140
Miller, George, 31, 35
Mitchelson, David, 113, 114
"Moderatism," 15–16
Moravians, 68, 139
Morice, Alexander, 35
Münsterites, 205n31
Murray, John, 139

Niebuhr, H. Richard, 171
Noble, Moses, 202n10

Old Scots Independents, 157
Oliphant, Andrew, 113
Osborn, Levi, 175
Owen, John, 34

Palmer, R. R., 4
Paterson, Archibald, 90
Patten, William, 125
Pease, Simon, 131–132
Peck, Ezra, 175
Pelagianism, 97, 197n6
Peters, Samuel Andrew, 134
Pietism, 19–20
Pike, Samuel, 78–79, 80, 81, 82–84, 87, 154; *Plain and Full Account of the Christian Practices Observed by the Church in St. Martin's-le-Grand, A*, 83–84, 118
Popkin, John, 87–88
Powel, William, 88
Presbyterianism, 11–18, 30, 36, 46, 97–98, 154, 155, 166, 179
Presbytery of Angus and Mearns, 35

Index

Presbytery of Dundee, 23–24, 26–28, 30–32
Primitive Christianity, 189n1
Prince, Thomas Jr., 99, 100; *Christian History, The*, 99, 100, 101
"Protestant," 128–129
Pynchon, Joseph, 134, 145, 147

Quakers, 2, 49, 96, 100–101, 103, 139, 161, 168–169, 171–172
Quebec Act (1774), 125, 135

"Reformed" Presbyterians, 16
Restoration, English (1660), 13
Restorationism, 180–181; "Christian Association," 180
Revere, Paul, 125, 135
Rhoden, Nancy L., 141
Rich, Elisha, 140
Richmond, William, 147
Rogers, Nathaniel, 202n10
Rogerenes, 196n4
Rowlands, Daniel, 87

Sandeman, Catherine, 68
Sandeman, David, 68
Sandeman, George, 113, 114
Sandeman, Gerald, 208–209n4
Sandeman, Margaret, 68
Sandeman, Robert, 2, 5, 37, 39–40, 63, 65, 66, 68–69, 71, 81–83 *passim*, 86, 93, 94, 104, 111–115 *passim*, 117–120 *passim*, 123, 126–127, 130–131, 133, 136, 137, 138, 150, 151, 153, 158–160 *passim*, 163, 165–167 *passim*, 170, 173, 174, 177, 178, 181, 182; activities in England, 81, 84; activities in New England, 93, 112–114, 200n34; controversy with James Hervey and John Wesley, 71–78; *Discourses on Passages of Scripture: With Essays and Letters*, 71; *Letters on Theron and Aspasio*, 40, 63, 71, 78, 79, 87, 90–92 *passim*, 93, 104; on assurance, 75–77; on faith, 75–77; on means, 71–75;

"Thoughts on Christianity in a Letter to a Friend," 69
Sandeman, William, 81
Sandemanianism, 2, 84, 119–120, 181–182; women and, 191n22. *See* Glasites, ecclesiology of; Glasites, practices of; Sandeman, Robert, on assurance; Sandeman, Robert, on faith; Sandeman, Robert, on means
Sandemanians, vii, 2, 6, 7, 182, 186n2; in England, 81–87; in Wales, 87–88; scholarship on Glasites and, 5–6
Saybrook Platform, 110–111, 199n22
Schwenkfelders, 141
Scotch Baptists, 89–90, 157
Scots Independents, 90, 91
Scott, Walter, 158, 179–180
Scottish Enlightenment, 62
Scottish Reformation, 10–14
Secession Church, 16
Secker, Thomas, 103, 104, 125
Seven Years' War, 102–103
Shakers, 136, 169–170, 171–172
Sherwood, Samuel, 135
Sibbes, Richard, 19
Simson, John, 15
Smellon, Jean, 189n40
Smith, Benjamin, 145, 147
Smith, Elias, 180
Smith, James, 90–91
Smith, Titus, 145, 147
Society for the Propagation of the Gospel in Foreign Parts (S.P.G.), 94, 96, 103, 104
Society of Friends. *See* Quakers
Socinianism, 97, 197n6
Solemn League and Covenant (American Nonimportation Agreement), 127–130 *passim*, 134, 202n10, 203n13
Sons of Liberty, 124, 134
Sparhawk, John, 144–146, 150, 161
Spener, Philipp Jakob, 20
Stamp Act (1765), 124, 125
Stayner, Charles St. C., 5
Stevens, Benjamin, 114

Stiles, Ezra, 93, 94, 103–104, 112, 113, 119–120, 140, 147–148, 162; *Memoir of Robert Sandeman on his First Coming to America 1764*, 93, 114; opposition to Sandeman, 114–117
Stone, Barton Warren, 180
Stuart, John (Earl of Bute), 125
Synod of Angus and Mearns, 9, 26, 35
Synod of Brechin, 26
Synod of Dundee, 25, 29, 32–33
Synod of Philadelphia, 99

Taylor, Amos, 169–170
Taylor, James, 104, 111
Taylor, Jeremy, 19; *Rule and Exercises of Holy Dying*, 19–20; *Rule and Exercises of Holy Living*, 19–20
Tealing, 18, 31, 34
Tennent, Gilbert, 97, 197n7, 197n9
Tennent, John, 97, 197n7, 197n9
Tennent, William Jr., 97, 197n7, 197n9
Tennent, William Sr., 97–98, 197n7, 197n9; "Log College," 97
Thirty Years' War, 19
Townshend Revenue Act (1767), 125–126
Traill, James, 20
Trenchard, John, 161
Troeltsch, Ernst, 170–173
Trumbull, Jonathan, 143, 147

Uffington, Thomas, 79
Universalism, 189–90n4

Vernor, Thomas, 88

Walker, Williston, 5, 175
Walkerites, 157, 195n46
Weber, Max, 173
Weigel, Valentine, 19
Wesley, Charles, 68, 167
Wesley, John, 68, 70–71, 77–78, 99, 159, 160, 166, 167, 172
Wetmore, Noah, 104
White, Ebenezer, 93–94, 104, 106–116 *passim*, 144–146 *passim*, 160
White, Ebenezer Russell, 160, 174–175
White, Joseph Moss, 114, 115
Whitefield, George, 56, 66, 70, 79, 99, 101, 139
Whittlesey, Chauncy, 115
Wilkes, John, 161
William III (King of England), 14
Williams, William, 88
Willison, John, 22–26 *passim*, 28; *Afflicted Man's Companion, The*, 25
Winslow, Isaac Jr., 131–133, 142, 143
Winthrop, John Jr., 96
Wodrow, Robert, 17, 30, 67
Wonderful Appearance of an Angel, Devil & Ghost, The, 121–123
Woodhull, Richard, 147, 148

www.ingramcontent.com/pod-product-compliance
Lightning Source LLC
Chambersburg PA
CBHW020649230426
43665CB00008B/369